To James -
lovely Wor)
with

Marie Cooo,
(caroline Rejdak).

C000186205

FOSTERING and US

US

MARIE COADY

authorHOUSE®

AuthorHouse™ UK
1663 Liberty Drive
Bloomington, IN 47403 USA
www.authorhouse.co.uk
Phone: 0800 047 8203 (Domestic TFN)
*   +44 1908 723714 (International)*

Published by AuthorHouse 05/20/2019

ISBN: 978-1-7283-8007-0 (sc)
ISBN: 978-1-7283-8006-3 (e)

Print information available on the last page.

This book is printed on acid-free paper.

Chapter 1

I looked at the newly decorated bedroom knowing that there would be no more furniture decorated by random carvings and stains of goodness knows what. This time the rooms were going to stay as they were. Getting ready to start on the next assignment got me thinking of all the children who had used and abused these rooms over the years. My memories took me back to that first phone call.

The call we had been waiting for had finally arrived. It was our social worker who wanted to know if a young Mum could come and meet us and have a look around our home to see if she would be happy to let us foster her two sons. We didn't know whether to be excited or nervous. A social worker accompanied her and did the introductions. I showed her around the house, hoping for her approval. How naïve we were! She agreed that she would be happy to sign her two boys into care, and arrangements were made to deliver them and their clothes the next day. Our social worker had advised us that we would be wise to provide ourselves with a stock of different size clothing in case of emergencies. That was the best advice that we have ever been given.

We had made sure that our spare room was spotless and child friendly, so we felt we were prepared for anything. The social worker arrived the next day, as planned, with Mum and her two sons, Mathew, who was three years old, and Steven, who was eighteen months old. Mum gave me a list of their like and dislikes, the main one being that they hated baths or being washed. Of course I didn't have trouble believing her when I saw the boys. I thought they were gorgeous—at least what I could see through the dirt. They settled in well after Mum and the social worker left. We decided not to push our luck, and we sent them to bed that first night without baths. I opened their case to get them some pyjamas and immediately closed it again. I shoved it under the bed where it could stay until such time as they went home. At least with it closed we wouldn't be subjected to the smell!

That first morning they got up bright and cheerful and went off out to play in the garden. It was early spring, and the weather was perfect. We had no problems with feeding them as they ate anything that was given to them providing Steven tried it first. If he survived, then Mathew would eat.

By bedtime, we realized that we should really get them washed somehow because, as much as we liked potatoes, we didn't think that the ones that could easily grow in their ears would be very appetizing. Well, in for a penny in for a pound. We ran the bath and got them undressed. Mathew looked at the water and said, "Steven first!" It was with bated breath that Robert lifted Steven into the bath and we waited for the screams. But there weren't any, so Mathew decided that it was obviously safe for him to get in with his brother. An hour later, we had to beg them to get out and get dressed for bed. Eventually they did as they were asked. We took them into the kitchen, sat them on the floor, and gave each of them a drink of milk and a few biscuits, and as soon as they were finished, I got the dustpan and brush and cleaned the crumbs off the floor before tucking them up in their beds.

The next week went wonderfully. They were a dream to look after. They didn't fight with each other; in fact, they were very protective of one another. At that time we had neighbours who had three boys. One of them happened to be the same age as Steven. One day when Steven and Matthew were playing with them, one of the little neighbour boys happened to take Steven's toy away from him. Before we knew what was happening, Mathew picked up a stone and was about to hit the little boy. We managed to stop him in time, so needless to say, we had to keep a sharp eye on our charges when they were playing with other children.

A few days into the second week, the boys' social worker came to see how they were getting on. After she had visited with them for about a half hour, she said she owed me an apology. When I asked her what for, she replied that, when she'd left the children with us, she went away thinking that she would be back pretty soon to pick up the pieces. She hadn't believed that I'd be able to cope with them because I looked so young and inexperienced. But when she saw the children and watched them play, she said they didn't appear to be the same boys that she had left with us. Little did she know that, being the youngest of sixteen children, I had always been around youngsters. From the time I was old enough, I did a lot of babysitting for many of my nieces and nephews. Even after we were married, some of them used to come and stay with us at weekends when we lived in Harrow. And when we moved to the village, they often came and stayed in the school holidays.

Two weeks went really quickly. Robert's dad, Jan, lived with us, and he loved having the boys around. He would play outside with them or take them for walks down the lane with our dog. I would take them for walks up to the village where everyone chatted to them. I even took them to the manor to meet Robert's employer and his wife, as they were very interested in the children who had been placed with us. They had been very supportive with our application and had provided us with a reference.

On the Wednesday of the second week, the social worker rang to say that the boys' mum and dad had sorted themselves out and would like the boys back at the weekend. It was Mathew's birthday on Saturday, so it was agreed that Mum would come and have tea with us to turn the occasion into a birthday and goodbye party. When Mum and a friend turned up at an agreed time, both boys were really pleased to see her. They took her outside to play while I got the cake and sandwiches ready. Well, what came back in wasn't our two boys; rather, there were two little monsters who were fighting and arguing all the time. They proceeded to stamp their food into the floor, and by the end of the festivities, when it was time for them to go, I couldn't wait to wave them off. I was still sitting in shock an hour later. I couldn't believe what I had just witnessed. How quickly their characters had changed! Was this what it was going to be like? During all those months of assessment we had gone through, at times we wondered if we were doing the right thing as it felt that our whole life was under a microscope. But we told ourselves that it would be worth it in the end. Life goes on, and we had a few weeks without a phone call. Maybe the next one would be different.

A phone call did come, but it wasn't exactly what I was expecting. This one was from the mother of Mathew and Steven. She asked if we could have the children back because she and her husband were having marital problems, and they needed more time to sort themselves out. If we could have the boys, it would be a great help to them. I explained that I couldn't do that without going through social services, and she explained that she had already asked them and had been told they couldn't help her. They told her she should ask her family for help. She then asked me to meet her in town to have a chat. Now a thought went through my mind—what was to stop her from just leaving me with the two boys and walking off? But I agreed to meet her the next day. I immediately rang social services to explain what had happened, and they advised me to keep to the arrangements. They would send a social worker along as well so that nothing could happen. The more I thought about it, the more I didn't know if I wanted the boys back. I was afraid they would probably behave the way they did on that last day, and I wondered if I could cope with that. The next day, I got a call from social services asking me to go to the offices instead of the coffee bar, as they had got in touch with Mum and asked her to come in to see them.

When I arrived, we were taken into a room for privacy, and it was agreed that I could take the boys as a fostering placement while the parents sorted themselves out. The social worker asked me if I would mind going back to their house to collect their clothes. I had no problem with that. What an eye-opener! I walked into a house that had so much litter—including dog muck—that there was nowhere to walk without stepping on something. My first thought was, *How did that mum have the nerve to come and inspect my home to see if it was good enough!* That did away with my naivety; I would be a lot wiser in future.

All the way home, I was worried about how it was going to be with the boys, but as soon as I stopped the car, they were out of it quick as lightning. They went straight to the bathroom and stood waiting for me to come and put the water into the bath. It took ages to get them back out again. As soon as they were dried and dressed, they went through to the kitchen and asked for drinks and biscuits. As soon as they finished, Mathew ran to get the dustpan and brush. So the scene was set for the next couple of weeks. It was as if they had never gone away. Robert's dad was pleased to see them as he had missed them. We had lots of picnics in adventure playgrounds and wildlife parks. They had a wonderful time, but like all good things, it had to come to an end.

Two weeks later, I received a phone call from their mum on the Friday asking me to take them back home. I explained that I couldn't do that without permission from social services, but she didn't want me to contact them. I told her that I would have to, and I asked her to call me back a bit later. I immediately phoned the social worker who explained to me that I didn't have to take them to her, but if she turned up, I couldn't stop her from taking them as they were in voluntary care. That was why the mum had rung when she did; if she had left it for another day, it would have been more difficult for her to get them back as they would have been in care for over fourteen days.

When Mum rang back, I told her that I couldn't bring them home until the next day as I had things to do, but she wasn't having any of that. She said she would come and get them herself; she would walk over with a few friends. I asked how she was going to get them back to town. It was a good six or seven miles from her house to ours, and there was no public transport. Surely she didn't expect the boys to walk all that way. She said she would be bringing some buggies for them. I told her I couldn't stop her, and I would have them ready for when she arrived. I rang the social worker to let her know what was happening and how concerned I was about them all walking that distance. She advised me to ring the police and inform them about what was happening. When I did, they told me they would wait for an hour and send a patrol car to ride back and forth to keep an eye on them to make sure the little ones were safe. We gave the two boys their supper and had them ready and waiting.

At about 8.30 that evening, we heard an awful commotion coming down the road. Between the swearing and shouting that was going on we guessed the group coming our way must have called in to every pub between their house and our village. They were certainly merry.

When I answered the door, Mum asked me if I could call a taxi as they didn't fancy pushing their buggies all the way back to town. When I looked to see what they had brought, I saw two old handcarts that had definitely seen better days. I agreed to make the call, but I had Mum and her friends wait outside while the boys waited indoors where it was warm. I then phoned the police to keep them up to date. While we waited for the taxi, I asked her if she and her husband had sorted themselves out. "Oh, yes. We had a wonderful rest, and we did a bit of re-decorating!" I was not amused. I told her not to call me the next time she needed a break as I wasn't there to provide a holiday for them. We finally waved them off in the taxi about an hour later. My husband and I went out the following morning, and when we came back both old carts were gone.

We did see the boys around town a few times after that, but they didn't recognize us, although Mathew kept looking as though he should know us but wasn't quite sure. The house was very quiet for a while. We certainly missed them. Robert's dad, Jan, had enjoyed their company and had got very attached to them, and Robert had become very fond of them too. Both of them were like lost souls for a while. All we could do now was wait for the next call.

Chapter 2

Doesn't time drag? We thought we had been forgotten. However, on December 7th we were back on track. A little boy needed to be looked after until his mum came out of hospital with his baby brother. This was the only eighteen-month-old we had ever seen who could eat a banana without stopping. He'd put it in his mouth, and he wouldn't stop pushing until it disappeared. The first time we watched him, we thought he was going to choke! But he obviously had been used to doing this as he had no problems at all. Sandy stayed with us for one week and three days. He was so good I couldn't fault him, and in some ways we were sad to see him go, but on the other hand he was going back to a loving mum and a new baby brother, which was nice to know. Helping in this type of situation was closer to the reason we had wanted to do fostering in the first place.

We had a quiet Christmas waiting and hoping for a call, but it never came. By the end of January, we were feeling ignored again. By the second week in February, at last we were needed to care for two girls, a three-year-old and a two-year-old. The younger was a doll. She had lovely long blonde hair, and she was so good we didn't know we had her, except for all the hair brushing and dressing up. I had plenty of volunteers to help get her dressed and ready to go anywhere. The three-year-old, on the other hand, was obviously more aware that she was with strangers and found it hard to settle. She caused us so many nightmares, we thought the sisters couldn't be related as they were so opposite to each other.

Although she was toilet trained, this didn't stop her from just wetting herself wherever she was. I would have to pick her up and put her straight into the bath to clean her. There were was endless disturbed nights and loads of screaming fits and temper tantrums. Being away from her parents was not a good experience for this child, and she needed to go home as soon as possible. Luckily, they were able to go home after just one week. Maybe it wasn't so bad for us to be ignored after all!

Chapter 3

A t the end of February, we were asked to take in Clint, a thirteen-month-old boy whose mum had just separated from his dad and needed breathing space to sort out a job and somewhere to live. This one we could have kept. He just seemed to blend in with the family. Jan used to love taking him for walks with the dog, and Robert enjoyed just chatting to him in the evenings before putting him to bed.

While we had him, one of my sisters was doing a move to Redruth in Cornwall. They couldn't have picked anywhere further away. They asked us if we could help them by taking their property down in a self-drive hire truck. After we delivered their belongings, we could then bring the truck back to the depot.

We agreed and were actually looking forward to it because we would be able to see where they were moving to. As baby Clint was so good, there should be no problem. We cleared it with social services and Clint's mum. Everyone was agreeable, so dates were set and arrangements were made.

We picked the truck up on a Friday evening so we could get an early start on Saturday. We arrived at my sister's house very early in the morning along with other family members. Together, we got the truck loaded. Robert and I made sure we had the address and instructions along with everything that we might need for Clint in the way of bottles, food, nappies, and extra clothes. It was like going on safari.

We arranged to meet my sister and brother-in-law halfway there at a service station, just to touch base and make sure everything was okay. What none of us took into consideration was that they were heading off in a car that could do over seventy miles per hour, but our truck couldn't do above fifty, even on the motorway. So when we finally arrived at the service area, they were waiting for us in the car park ready for the second half of their journey. They'd already had had their lunch and toilet break. We waved them off saying we would meet them at the house sometime in the evening.

We eventually set off again when we were fed and watered. By the time we got to Bodmin Moor, we thought we were doing well until we ran into some patchy fog. Add that to the darkness that was now descending, and we were no longer speeding at fifty. We were doing a steady twenty miles per hour! Even so, we really were enjoying ourselves. While all this was going on, Clint was sitting quietly enjoying his bottles and food. We thought we were never going to get there, but we eventually arrived at about ten in the evening, tired and hungry. I saw to Clint while everyone else unloaded the truck. After we had some refreshments, we got everything ready for the journey home next morning. We knew it was probably going to take as long to get home, so again we planned a very early start.

The next day, we stopped after driving two hours to have a drink and freshen up, but when we got back into the truck, it wouldn't start. Luckily, there was a good old AA man having a tea break. As we were members, he got us going again with instructions not to stop anywhere on the way because we would not be able to start the truck again. I made sure we had enough of everything we might need to get us home. Off we trundled. Just as we got to the outskirts of Reading, the heavens opened. With the wipers on, along with the lights, we hadn't done many miles before the battery zonked out. Luckily again, we broke down near an emergency phone. This, of course, was in the days before mobile phones. We tried to get hold of the company we'd hired the truck from, but all their emergency engineers for that size vehicle were gone off duty. Obviously, they didn't expect emergencies to happen during their off hours.

While we were racking our brains trying to come up with a solution, the police came along and made sure we were okay. The officer said they would go to the next turn-off and come back. If we were still there and hadn't managed to get hold of anyone, they would call a local garage to come and tow us off. Needless to say, we were still waiting patiently when they came back. They organized a breakdown lorry to come and take us off the motorway and take us to the nearest station, which was Reading. We were dropped off at the train station where we managed to get in touch with a very close friend who came all the way from Hayes to pick us up. In the meantime, Clint was having the time of his life. He loved the flashing lights he could see as we travelled in the tow truck. While we were waiting, we thought we would have a cup of coffee. I asked a waitress if she could heat a bottle for Clint, which she very kindly did for me. I took it back to our table, but when I shook it before giving it to Clint, the hole in the teat expanded, drowning both myself and Clint. If it hadn't been for Clint going into fits of laughter, I think I would have burst into tears. We finally ended up at my mum's in Harrow where we stayed the night. The next morning, we got in touch with the truck-hire company. They were very apologetic and sent a car to collect us and take us back to where we had parked our own car. We finally headed home, shattered. Luckily it didn't have any lasting effects on Clint.

Unfortunately, it was soon time for him to go home, but this was a lovely ending. His mum had got herself a job a job, settled in a new flat, organized a child-minder, and couldn't wait to get him home. I can't say I blamed her.

That was one trip to Cornwall that we will never forget. When my sister moved back nearer to London, we politely declined their request for help.

Chapter 4

Back while we were waiting for our first placement, we attended a few information evenings. It was at one of these that someone asked if there was an age barrier for becoming foster carers. We were told that there wasn't any for fostering, but adoption could be a different matter, especially with younger children. We had been trying for our own family for some time and thought maybe we should have a word with our doctor. At the time, I was twenty-six and Robert was thirty-one. The doctor was very understanding and sent us for some tests. The results were that Robert was fine, but my fallopian tubes were blocked. They could be cleared with a minor operation, which I went along for. But, when we went back to get the results, it appeared that they were well and truly blocked and couldn't be cleared without a more major operation (bring in dyno-rod).

The reason they were blocked was that I had suffered from Crohn's disease in my teens. The illness had agitated my appendix causing it to become perforated, which resulted in the poison running into my tubes creating the blockage. I had been lucky enough to have had an exploratory operation during which they had removed the diseased part of the bowel, which put the Crohn's into remission. Doctors at the hospital said they would do the operation to clear my tubes only if I would sign a form saying that I would not hold them responsible if the Crohn's disease returned. Anyone who has suffered from this will understand my decision not to have the operation if there was even the slightest chance of this happening.

We now had to come to terms with the fact that we were never going to have our own children. Luckily by the time the tests were carried out, we had already had our first placement, so at least with the fostering we could make sure that our home would ring with the laughter and tears of children. When we felt we had come to terms with our situation, we made enquiries regarding adoption. Social services informed us that there was a seven-year waiting list, so we knew we had to find other options. We wrote to and phoned some private agencies, National Children's Home (NCH, now known as Action for Children), and Barnado's adoption agency among them. They all responded that either their lists were closed, or the waiting time was so long it seemed a lifetime away. One of my sisters-in-law suggested that we consult our parish priest and find out about Catholic adoption agencies. She thought they may be able to help us because so many Irish Catholic girls were coming over to England to hide their pregnancies. They would give their babies up for adoption and then return home.

We thought we would give it a try, so we got in touch with our local priest. We knew him quite well as he had been to our home to give it a blessing when we first moved in. He was very helpful, and he asked us a lot of questions, one of them being had we been married in the Catholic Church. Of course we might have known that question would be coming. We hadn't been able to because Robert had previously been married in an Anglican church, and the Catholic Church wouldn't even consider us. But thanks to some very good and close friends, we had been able to organize our marriage eventually in a Baptist church. But obviously, that wasn't going to be good enough for the Catholic Church as they didn't recognize the Baptist faith as they did the Anglican faith. However, what the priest did suggest was that Robert's first marriage had lasted only for six months, and I hadn't met him until he had been separated for two years. There might be a chance, he told us, to get that first marriage annulled. He filled in all the necessary forms and wrote the appropriate letter, which he sent off to Westminster. Now all we had to do was wait.

In the meantime, we carried on with the fostering, and our support worker asked us if we would consider long-term fostering as an alternative. We weren't too keen because, around that time, there had been an article in the papers regarding a young girl who had lived with her foster parents for five years and was then made to return to her birth parents. We didn't think we could cope with that happening, so we said we would have a long and hard think about it.

Eventually the answer came back from Westminster that we were not going to get the annulment. It was back to the drawing board. Our support worker had another word with us he could see how upset we were, and he told us that, although he couldn't promise one hundred percent a child would not go back to his or her parents, he would do his best to find us one that he could place in the ninety-nine percent category. We decided that might be our only option if we couldn't adopt, so we agreed to give it a go.

Chapter 5

Our support worker came back to us to say he had been to a meeting at which he met a social worker who was trying to find long-term carers for a little boy who was nearly a year old. She had been interviewing couples in an effort to find the people she felt would be right for him. She came to see us, told us his history, and asked a lot of questions about our way of life and backgrounds. She said she would let our support worker know when she had made her final decision.

A week later, he phoned to let us know that she had decided to take a chance with us. He asked if we would like to go and meet this little boy. We agreed, and he said he'd make arrangements.

The day finally arrived. Robert, his dad, and I set off to meet this child. We arrived feeling very nervous. We had brought along a little toy for him. Soon we walked into this massive room and saw a wonderful chubby, blonde-haired, blue-eyed little boy sitting on the floor playing. I remember that he looked up at us and smiled. We didn't want to crowd him, so we sat down on nearby armchairs and spoke to him for a little while before I went over and sat on the floor next to him. I played with him for a few minutes, and the next thing I knew he was putting his arms up for me to pick him up. The house-mother gave a small gasp, and when I turned around to look at her she had tears in her eyes. She went on to explain to us that he had been in the home for about three months and was the centre of attention, being the baby of the unit, so anyone who came to visit the other children always made a fuss of him, but never before had she seen him put his arms up to actually go to anyone. Well, what can I say? How could we not fall in love with him?

It wasn't a case of now the decision has been made, and we could take him home. We had to go back and forth to let him get to know us and be comfortable with all of us. We had to feed him, bath him, get him ready for bed, and take him for walks on our own so that we were all comfortable with each other. I went shopping with the assistant house mother to get him his very first pair of shoes. We have since experienced other couples coming to us and getting to know the children they are adopting. We know exactly how they are feeling, so we take a step back and let them have lots of hands-on experience so they feel the child really is theirs. Things were ready just a few days before his first birthday for him to move permanently to our home, but as he was going to be missed by the other children in the home, everyone agreed it would be nice for him to stay and have his first birthday party with his friends and to turn it into a goodbye party at the same time.

The following morning, his assistant house mother brought him along with his little bag of clothes. Because we all needed time to let him settle and so that we could give him all of our attention, we had to stop fostering the short-term placements and just concentrate on our son. That was a very special time in our lives. We knew we could relax and shower him with as much love as we had to give. We knew that Dean was going to be around for a very long time. Mind you, there were times in his teenage years when it was touch and go. I swear he gave us more headaches than the majority of fostered children. But I don't mind saying this as it proves what a normal relationship we had with him. I don't think there are many parents who, at one time or another, hasn't felt the same. Along with the headaches and heartaches, there were so many good times. And over the years, he has been so supportive and helpful with some of our troubled teenagers that dare I say that we actually missed him when he finally moved out. Not that he still doesn't give us grief, but we wouldn't have it any other way and we are very proud of the life that he has turned around with the help of his partner, who has been very good for him. They have given us a wonderful granddaughter, and for that we thank them.

Chapter 6

As time moved on and Dean settled in, it was time for us to get back to fostering. In January 1979, a baby girl was placed with us. I was really looking forward to this one as she was another doll. The only thing that made me nervous was her hair; she was mixed race and had the most glorious head of curls that I had ever seen. Because it looked a mass of tangles, I was reluctant to brush it in case it hurt her, but when I did eventually plucked up the courage, I found it was so soft that the brush just flowed through it. I thought, *I am going to have to get more confident with this sort of thing!* It's amazing the things that make you nervous when you are dealing with children who are not related to you. However, this placement didn't last long enough; it ended rather abruptly after just one week.

On 9 January, I was planning to go shopping. The weather was very cold and frosty, and our car wouldn't start. Robert had to go and get a few things for the farm, and he asked if I would like to go with him. I decided that I would go. I thought about taking Dean but decided I would be quicker on my own, so I left him and the baby with Robert's dad, Jan.

We were nearing town when a car came around a bend in the opposite direction and lost control on a patch of black ice. It narrowly missed a mini that was in front of us, and the last thing I remember was seeing it coming straight for us. My next thoughts were totally confused. I remember coming round in complete darkness. My thoughts were all fuzzy as I was trying to piece together who I was and where I was. I could remember that I had a son called Dean. I knew I'd left him at home with his granddad. Then it came back to me that I had been with Robert on our way to town. But I couldn't understand why I couldn't see! I could hear voices. One was saying, "Is she okay?" and another one answering, "She'll be fine. We'll get her to hospital." I tried to open my eyes, but I still couldn't see. By that time I was starting to panic thinking that I had gone blind. I put my hands up to feel my face and realized that someone had put some kind of bandage around my eyes. When I pushed it up, I could see daylight and felt enormous relief. I could still hear the voices, and then recognized that one of them was Robert's, and he was really worried about me. I thought I would open the car door, but before I could move, I felt myself being lifted. I heard a man telling Robert that they were taking me to hospital and that I would be in good hands. Robert sat beside me the whole journey holding my hand.

When we arrived at the hospital, I was taken to a cubicle where a team of nurses and doctors gave me a quick check over. One of them had to cut my clothes off and get me into a gown. They said there were no bones broken, but because I'd gone through the windscreen, I would need stitches in my face and neck. I was taken to a side cubicle where a nurse cleaned me up and said as the cuts were all over my face and neck. She would have to put the stitches in without a local anaesthetic. She then proceeded to do just that. As she got to the last painful two, a doctor came in to see if everything was okay. When he saw what she was doing, he asked if he could do the last ones. Boy, was I glad that the nurse had only two left to do. Otherwise I would have made a miraculous recovery and dashed out of the hospital. Those two hurt more than the other twenty-eight. When the nurse finished cleaning me up, she took me to the emergency ward for overnight observation. I was pleased to see Robert was in the ward next to me. He was also in for overnight observation for a possible concussion. He was allowed to come and sit with me, but before they let him come in, they warned him that my face wasn't exactly looking its best.

Either the police or someone at the hospital had gotten in touch with Robert's boss, and he let Jan and my parents know. The hospital dentist came to see me and check my teeth as my bottom teeth had been pushed up out of my jaw. My top front ones had been broken. He said not to worry as he could replace them with capped ones that would be the same as my original ones. I nearly had a panic attack as I had always hated my teeth because they had been slightly protruded. I asked if he could take them out and replace them with straight false ones. He laughed and said they would make sure that the new capped ones would be straight. My heart rate came back down to normal, and I agreed that would be okay. He then asked if I had looked in a mirror to see what damage had been done to my face. I told him that I hadn't even thought of it, so he asked one of the nurses to get me a mirror. It was a good job I wasn't squeamish as I was not a pretty sight. In fact, if one of my brothers had rung me then and asked, as they usually did, if that was "meself" they were talking to, I would have said I didn't think so because if it was then someone had stolen me beautiful face and left me with an "ould" cracked one!

My sister Liz arrived with my parents. The looks on their faces told me how worried they had been, but they did put our minds at rest because they had been to see Jan and Dean to make sure they were okay. Between them and Mrs Jim—Robert's boss's wife—they had got in touch with social services who had taken the baby to another carer. My parents would stay with us in the village, and Mrs Jim's daughter would pop in every day to get Dean washed and dressed. She would also get any shopping that was required. It was quite a few months before we were anywhere near ready to start fostering again as I had a lot of work done on my teeth, and I was in considerable pain for a few months. But time does heal, as they say, and by late October we felt able to continue.

Chapter 7

In November 1979, Dean's older sister came into care. It was thought it would be best for them to be kept together. When she arrived, there was an immediate bond. They played together and enjoyed each other's company. But Dean had suffered from malnutrition when he was only a few months old, and there had been grave concerns over his ability to progress. In fact, he never started to walk until he was eighteen months. When he first came to us, he couldn't crawl, mostly because they'd had him in a baby walker every day so there was never a need for him to crawl or walk to get about. We had to put his toys just out of reach so that he had to stretch and finally move to get hold of them. Each time he managed to reach one, we would move it a bit further away until he eventually learned to crawl to get them. Once he started to move, he then very quickly learned to walk.

It was lovely to see them playing together until we all realized that Maxine was so damaged emotionally that her playing ability was at even younger level than her younger brother's. Dean started to try to copy her, and as a result, he started to go backwards in his behaviour. We had meetings with social services and various professionals; the outcome was that everyone thought that, in the interest of both children, they should be separated to give them an equal chance to thrive. We were very lucky we had some friends in the village who were interested in fostering Maxine, so although they had to live apart, they were actually brought up within the village together knowing that they were brother and sister. For many years, they had a very close relationship.

Before we knew it, 1980 was upon us. Maxine moved to her new carers in January, and at the beginning of February, we were asked to take an emergency placement—a thirteen-month-old boy, Peter, whose mum had just been rushed to hospital to give birth. Dean and this child got on really well; in fact, they became very close and played together all the time. The boy's social worker came to visit on a regular basis, sometimes bringing his mum to visit. As his mum and dad had separated, a visit was arranged for his dad to visit separately so that he could have some one-on-one time with him.

The social worker came to let us know that there was a possibility that the placement could be longer than first anticipated because his mum had made the very difficult decision to place her new baby up for adoption. She had six weeks to think about it before making the final decision. When she came to visit, we could see that she loved him very much. We became quite friendly during this time, and we were hoping to stay in touch and give her some moral support when they settled back home. She made the decision to let her daughter go for adoption. She reasoned that she loved her son very much, and while she felt she could just about cope with one child, she didn't think she could cope with two. She stood a good chance of ending up losing both of them. It was a very hard decision, but once she made it, she was very determined to go through with it.

During one of the social worker's visits, I said to her it was a pity we couldn't adopt the baby as we would love to have a little girl. At first she said there would be no chance because both parents knew us and knew where we lived. After thinking it over, she asked me if I had been serious. Obviously, I said I had, but I could understand the problem. But she said the more she thought about it, the more she liked the idea. She had decided to ask more senior management what our chances were. She came back a few days later with the news that we really shouldn't be allowed, but if both parents agreed and we were willing to take the risk of one of them turning up at a later date wanting the child back, then they would support it.

Both parents were asked and agreed. The mum said that, although she had hoped to stay in touch with me, she would be happier knowing where her daughter would be. She could live with the adoption plan. We did keep in touch over the years. I sent photos of Marie as she was growing up, and she sent photos of herself and her son as he was growing. Eventually this communication expanded when Marie wrote to her mum to find the answers to questions that we couldn't hope to know. They finally met when Marie was fourteen years old.

Marie's birth father also agreed to the adoption, but he said he couldn't promise he wouldn't turn up when Marie was approaching seventeen or eighteen years of age to see how she was getting on. However, he never did. Marie and I and Robert tried to contact him, but we had no luck.

Marie's brother, Peter, was with us until June 1980. During that time we carried on as normal as possible. We had to wait until Mum got herself sorted out and was able to take Peter back home with her. We were allowed to visit Marie where she was living with a set of foster carers who were looking after her; she couldn't come to live with us while we still had Peter because it wouldn't be fair for her mum to have to see her when she came to spend time with Peter. We did manage to take Peter on holiday with us to Great Yarmouth. We had been there for only a day when Peter came out in loads of spots and we had to take him to the local doctor. It turned out he had German measles, but after a few days he settled and had a lovely time on the beach knocking down every sandcastle that Dean made.

Pretty soon, in June, Peter went home, and we could now concentrate on the arrival of our perfect china doll. I tell her now that she has since grown up to be our raggedy doll, but you can't have everything. Once again, we had to stop fostering short-term placements so that we could take time to get used to being a family. We couldn't have been happier. I had my little doll, and Robert had his little helper. Jan was over the moon having two grandchildren and was kept busy playing with them. That summer, two of my nieces, Babs and Annette, came over from Ireland, and we spent the summer going for walks and picnics. They thought it was wonderful to be pushing a pram up and down the village. When people stopped them and asked to see Marie, they felt very important.

Chapter 8

Dean and Marie not only filled our hearts; they also filled our bedrooms, which was going to make it more difficult to carry on short-term fostering.

We didn't own our cottage; it went with Robert's job. Luckily, his employers had been very supportive of our fostering; in fact, they had given us a reference when we first applied to foster. We had no difficulty going to them and explaining our problem. They were very understanding, and we discussed potential options. There really wasn't a bigger house in the village. Some may have had larger rooms, but ultimately there would still be only three bedrooms. One option was to have a three-bedroom house next door to a two-bedroom one, which Jan could live in. The thought of running two homes was a bit daunting, and Jan would have felt as though we were pushing him out. As he idolized the children, that wouldn't be fair or practical. Robert remarked that the ideal solution would be to add an extension to our existing cottage. Mr Jim asked him to put something on paper, which he did, and some time later, Mr Jim returned with plans he'd had drawn up by an architect. We came to an agreement: if Robert was prepared to build it himself in his own time, then the estate would provide all the materials.

We have been very lucky in the support that has been given to us over the years from all our family members and friends, but none have done as much as Mr and Mrs Jim; if it hadn't been for them, we would have got no further than adopting Dean and Marie. Mr and Mrs Jim not only provided our living accommodation, but when we had our car accident, without their help and the help of their oldest daughter, Dean would have had to be placed temporarily with other carers while I recovered.

While all this was going on, 1980 turned into 1981. Marie's adoption went through without any problems. Robert, Dean, Jan, Marie, and I turned up at the court house in Hitchin and sat in a very large courtroom. The judge read through the papers and asked each of us how we felt about the adoption. He especially asked Dean how he felt about having a baby sister. The judge then looked at us and said, "Right. That's it!" We looked at each other and then at him. Our faces must have looked blank because he then told us that we could take Marie home or go and celebrate. She was now ours! Dean let out a cheer. The judge remarked that he was glad to see that Dean was so pleased. Then he wished us luck and said goodbye. We came out not believing how quick and easy it all had been. I don't know what we'd been expecting, but it certainly wasn't anything that was that quick. We all went and had a cup of coffee to celebrate.

Marie settled down with us very quickly. The only problem we had was that she suffered from colic and would wake up three or four times a night screaming in pain. She wasn't much better during the day. It got so bad that I couldn't leave her down anywhere and ended up getting a sling to carry her around even when I was doing the housework.

Our support worker came out to see us a few times and suggested we try her on goat's milk. We found a farm near us that sold it in pouches. We boiled it with water to weaken the strength, and within days Marie was much calmer and not doubling up in pain, but that didn't stop her from crying every time I tried to put her down; neither did it stop her from waking up in the night. But we endured it as long as we could before finally putting her in a single bed from which she could walk into our room and crawl into our bed.

We were still busy with building the extension, so we weren't taking any other children for the moment. It was nice to be able to spend time with Dean and Marie. We were still in the process of seeing a solicitor regarding the accident that we had been involved in. Although most of my injuries had cleared up, I was left with a couple of bumps, one on the side of my nose and the other on my forehead. Our solicitor recommended I have plastic surgery. Arrangements were made for me to stay in Mount Vernon Hospital to have it done. This meant time away from home, so one of our friends, Donna, moved in to look after Dean and Marie while I was away. I was away from home for three days. Because of Donna's help, Robert was able to continue with the work on the house.

Other friends came and helped with some of the building work. One friend in particular, David, would come for the weekend with his wife and really get stuck in helping Robert. He was a builder as well, and Robert had worked with him when we lived in Harrow, so they were used to working together.

Our very good friends George and Trudie had sadly lost their wonderful son, Alan, which affected all of us as we had all grown to love him. Actually it was mostly because of Alan that we became foster carers. We used to look after him to give Trudie a break, and we thought that there must be other people who could use the same sort of help, which is why we got in contact with social services. As they came to terms with their loss, a cottage became available just a few doors away from us, and they were lucky enough to be able to move in and rent. Trudie loved being able to just pop down and get involved with the children, especially Marie. She spoiled her rotten. One day when Trudy was visiting, Marie wanted my car keys to play with. I had already said no, because the men had the footings ready to be filled in with cement, and I was a bit concerned she might drop them into the wet cement! But Trudie wasn't aware of this and handed them to her. That afternoon I needed to go to town, and when I went to get my keys, we realized they were missing. Trudie told me that she had given them to Marie, so George came down with a metal detector. He had no luck with finding them, and by now the cement had been poured and smoothed over. So we assume that somewhere beneath our extension is a set of old keys that cost me a fortune to replace because the ring also contained all my house keys. We often laugh about it now. Trudie's face was a picture when she realized what had happened.

That summer rolled on. Babs and Annette came for the holidays again. Dean started school in September. We had applied to adopt him because he had been with us long enough for us to stand a chance of getting approval without parental consent although we were being informed by his social worker that his parents were going to turn up in court and fight it. But we didn't have any dates for that yet, so we had to carry on and try not to worry too much. We knew that the longer it took to get a court date, the harder it would be for his parents to fight our adoption.

It was so difficult taking him to school and leaving him there for the whole day and realizing that he now had to do this for the next ten years at least. I would no longer be able to take him and his invisible friends for a drive to the next village to pick up bits of shopping or a paper, although I had put a stop to taking all his invisible friends when I had to wait with the car door open until all sixteen of them were safely inside. Now it was reality time, and all we could hope was that he was going to enjoy school and be happy there. We did worry a bit when he came home one day and asked if the next school that he went to could be round. When we asked him why, he said that he was fed up having to sit in the corner all the time. I thought we were going to be in for some interesting times over the next ten years.

Dean's court date finally came through for May 1982. We fretted and worried that we would turn up for court and find his birth family waiting there. This time we knew where to go and more or less what to expect, but with the added worry we couldn't relax.

When we arrived at the court, we kept looking around to see if we could see anyone who looked like they could be Dean's parents. We didn't have a clue what they looked like. We had never met his dad, and we had met his mother only once and that was within the first year of his time with us. As we were asked to enter the courtroom, we were still looking around, but no one seemed to be bothered when the names were called out, so we just followed the clerk, found our seats, and waited. It was the same judge who had presided over Marie's adoption, and he recognized us, which was lovely. We actually relaxed a bit. He asked us how we were feeling, and he asked Dean if he was happy to be having us as his parents. He, of course, replied that he was. Marie piped up to inform him that we were her parents too, and she was adopted as well. This time, too, the procedure was over within ten minutes. Again, he wished us well before he said goodbye. We came out feeling it had all been a bit of an anti-climax as had been expecting to have to fight for Dean. We couldn't believe our luck when it was all over. Again, we went off and had a coffee to celebrate. We then made arrangements to have Dean baptised in our local church, and we had a big party afterward to celebrate both events. It was such a relief to have all the legal issues behind us. Now we could get on with the rest of our lives.

Chapter 9

By the summer of 1983, we were ready to start short-term fostering again. All the building work had been finished. We had a new and bigger kitchen and a dining room downstairs. Upstairs we now had three bedrooms instead of two. Jan's bedroom was downstairs.

This new placement gave us our first experiences in many things including our biggest nightmare. They were a brother and sister, ages twelve and fourteen. They were of the Sikh religion, which we had to learn and respect. Their dietary needs had to be catered for. They could not eat beef, so our menus had to be altered. I had never realized how much beef we ate in our house—from basic roasts to things like cottage pie and Bolognese. The list seemed to be very long, and shopping took on a whole new meaning. The time of year they stayed with us happened to be during the harvest when Robert would have to leave his usual job of estate maintenance and help with corn carting. This meant he started work at 7.30 every morning, and more often than not wouldn't finish until near midnight and sometimes later. He did come home for lunch at the usual time of 12.30, but I would have to take his supper to him.

Most evenings, we would all go together and have a picnic at the side of the field. If he couldn't come and join us, I'd have to carry food across the field to where he was waiting in the tractor. Bal would volunteer to do this. I swear she had leather soles on her bare feet because before, they set off, she would remove her shoes and run barefoot across a field full of stubble. Just watching made my eyes water. I always wore my wellingtons because I knew the stubble could have very sharp spikes.

During the summer holidays, I would try and take the kids to the coast for a day if I could. One year, only my niece Babs came to stay for a few weeks. One of my brothers owned a caravan near Great Yarmouth. He asked me if I would like to take all the children there for a weekend, and he would meet us there and join us.

We set off on a Friday morning and had a lovely weekend. Everyone got on really well together. There were no problems at all. When we returned home on Sunday evening, the kids went for a walk while I unpacked and my brother set off for home.

That night when they had gone to bed, Babs, who was sixteen then, stayed up later to keep me company while Robert was working. She told me she'd had a strange conversation with our foster girl. She had wanted to know what would happen to me if anything happened to her while she was in my care. Babs told her that she didn't really know but would assume that we would be stopped from fostering. We thought it an odd question but dismissed it as we have always been asked all sorts of things.

A few days later, the girl's social worker came to collect them to take them to have contact with their parents as they would shortly be going home. I repeated the conversation with her, and she said she would let me know if the girl said anything to her that day. Well, I certainly wasn't ready for what happened.

The social worker phoned me at lunchtime to say that she was taking them to the local police station because the girl had made an accusation against my brother. It would have to be taken seriously. She would ring me from the police station as soon as the interview was over and she knew more about what was going to happen. I could have dropped through the floor. The police rang to ask if they could come around straight away to take statements from everyone. In the meantime, I was not to speak to my brother because he would have to be interviewed by officers from where he lived. I can't describe how awful I was feeling. I knew nothing had happened, but how could we prove it? I was lucky to have Babs with me along with several very good friends stay with me throughout the day. It seemed so unfair. My brother had only been helping us, and it was our choice to foster, not my family members'. They gave us their total support and accepted all the children as part of our family. I had never realized how much danger we were exposing them to. We had always taken it for granted that we were at risk from allegations, and therefore we covered our backs as much as we could and still do the job to the best of our ability. But we had never thought of family members as being at risk. We did from then on.

Two police officers came to see us. They were very good and put us at our ease, telling us that they thought the girl was lying because of the things she was saying. But they needed to do everything by the book. What shook them the most was that a girl of fourteen knew about some of the things she was telling them. One of the officers had a daughter of the same age, and he wondered what things she knew. They took statements from me and from Babs and a student friend who had been with Babs when they had been for the walk during which the conversation with the foster girl had taken place.

We waited all afternoon and evening. I don't remember praying so much in my whole life. I couldn't focus on anything. I went through the motions of feeding the younger ones and getting them ready for bed, but all the time my mind kept going over the weekend and what my brother might have to go through. Eventually, at around 11.30 that evening, the social worker phoned to say that the girl had retracted her statement and admitted that nothing had happened. The reason she had made the allegation was that she thought, if something like that happened to her while she was in my care, I would be restricted from fostering. She knew she was going home shortly, and I had been a better mother to her than her own. If she couldn't have me, then she didn't want any other child to have me.

What had brought it to a head was that she kept asking the social worker what was going to happen to me. The social worker had been saying that what happened to me was our worry and not hers, but eventually she told the girl that nothing would happen to me because I hadn't committed an offence. I would carry on as before. When the girl realized that I wasn't going to be prevented from fostering, she burst into tears and admitted what her plan had been. The brother and sister were placed in a local residential home for the rest of their time in care. Their belongings were still with us, and that had to be sorted out. The social worker suggested that she bring both children to our house. The boy was feeling awful because he hadn't got a clue as to what had been going on. The girl was feeling very sorry and looking lost. At first I felt I never wanted to see her again, but on reflection I thought that perhaps we both needed to finish on ground that was a bit more positive. They came over that afternoon. The first thing she did was to fall into my arms and sob her heart out. At the end of the day, everyone was feeling they could move on from the unfortunate situation. This was one lesson we were never going to forget in a hurry. I did meet her again about five years later. She told me she was getting ready for an arranged marriage and was looking forward to it because it meant she would be leaving home and going to live with her new husband in his country.

Chapter 10

A few days after the brother and sister left us, two sisters were placed with us, and we found that, by putting our thoughts and energy into them, we were able to put the previous incident behind us.

These two were nine and eleven years old, Rose and Ellie but because they had lived and gone to schools far away from our area and no one knew how long they would be with us it was felt that they would be better off going to our village school. The nine-year-old was no problem and fitted into her year group. The eleven-year-old should have been starting secondary school, but again, because no one knew where they would eventually be living, it was decided that another few months as a year six would not go amiss. She was over the moon because this solution would keep them together. They would make friends in the village, but more importantly to her, having to repeat that year meant she would be familiar with the work and should be top of the class, or so she thought. After several weeks, she came home laughing and said they were doing work that she hadn't done before. And when she asked, she was told that our village school liked to get all the students a year ahead so, when they left and moved on to secondary schools, they would be familiar with the work and could settle in better and take time to find their way around a much larger building and make friends without worrying so much about keeping up with their schoolwork and homework. She took to this situation really well and settled down easily.

They did have a younger brother with whom they had contact at the same time they were visiting their mum. Each girl had fantastic personality and a good sense of humour. They used to dress Dean, Marie, and themselves in weird and wonderful outfits and put on plays for us. They loved to sing and dance and were very much into Boy George.

This was a lovely time for us. The children got on well together and everything was very peaceful. The girls eventually stayed with us for about three months and were all set up to go home for Christmas. Although they were looking forward to being back with their mum, they were disappointed not to be having Christmas with us, as we had all grown very close. The obvious decision was for all of them to come and spend Christmas with us. We are constantly being told not to get emotionally involved. It is good advice and, in most cases, should be followed, but there are times when certain children get under your guard. This family was in that category, and we have nothing but good memories regarding their time with us. We have no regrets about keeping in touch over the years. They have attended some of our celebrations, and we have also been to a few of theirs. I think these girls were certainly sent to us at the right time and restored our enthusiasm for fostering.

January 1984 brought us two short-term placements, each two weeks. The first was a ten-year-old girl. Although she had not been abused, her older brother and sister had. Their father was being released after serving his time in prison. Mum had been told that, if she accepted him back into the family home, the children would have to be removed. She chose to be there for her husband because she could cope without the children but not without him. It never has ceased to amaze us over the years how many mothers will support an abusive father. They even see the abuse as a lesser crime than an extra-marital affair. It is almost as though they can handle it because it is something that is kept within the family. All of the family members can be very loyal to each other and see no wrong; to them whatever has happened, no matter how bad, is a way of life. This girl was more worried about how her father was feeling. She worried about whether he would be able to find his way home okay.

When he returned home, he came to visit his daughter. Regardless of our feelings, we had to make him feel welcome as it was important to the girl. There are a lot of times when foster carers have to put aside their own feelings for the sake of the children. When he was finally settled back at home, the children all went to stay with a relative who was prepared to look after them.

The second placement was a young boy whose father was working away from home and whose mum had to go into hospital. But when Dad returned, he came to collect his son. Neither of these children made much of an impact on our way of life, and things carried on as normal. Dean and Marie got on with both of these kids, and the time they spent with us didn't interfere with anything that was happening for them. Marie was still able to go to her ballet lessons, and Dean had joined the Cub Scouts and was making his own friends.

There are so many reasons why children come into care. We never knew what the next call would bring, and sometimes it was just as well.

It can be very lonely for a teenager living in a village. Because we understand this, we don't have a problem with teens having friends over to stay. What we didn't expect was a friend that ended up staying the two entire weeks of the placement. In February of 1984, we had a call asking us to take a fifteen-year-old girl who wasn't getting on with her parents and had a tendency to continue to get into trouble and stay out all night. This was a case of the usual arguments with her parents. As to be expected, her parents didn't understand that she needed to be out late, and at fifteen she felt she was entitled to make her own choices. After all, parents were never teenagers so how could they hope to understand? Because we weren't emotionally involved, we could take a step back and put things into perspective. Also, if she wanted to go anywhere while she was staying with us, the only way she had of getting there and back was for us to take her and collect her. It was a very long walk from town to a village with no public transport. However, she gave us no problems. She asked if her friend could stay for a couple of nights. We agreed that she could on the understanding that, when they went to their youth club, they had to be where we arranged to meet them at the right time. They were always there waiting for us. The biggest problem was getting them both to move back home when the placement came to an end. They had both been good company and behaved around the house. Her friend wanted to know if she could stay with us indefinitely, but we had to say no. I must admit that, as much as I missed the little ones when they moved on, this was the first time that I shed a quiet tear over older children as they were being driven off by the social worker.

Chapter 11

We had several months to ourselves and managed to do things with Dean and Marie. We went on holiday to Great Yarmouth, we managed trips to London Zoo with some friends, and we had a few more odd days out.

By April 1984, we had been fostering for seven years, and all the placements apart from Dean had been short term placements. But the next lot of youngsters that arrived turned out to be very long-term visitors. Vicky, Chris, and Nicole became quite close to being family without adoption papers. Both Dean and Marie thought of them as their brother and sisters and still do.

We received a phone call asking if we could take three siblings for a few weeks while their mum went into hospital for bed rest as she had ovarian cancer. We agreed to have them. I went with my friend one Sunday morning to collect them. We brought them and their belongings back to our house. As it was during the Easter holidays, we didn't have to worry about school for a few weeks.

Their mum was admitted to our local hospital, and for the next two weeks, we took the children to visit her several times each day. As the first fortnight was coming to an end, the doctors at the hospital had a word with me and the children's social worker. It seemed unlikely that the children's mum would be coming out of hospital anytime soon. Arrangements were made for the children to go to school from our house. We carried on taking them to see their mum every evening and at the weekends, as it was important to her and also for them. Marie's ballet lessons went on hold as we didn't know how long we would have to be going to the hospital. She wasn't too bothered as she was getting fed up with them anyway. Social services organized a meeting to which we were actually invited. Back then we were not normally included in meetings for any of the children in care, although a lot of carers were trying to change this because the carers were the ones who were responsible for the daily care of each child and knew better than any one of the professionals how the children were feeling. Carers could also be a voice for the children. It is now normal practise for carers to attend children's review or planning meetings.

It was decided at this meeting that the children would remain with us because no one knew the whereabouts of their father. Their aunt and uncle were a great support for them, and we all worked together to help them through a very difficult time. We managed to keep them in touch with their next-door neighbour, who had been very fond of them and had kept an eye on them when they were living at home. Over the next few weeks, Robert and I took turns to accompany them to visit Mum in hospital every evening, as one of us had to spend time with Dean and Marie, who, at this time, had to take a back seat. But they were very good, and we tried to spoil them a bit when we could. I think because the relationship between them all was very close, no one felt left out; in fact, Marie's name was changed to Midge—short for Midget—as she was the smallest in the family. As the evenings were getting brighter and longer, the children wanted to play outside and would get very fidgety at the hospital. We organized it so that they visited in turns. That gave each of them time out to have a good runabout and enjoy their lives in the countryside. It soon became apparent to everyone that their mum wasn't going to be around for much longer, and the children had to be prepared. This is not an easy thing to have to explain to anyone, let alone three young people who adored their mum. Our support worker came over, and we sat them down to explain what was going to happen. They were very upset as could be expected. They comforted each other, the older two being particularly gentle with the youngest. All three pulled together and carried on with their lives as normally as they could under these circumstances. The staff members at their schools were told of the situation and were very supportive; in fact, they began allowing the children to skip their homework, which we felt was probably not the best thing for them as school routine often helps to keep children within a net of security. Also, they didn't need other children pointing them out as being any different.

The time soon came when the hospital staff members were talking of days and not weeks. We received a phone call early one evening and learned that we now only had hours for a final goodbye. The children couldn't face going to see her because they wanted to remember her as she had been and not the way she now was. Although at first, Vicky, the oldest girl, wanted to rush off to see her. But all three talked it over, and we felt nothing but admiration for them when they asked if I would go in their place.

That was the first time I had ever sat with a person who was taking that very last breath. What I had to report back to the youngsters the following morning was how peacefully she had passed away. They in turn were aware that she had not been on her own. I was able to tell them that a close friend of their mum had also been with her, and that made it easier for them to bear the sad news.

Their aunt and uncle made all the funeral arrangements. That was a comfort for the children because they did not have to make any final decisions, although they were kept informed of what the arrangements were going to be. Nothing, however, was going to make the day any easier. They felt very much that everyone's eyes were going to be on them, and it made them very self-conscious. They didn't think they could handle the actual burial while everyone else was there. We ordered the usual floral arrangements plus three red roses. On the day of the service, at the graveyard, Robert represented the three siblings. He was there for the lowering of the coffin. I stayed a distance away from the graveside with the children waiting until everyone else had gone. We then walked up to the grave so they could say what they wanted to say to their mum. Each child threw a rose down on the coffin. We stayed until they felt ready to leave.

Life goes on, and the children settled down, Vicky taking on the role of mothering Chris and Nicole. We had to try to get her to ease up and have a life of her own. They had then and still have today a very close relationship, which has seen them through some very tough times.

After everything they had been through, things started to settle down and we all felt they could do with a good holiday; in fact, we all could. We made arrangements with a friend to use their caravan near Great Yarmouth. The only problem we had was how to get everyone there, as this was in the days before people carriers. Social services were very good, and we were able to come up with an agreement to hire a mini-bus, which all the kids loved, although, even with all those seats, there were still the inevitable arguments over who was going to sit where.

We arrived safely and in a holiday mood. The kids sorted out where they were all going to sleep. Once that was decided, it was down to the clubhouse for them while we sorted the luggage. Then we met down on the beach to find our way around and see what was on offer for them.

We all had a wonderful, carefree week. The weather was dry and sunny, which enabled the children to go out and enjoy themselves building sandcastles and playing sharks in the local swimming pool. We had a day out at Pleasurewood Hills Family theme Park, which had newly opened, and we had a picnic at Fritton Lake. We enjoyed dancing in the clubhouse every evening and taking fish and chips back to the caravan before bedtime. Too soon it all came to an end, and it was back to reality.

While the three children had been living with their mum, they'd had no contact with their father. Now that she had gone, they felt they might like to have contact with him. We managed to trace his family, who lived in a neighbouring village. They couldn't really tell us much about where he was living, but when Vicky went to a family party, she met him there. In the meantime, she had reached her sixteenth birthday, and back then, once a young person became sixteen, he or she was usually moved to a part of fostering called Teencare, which was intended to work on getting teenagers ready to leave care. However, we did maintain close contact, and through this contact, the children spoke about getting to know their father. They wondered if their mum would have approved.

It was near to Christmas when we finally managed to get their father's address. There was still some hesitation on their part, which was good as it meant that they were really taking it seriously and not just rushing into it. Chris especially had doubts; he was the one who always thought first then acted. The girls were more inclined to act first then think about things. One of Chris's friends in the village had just seen his parents split up, and that served as an example of how two people might not be right for each other, which can cause problems within a marriage. We told them that that sort of situation doesn't always make people bad parents. The only way to find out would be to meet him and make up their own minds. There was no pressure put on them from us or from social services. They eventually decided that they would like to meet him, which is what happened. They slowly built up a close relationship with him, and after all these years that still holds good. He has been there for them when they needed him.

The most endearing thing about these children was their ability to just be children and have a good time, which leaves us with some wonderful memories. Every year at the beginning of the school holidays, we would put up an eight-person tent that was given to us by one of my nephews. The children loved sleeping in it. They would take it in turns—boys one night, girls the next. During one of the summer holidays, the two girls that we had previously fostered arrived at our house along with their brother and stepfather. Their mother had been taken ill, and he didn't know who else to turn to for help with the kids. We said we would keep them overnight as we had the tent and there weren't any problems regarding sleeping space. The kids all knew each other because we had been keeping in touch, so they were quite happy with sharing. It didn't stop there! Children of some of our friends were staying for several days, and one of my nieces, Sandy, was staying over as her grandmother was very ill. My sister-in-law was staying with her in Edgeware in Middlesex, so it was easier for Sandy to stay here with us. Chris's two friends from the village were sleeping over too.

The following day I contacted social services and explained the situation of the children whose mother was in the hospital. I was told someone would get back to me as soon as they had found somewhere for the three of them to stay. The kids spent the day running across to the woods to make a camp. By late afternoon I received a call to say they didn't have anywhere for a sibling group of three to be kept together; they would have to be split up. The children weren't happy about that and wanted to stay with us. It was agreed that, as we had the tent and the kids were happy and we could manage, they could stay with us until somewhere became available. Our friends did come to collect their two, who went off protesting that it wasn't fair. The children whose mum was sick ended up staying for a fortnight. That was the best two weeks ever! They all amused themselves in camp they had made in the woods. The older ones watched out for the younger ones. We would see them walking down the road. Someone always held on to Marie's hand. If the weather was bad, they were allowed to use the village youth club hall during the day, which had a mat for their breakdancing. They also had the use of table tennis equipment.

One of the days, Trudie the friend who got us into all this by having such a wonderful son, came with me and another friend, Fiona, to take them all along with one of the boys from next door to the local beauty spot for a picnic. The last thing my next-door neighbour said to me was not to let her son get wet. They were going on holiday soon, and she didn't want him catching a cold before they left. "Trust me," I said. Famous last words. We got everyone there in three cars. When we arrived we walked to the top of the hills, and all the kids went off to enjoy themselves. I reminded them not to let the little boy from next door get wet. We got the food ready and called them back to eat. When we had finished, off they went again, some of them climbing, some swinging on a rope over the water, and others paddling in the stream. When we had cleared everything away, a few of them still wanted something to drink, so I gave each of them a paper cup, I then went to get myself a cup of the fresh spring water because I wanted to wash my hands. Suddenly, one of the older boys threw his remaining half-cup of water at me I instinctively threw my water at him! Big mistake! The next thing I heard was shouts of "Water fight!" The adults joined in, but we had to keep shouting out warnings not to throw water on the little boy from next door. We should have known better because Nicole finally up-ended her cup on top of his head. It was like musical statues when the music stops—everyone froze with mouths open. Time to go home. They were all quite adamant that none of them was going to go next door with me when I took the damp child home, adults included. I knocked on the door. When my neighbour came out and looked at her son, and then saw my face, all she could do was laugh. So it didn't end too badly.

Some nights all the kids thought they were being sneaky and getting one over on us. We could hear whichever lot was sleeping in the house trying to go downstairs without making a noise. Of course, a herd of elephants would have made less noise. We could hear them going out of the back gate and giggling as they tried to creep past the front of the house to go for a walk down the lane. We let them think we didn't know what was happening. They weren't doing any harm. We all live only once, and after all, the reason we were fostering was to try to give some children a happy childhood.

The fortnight came to an end too quickly, and three children had to go home. They were pleased that their mum was better, but they were reluctant to leave us because they'd been having such a good time. We had them back for a few days at a time during other summers.

Chapter 12

By 1986 Chris and Nicole had been with us for two years. In that time, Marie had started school, and both Chris and Nicole had changed schools. Nicole left primary and started secondary, and it was felt that, as they were both settled, Chris may as well go to the same school, so they both started at the secondary school in town.

Another of my nieces, Kathleen, was getting married and asked both Marie and Nicole to be bridesmaids. This was the extent to which my family had accepted these children as part of our family. There was never a problem with attending any family gathering. Our invitations always included any children that we had living with us. We were so proud of Marie and Nicole. I had been up to all hours making Marie's dress. She was so pleased with it she wore it to school on the Monday after the wedding. None of us had ever seen Nicole in a dress since she was always more comfortable in a pair of jeans, so it made it all the more memorable to see her looking very feminine.

We had all built up a good relationship with the children's dad. Vicky had already moved into a bedsit in the house where he lived, which made it easier to keep in touch. They all felt ready for the next move, which was for Chris and Nicole to think about going to live with them. The father had now come to the top of the housing list and was offered a flat that would enable them to get back together as a family. Both Chris and Nicole were given the choice. Nicole did not hesitate. She wanted very much to live with her father. It was a lovely ending to her placement with us, but not an ending to our relationship. Chris was given the same choice, but he felt that as he was going through enough pressure at school and would be happier to stay with us until he had finished his schooling. Then he would think about moving in with his dad.

As Nicole moved on, my niece Babs wanted to move to England and needed an initial base where she could stay while she sorted herself out with a job and somewhere to live. Having her with us was a heaven-sent blessing because our next placement was two-and-a-half-year-old twin girls. They were little angels, but more the kind you would class as hell's angels. I know I can safely say this as both they and their mum would agree with me. Their mum, Toni, had to spend some time in hospital, so again we made trips back and forth to the local hospital. We didn't do it quite as often this time; I don't think the nursing staff could have coped with them visiting too often, and we also wanted Mum to get better not worse. After six weeks of having them, I was ready to swap places with her, except I would have been asking for a bed in the psychiatric unit. It is a good job we hit it off with Toni from the word go. What one of the twins didn't think of, the other one did. Linda slept most nights; Veronica didn't. This was when

Babs earned her keep. She took night duties, and I took days. When we took them shopping, we had to be careful not to walk directly behind anyone or one of them would shout, "Move out of the f-----g way!" Needless to say, we would beat a hasty retreat. Buying shoes was a nightmare; we had to take them in the shop one at a time because if one sat still, the other would run away. How on earth Toni managed on her own I'll never know. I think even today no one can believe how she survived as well as she has.

We used to have chickens caged up at the bottom of the garden, and most days we spent chasing them around as one of the girls would open the gate to the run and let them out.

Marie was fascinated by them. It was very difficult to tell them apart. After a few days, Babs and I didn't have a problem, but Robert, Dean, and Marie were constantly asking us which was which. Chris didn't have much to do with them as he was out and about with his friends mostly or busy doing his schoolwork. Marie found them hard work as they would very rarely sit quietly, but she used to bring her friends home to meet them, and she loved it when we went out anywhere because people were constantly looking at them.

I won't say the six weeks dragged because we were so run off our feet that time meant nothing. Toni was discharged from hospital, but she had to spend a few weeks settling in at home before finally having the girls home. They had an older sister, Patricia, who was a big help to Mum, which she certainly needed.

Chapter 13

Once Veronica and Linda had gone home to Mum, we had a much-needed holiday. It was rather a special one too. An endowment policy we owned had matured earlier in the year, and we wanted to do something special with Dean and Marie. One of my brothers lived near Atlantic City in America and had been asking us to go over and spend some time with them. We thought that, while we were there, we could spend a few days at Disney World.

Chris was still living with us, and we were quite prepared to take him with us. We booked everything in the month of June. What we didn't take into account was that Chris would be leaving school and starting a job. Normally this wouldn't have mattered, but he had worked hard and had done well in his exams, and because of this, he had managed to get an apprenticeship with an airline at our local airport. As luck would have it, his starting date coincided with our holiday. They told him that the first week was the most important of all and it really would be unwise to miss it, so we had to do a swap and change his ticket so we could take my niece Mandy while her parents looked after Chris for us. We felt so sorry for him as he had been looking forward to the trip, but he was very grown up and realized that his future had to come first. We did promise him that, if we ever got another chance to go again, we would try to take him with us to make up for it.

It had taken most of the summer to get our visas and passports sorted out. First I applied for my passport and was told that, because I wanted an Irish one, I couldn't have Dean and Marie put on it because they had been born in England. They would have to go on Robert's passport. That meant that we had to reapply for both of them. Robert's came through okay with Dean and Marie's names on it. Mine seemed to take ages. It was getting to within a few weeks of our travelling dates, and we were getting worried. This was where having Babs with us was a godsend. Because time was getting short, one of my brothers said he would take me to the Irish Embassy in London to get it sorted. So Babs had charge of the kids, leaving me free to go with him. When we finally got the passports, we realized that we didn't have the visas, and that could take weeks because of some strike or other. My sister-in-law's nephew worked just around the corner from the American Embassy, and he went along and got them organized for us. We thought we were never going to get there. By now we were so grateful to Babs that we felt she was the one we should be taking, as she certainly deserved it, but everything was now booked and paid for.

It was lovely to think about having some time with Dean and Marie. We always tried to spoil them between placements, but it was getting to a point where we nearly always had a child placed with us. When we could, I would do special dinners with flowers and candles on the table. Marie and I would have melon balls as a starter. Robert and Dean would have prawn cocktail. We would all have steak with a special sauce that I used to make. And there was always ice cream for dessert. Sometimes, if the weather was bad, we would spread a blanket on the living room floor and have an indoor picnic. These were our special times with them.

In a lot of ways, having Dean and Marie made fostering easier because very often children relate more easily to other children than they do to adults. When children first arrived, Dean or Marie would show them to their room and help them to settle in. Dean or Marie would explain the house rules. Often foster children had problems that they felt they couldn't talk about with Robert and me. But often they would talk to Dean or Marie, who would then pass the information on to us, and we would sort the problem out, put the youngsters' minds at rest, and let them know we would be doing our best for them. Our children also played the role of super spies. When children did something they shouldn't, one of them would come and tell us. We always approach the misbehaving children as though we found out through some other means. At one time, the children currently living with us thought that I was a bit of a witch because I knew everything that was going on. They didn't know that we had spies everywhere. The children from larger towns didn't realize what a village community was like. We allowed our children to go out around the village. We told them not to go certain places, and quite often we would get a phone call from one of the villagers to let us know they had seen one or two of our kids somewhere they shouldn't be. When the kids came home, we would ask why they had gone to a forbidden place. It was so funny to see their faces while they were trying to work out how we knew what they had been up to. That is the nice thing about living in a small village where we all look out for each other. If any strange children were seen wandering around, we would get a call asking if they were ours. It certainly made life easier, and the children were more wary of where they went.

Chapter 14

Once we had recovered from the twins, we were more than ready for our holiday. Jan went to stay with some friends in Hayes, and Babs moved to Robert's sister who lived in Harrow as she was having no luck finding a job in our area, and without a job, she couldn't get anywhere to rent in our local town. Also, she had no means of travelling to a job every day. So, with some regret, we took her to Chris's the week before we went on holiday. I knew I was going to miss her. She was good company, and we had lots of laughs together. We had spent a lot of good evenings dancing around the kitchen. But I was hopeful that I would see her often.

Dean and Marie were excited about our trip. My brother hired a mini-bus to take us to Gatwick Airport as they wanted to wave us and their daughter off. We loaded everything and were ready to go. When we went outside to hop onboard, we found a few of the neighbours waiting outside to wave us off. It was lovely to drive away to the sound of them cheering and calling out for us to have a good time. Now surely nothing could go wrong, and we could relax and enjoy ourselves. After we arrived at the airport and booked ourselves in, we sat and had coffee with my brother and sister-in-law while we waited for the boarding announcement. Finally it came, and we headed off to the proper boarding gate. Our belongings went through the machine. "Sorry, but gas-heated tongs are not allowed inside the aircraft. Would you like us to find your luggage so it can be put in your case?" "No, thank you. There is no way I'm going to hold up the flight for curling tongs. I shall just pass it back to my brother who is waiting by the departure gate." This was a good start. It could only get better. We were called on first as we had two children. We settled down nicely and were ready to go. Dean and Marie had been given goody bags with things to do to stop them getting bored throughout the flight. The air hostess went through her safety speech and told us where our life jackets were stowed. The next thing we knew, Dean was trying to get under the seat. He was looking for his as he thought the plane was going to crash. "Dean we haven't even left the airport yet!" The rest of the journey was uneventful. The hostesses looked after Dean and Marie making sure they had plenty to drink.

Nearing landing time, we had to fill in customs forms and report if we had been on agricultural land. Of course we had to say we lived in a farming village. We got off the plane and went through passport control and customs. We were just going towards the exit when we were approached by a customs officer who asked us to follow him to a side room. This could only happen to us. They wanted to know what kind of farm we lived on. Did we have any clothes with us that we had been wearing on the farm—especially footwear? We explained that we lived in a village and not on a farm, and although Robert worked on the farm, he didn't come into contact with any animals. And no, he didn't have any of his work clothes with him. We eventually got out to my brother Tony who was waiting patiently as we were the last out.

We then had a two-hour drive from Newark Airport to Atlantic City where he lives. By the time we got there, we were totally shattered. The kids went to bed and slept for hours. Robert and I had a lot of catching up to do with my brother, so it was another few hours before we got our heads down. It took me several days to recover. The first day we went out to a local travel agent to book a week in Disney. What we hadn't realized was that it was Columbus Day week, which is a big national holiday over there. We managed to book in to Disney for only three days. After travelling all the way across the Atlantic, there was no way we were going home without taking them to Disney! We spent our first week with Tony, getting to know his local area. We could walk to the local mall, which was about a mile away. We wondered why we were getting funny looks as people passed us in their cars. But Tony pointed out that no one walked over there. Even if they were just going around the corner, they took the car. But we were happy in our own way and carried on. Tony took us into Atlantic City one evening to have a look in the casinos. We managed to have a few games on the machines, which we enjoyed. We won a lot of money and then lost it in another game. Then it was back home to the children, who were safely tucked up in bed.

Our journey to Disney World was fine. Tony took us to Philadelphia International Airport. It wasn't a long flight to Florida. Dean and Marie were really excited; they were going to see Mickey Mouse at last! We got a cab from Orlando Airport to our Holiday Inn Hotel. We went via the toll road not realizing that we had to give the cab driver the dimes for the booths. Luckily he had some, so we just repaid him when we got out. We booked in and went to our room. The kids thought it was great because we had a massage bed, which they insisted was "theirs"! In the end, we turfed them off and bagged it for ourselves. Disney was fantastic. The kids managed to see lots of characters and go on loads of rides. We managed to get around the Epcot Center. The only thing we didn't get to see was the firework display at night as the courtesy coach from the hotel left the parks at six o'clock. But we all enjoyed ourselves. We spent the last day in the hotel swimming pool because we were all too worn out to manage another day rushing around.

We started the journey back to Philadelphia by boarding the plane in Orlando. It taxied out to the take-off point, but then suddenly started going back to the boarding bay. The captain then announced that they were having engine trouble and would have to have someone take a look to make sure we got home safely. It took us a little while to get Dean out from under his seat. The hostess had to promise that she would sit next to him for take-off and landing before he would sit back in his seat.

All too soon, our time in America came to an end, and it was time to go home. It was with bated breath that we started the journey home, but we managed to get back to Gatwick in one piece, much to Dean's delight.

We were met back in the village by the same neighbours who had waved us off, which made the kids feel very important. Then it was back to normal.

Chapter 15

We had a quiet Christmas that year. Chris's Dad, Vicky, and Nicole came over for the day. We took them home in the evening. It is my birthday on Boxing Day, and our next-door neighbours wanted to thank us for something that we had done for them, so they offered to take us out for a meal that day. They paid for Robert and I, and we paid for the children. We enjoyed it so much. After the hassle of Christmas day, it was nice not to have to worry about cooking again. We have since made a Boxing Day outing an annual event, which makes Christmas more relaxed for me, knowing that no matter how many I have to cook for one day, at least I can relax the next.

Toward the end of April in 1988, I received a call from our support worker asking if we could take a fourteen-year-old boy who needed to be moved out of a residential home very quickly. Apparently there had been an incident between him and a social worker that resulted in the need to get him moved as soon as possible. I received the call on a Friday, and he had to leave his present place by Sunday at the latest. The support worker went through a brief history of his background, which consisted of a lot of violent behaviour. We are usually told a bit of what we are letting ourselves in for, and we have the right to say no if we don't feel comfortable. By the time she had finished filling me in, I was wondering why I was going to say okay, but when she said his name, I thought I recognized it, and I realized that he had spent a day with us during that eventful fortnight with one of the boys. I remembered liking him. One of the things we have tried to do is not to judge by past history as sometimes chemistry matters. Just because a child doesn't get on in one placement doesn't mean he or she won't successfully fit into another, so we try to give each child a fresh start when he or she comes to us. We agreed to give it a go.

We went to the residential home to collect Don and bring him back to our home. He soon settled in, sharing a room with Chris. He very quickly became part of the family. He arrived about a week before his fourteenth birthday. We made a big deal of this because we wanted him to feel as much a part of the family as the others. We wanted him to know that he was important to us. He had been going to Army Cadets twice a week. We managed to keep this going for him. We would get him there by seven in the evening and collect him at ten. This was a very important part of his life. Later on we would learn just how important. The Cadets often went away to camp at weekends and school holidays. Every time he came back, the phone would continually ring. It was always a girl for Don, and sometimes more than one would call. He was like a magnet to them. Considering his personality we weren't surprised.

Don mixed well with fellow cadets outside of formal meetings and would often meet some of the others in town. Whatever time and place we arranged to meet him, he was always there. One memorable weekend was so different. He wanted to go to a party in Enfield with a few of his mates. We agreed he could go as long as he was back at the train station at 11.30 p.m. We would be waiting for him there. As he had never let us down before, we were quite happy for him to do this. We duly arrived at the station on time. We waited just over half an hour until just after midnight, but there was no sign of him. We then went knocking on the doors of a few of his friends' houses where there was a slight chance that he might be, but to no avail. All we could do was report him missing—to both our emergency duty team and the police. Then we went home to wait. At four in the morning, the telephone rang. It was the Enfield police asking if we were the carers of this boy. We said we were and had reported him missing. By now my heart was in my mouth; I was imagining the worst possible scenario. But they said they had him in one of their cells and would like us to go and collect him. Feeling very relieved and shaky, I asked if we could come in the morning when we were more awake, but the officer told me we couldn't do that because Don was only fourteen, and they couldn't keep him there without an adult. Luckily, with Jan living with us, we were able to leave the other children asleep and set off.

It took us over an hour to get there. We were stopped by a patrol car the other side of town wanting to know what we were doing out at that time of the morning. We were asked to show some ID, which we did as we explained where we were going. So they let us off again. First we went to the wrong police station, not realizing that there were two. We eventually found the right one and went in to claim him.

The officer in charge filled us in on the details of the previous night. Apparently a patrol car was doing the rounds of the town and saw a group of youngsters walking towards the train station at approximately ten in the evening. The group spotted the car and started shouting out insults and making rude gestures. The driver stopped the patrol car, but by the time the officers got out of the car to approach the boys, there was only one person left standing there. Don hadn't realized all his mates had done a runner. The officers tried to get him in the car, but there was no way he was going. They called for back-up, which came in the form of a Black Maria, and it took six of their officers to get him in the back. When they finally got him to the station, he was in a fighting mood and managed to clear the sergeant's desk of everything that was on it. Somehow they managed to get him under control and put him in one of their cells. He was then sick all over it. Someone cleared it up, and they then left him to sleep it off.

When he eventually woke up at about three in the morning, they sobered him up enough to question him. It was then they realized he was only fourteen, although he did look older. That was when they then phoned us to go and collect him. I just wondered why he hadn't slept until a more reasonable hour!

We signed the papers to say he was now our responsibility and he would have to appear in court. As we walked out to the car, he looked very pale—not an easy thing considering he was black. I said, "Get in the car and don't you dare get sick in it." There wasn't a word out of him all the way home. Everyone else was just getting out of bed as we went in. Of course, they all wanted to know what had happened. Don rushed off to the bathroom. When he came out, I told him to go upstairs and sleep it off. Our next-door neighbour came around to see what was going on as some of the children had gone there to tell them about the arrest. The friends we had called the night before got in touch to see if he was okay. I went upstairs to see if he was feeling any better. I wanted to offer him something to eat or drink. He looked very sheepish and couldn't understand why we weren't bawling him out. I explained that, yes, we were very angry, but our fears had overtaken our anger. We were now just very relieved to see that he was okay. We wanted to hear his side of the story, which turned out to be more or less the same as what we had been told by the police. We then told him how people were getting in touch to see if he was okay. We told him there were a lot of people who cared about him and had been very worried. He found it difficult to believe that anyone cared enough to worry. I put my arm around him and explained that he had better get used to it because, with his personality and character, there would always be people who liked and cared for him.

We soon got over that situation, and never in the time he was with us did we have any more problems. We had plenty of laughs, maybe, but no problems. We all used to like practical jokes. One night before bedtime, I put fake poo in his bed. When we all went up to bed that night, there wasn't any reaction from him, which we thought was odd. But Lee let out a shout! Don had found it, said nothing, and transferred it to Lee's bed. The next night when we went up, I tried to put my pyjama jacket on and found the sleeves knotted. I would do them apple-pie (short-sheeted) beds and in retaliation would find small toys in ours. This was the sort of atmosphere that was in our house. For Marie's ninth birthday, Don gave her a card with instructions on how to find her present. She had to follow a trail of clues until she found it.

Don had an appetite the same size as his personality; it was enormous. One Saturday we invited some friends to stay for dinner. I cooked toad-in-the-hole—sausages baked in batter. I made it in two dishes. There was plenty in one of them for everyone. After I dished it out onto the plates, my friend asked if I was saving the spare one for the next day. I told her that one was for Don. She didn't quite believe me until he came home, sat down, and proceeded to clean his plate. If anyone had leftovers on his or her plate, all eyes would be on him as we knew what was coming: "Have you had enough? I'll finish that if nobody minds." He wasn't overweight. He did look after himself, going to the gym regularly. He had a very good physique as he never tired of telling me.

Shortly after Don came to us, we heard that Ros, one of the girls we had fostered, was staying at a local residential home. Marie and I made arrangements to go see her one evening after we dropped Don off at Cadets. As we turned into the lane leading up to the home, something small and white flashed in the car headlights. I stopped to see what it was and realized it was a little animal. I picked it up because I knew that sometimes a child can have problems communicating with adults but will talk to a pet while an adult is close by. So this little animal might have been very important to some child in the home. I asked Marie to hold on to it while I drove the rest of the way to the buildings, but she was having none of it. (Very brave is my Marie!) I had to leave it in my lap, so it was just as well I didn't have far to go. When we reached the house Ros was in, I carried the critter with me and knocked on the door. Ros and a group of young girls came out. When I asked if anyone had lost a pet, they all shouted in unison, "That's A's pet rat!" Well that was one lucky rat—because I didn't drop him then and there. I thought to myself, *I've been carrying it all the way up the drive and it hasn't bitten me, so be very brave and hold on to him and don't show yourself up in front of these kids.* A staff member was standing behind the girls, and she wanted to know where this girl "A" had been keeping him because no one on the staff had known about him. They told her that he had been kept in the airing cupboard during the day and in her pocket when any of the staff were about. *At least it has an owner and I can soon pass it over*, I thought. I will never learn not to have these positive thoughts. The kids all said that A wasn't there. She had run away and no one knew where she was. The staff member said they would not be able to cope with the rat and asked me if I could possibly hang on to it until such time as they found her. Well, I suppose fostering a rat can't be as bad as fostering some of the children we had met. When we got home, we had to find a box to keep him in until Robert could make something a bit stronger. The girl eventually turned up and went to live with her sister, but she could not keep the rat—Adolph was his name. She asked if we would mind looking after him permanently. By then I had actually got quite attached to him. As Don and I were the only ones brave enough to pick him up and talk to him, it was left to us to look after him and clean his living quarters. Staff members at Don's school were trying to start a hands-on zoo to teach children how to look after small animals. Don asked if he could take Adolph in to join it as they had a female rat and were hoping to mate them. I agreed because he was becoming a bit smelly, and the only place we could keep him was a bit too near the kitchen. So it was with mixed feelings that I delivered him to his new home where he would have lots of company. Ah, another positive ending to a foster placement.

Soon it was time for our annual holiday. This time we weren't provided with a mini-bus so we had to make our own arrangements to get us and all the kids to Yarmouth where we had use of the same caravan. Several of our friends came to the rescue. One couple offered to drive down with us on the first weekend and stay overnight. The following weekend, another friend came down and stayed from Friday until Sunday and took some of the kids home. We were okay when we were there; it was transporting all of us and our luggage that caused the problem. But with the help of our friends, we had another good holiday.

In November of that year, my parents celebrated their sixtieth wedding anniversary. Chris made a giant family tree for them. He had his work cut out as there was so many of us. Along with sixteen children (I'm the youngest) my parents now had fifty-four grandchildren.

But what made it really awkward was the fact that some of my brothers and sisters had been through divorces, so some of their children had different mothers or fathers. There were also about six or seven great-grandchildren. Chris did a marvellous job, all in italic writing, which really gave it the finishing touch. On the night it was unveiled, everyone was duly impressed. Christmas came and went, and soon it was another new year.

Chapter 16

O ver the years, Dean was having problems of his own. He was feeling angry and frustrated. He wanted to know about his birth family. He often said he wished he had been our birth son, not our adopted son. We tried to help him as much as we could, and we answered any questions he had. We even managed to get in touch with his old social worker who came to see him and talk him through his past history. Things were getting difficult for him at school. He was also dealing with the normal teenage hormones, which didn't help. Unlike a fostered child, we couldn't get him counselling except by going through our own GP, and the only thing that he could offer was family guidance.

To try and help him, we thought that perhaps, if we had a break from fostering, we could concentrate on him and give him more of our time as both he and Marie had shared not only their bedrooms and toys but us as well. Maybe it was time to put them first. As much as we had enjoyed fostering and had been very lucky with all our placements, Dean and Marie must come first. It was with a heavy heart that we asked for Chris and Don to be moved.

Chris was approaching his eighteenth birthday and was placed in supportive lodgings, which is what would have happened anyway, but Don was placed with another carer in a nearby town that wasn't too far away, so we were able to keep in touch with him. He eventually left care and joined the army. He got married to a lovely girl and has two wonderful children. I used to write to him whenever he served abroad.

The house seemed unnaturally quiet. Our washing machine and tumble dryer must have thought they had reached their retirement as they weren't being used night and day. I got myself a part-time job. Unfortunately, within a few weeks of this change, Robert's dad, Jan, died. It was a very sad time as he had lived with us for fifteen years. Dean and Marie had been very close to him; he had always been there for them. We got on with our lives and redecorated their bedrooms the way they wanted them as they would not be sharing with anyone else. We attended family guidance together. During one of these sessions, Dean was asked how he felt now that we had stopped fostering. He said he didn't like it because the house was too quiet. Marie was asked the same question, and she gave the same answer! They both said it didn't feel right, and somehow it didn't feel like their home anymore. When we got home, we asked them if they really felt like that or if they had responded the way they thought everyone wanted them to. They were both quite adamant. They had meant it but hadn't liked to say anything because they thought we were the ones who didn't want to foster anymore. We talked it through with them some more and decided together that, if that was what they really wanted,

I would ring social services. We made an agreement with them that, this time, we wouldn't accept a child until we talked it over with them first. Additionally, they wouldn't need to share a room because we now had a spare room, which used to be Jan's. We agreed that I would contact social services to get the ball rolling.

There were no problems regarding our return to the system. I decided I would have to give a month's notice at work, but I should have known better. Our supervising social worker said she had two girls who needed somewhere within the next several weeks. She asked if I could run the placement along with my job or leave my job early. Luckily I had an understanding manager as he let me off with a fortnight's notice. We were back in action.

We had never been taken off their books as our supervisor had kept on asking us to go back, and she lived in the hopes that I would cave in, so we didn't need to go through the lengthy assessment process. They just had to do a quick update and police check, which was much less complicated than the initial assessment.

The initial process, when we first went into fostering, started with an interview with both Robert and me together, and then one each on our own. Jan also had to be interviewed as he was living with us. We had to provide references from people who weren't family members. We then had to write near enough our life history, starting with where we were born, how many siblings we had, their names and ages, what schools we attended, and a list of jobs we had after leaving school until the time of our application. My parents were interviewed as we were a close family and had regular contact, and they could possibly have negative feelings that could affect the children. Mr and Mrs Jim gave us a written reference and were also interviewed. We had to share our thoughts on discipline, a child's place in the family, how we would feel and cope if we had a child from a different race or culture, what we would be expecting from the children, why we wanted to foster, and what we expected to get out of it. Then we had to endure medicals, which were very thorough, although not as intrusive as the one we'd had for Marie's adoption. Our medical history was discussed, and we decided how we would cope if one of us were ever ill. The only thing that wasn't important was how we were financially situated because they provided a small maintenance. We didn't realize we would be eligible for that until we applied, not that it would have mattered. There was also a police check. Then, when everything was ready, all our papers went before a panel of people who decided if we were suitable to become foster carers. This was carried out over many months. It wasn't until it was all over that we realized how much we actually remembered of our own history, especially employment details, as I'd had seven permanent jobs. Also I had done some agency work within a ten-year period. Robert's work history wasn't so bad as he'd had only four jobs since leaving school. We got through it all, and as anyone who fosters will tell you, it was worth it. Now prospective foster carers take a skills-to-foster course while their assessment is being carried out. Back when we applied, we did not do any training until we were approved.

Chapter 17

The two girls arrived with their social worker at the end of January in 1990. We had a completely new lesson to learn with these two, as the older girl had an illness called phenylketonuria known in short as PKU. Her body was unable to break down protein in food, so once again, food shopping was an education. I had to check every tin and packet to see how much protein the contents contained. She was allowed only ten grams a day, so each meal for her had to be measured out, with a portion of her daily ration at each meal. She did have special bread and milk, which she was allowed freely, but it did mean she had to have a packed lunch for school. We also had to be careful when she went to visit friends for tea. We had to make her hosts aware of the problem without making too much of a fuss. If we weren't watchful, she would help herself to foods that were not allowed, which we understood. We often felt sorry for her; it can't have been easy at ten years of age to watch your sister and your friends eat crisps and things. She had to attend Great Ormond Street Hospital for check-ups every three monthly. In between she had to have a blood prick tests, which her dad used to do on contact visits. The girls were a bit of a handful, and we used to dread the hospital visits. Both Robert and I had to go because, if we weren't on our toes, the girls would try and run off and get on a different train carriage. But we managed never to lose one. On one particular visit, we were talking to the specialist while the girls were behind her playing in her sink and getting water everywhere. Luckily she was used to them and just laughed when she realized what was going on. She could see we were trying to listen to her but also trying to look over her shoulder without drawing too much attention to the girls.

The doctor was telling us that they didn't know enough about the illness to say how it would affect her in adulthood as their research records went back only slightly over twenty years. They were hoping that, as people got older, their bodies would adjust and enable them to increase the amount of protein they consumed. The oldest person on their books was in his or her twenties and had managed to increase the daily allowance, so this was a positive outcome. Of course, this was over twenty years ago, so I would imagine research has come a long way forward.

While the two girls were with us, they went to our local village school along with Marie. She did find it a bit strange at first as normally the school-age children we'd had until then had gone to schools in the local town. But as the girls were several years younger than Marie, they mixed with different friends, and they didn't intrude on her social life.

In September of that same year, we had our first new-born, pre-adoption baby. We had to go to the maternity unit to collect her. She was only two days old, like a little doll sleeping in her cot waiting in a side ward. It was not easy changing her nappy and dressing her for the first time while a midwife and social worker were looking over my shoulder. It wasn't that they were watching to see if I was doing it right; they were only trying to talk to her, but I felt as if I was under scrutiny. As this was our first new-born, I felt I had to get it right and not break one of her arms in the process. It is amazing how the whole dynamics of the house changes when there is a baby living there. Everyone competes to see who can be the most helpful.

A pre-adoption baby is usually in foster care for only six to eight weeks. The birth mother usually has six weeks to make a final decision so she's not pressured into making a hasty decision and regretting it afterwards. She can also see the baby if she would like to. Some mums do, but most often they don't as they feel this would weaken their resolve. In the meantime, the social workers choose the family that will be lucky enough to go to panel as prospective adopters. They are not allowed to visit until the mum has made her final decision and signed the appropriate paperwork. In our case, while all that is going on, we made the most of our time by making a fuss over the baby. It was lovely when we took her out; she attracted so much attention because she was so tiny. I used to love the night-time feeds. Everyone would be asleep, so I had the downstairs—and the baby—to myself. It was so peaceful—no arguments, no television blaring, and no one wanting to take over and feed her. We could sit and chat without interruption.

She stayed with us for a total of eight weeks. During the sixth week, social services rang to say that introductions to her new parents would start the following week. Arrangements were made for them to come and meet her. I think I was as excited as they were because we had been through their side of it when we adopted Marie. I knew exactly what they were going through and how they would be feeling. As soon as they walked into the house, we handed her over to them because, until the child is in your arms, you don't really feel that she is yours. With Dean it had been slightly different because we didn't know if we would ever get to adopt him or if he would have to go back to his birth family.

The next ten days were taken up with the new parents coming to visit and getting lots of hands-on experience. This was not just for their sakes, but also for the baby as she had to get used to someone else handling, feeding, bathing, and dressing her. They were a really lovely couple. They already had a young adopted daughter, and for me it was a nice feeling handing her to a ready-made family. As we stood back and watched them go, we were feeling a little sad, but mostly we were pleased to see the look of joy on their faces as they drove away. They did send some lovely photographs the following year, which was really nice of them.

The two older girls were soon due to go home to live with their dad. They had been with us for almost a year. We met them several years later, and they looked healthy and happy so hopefully everything worked out for them.

At the time, we felt the two girls were hard work, but when I think back over the years and compare them with some of the children we had in later years, I realize that they weren't that difficult and were actually two very nice girls. I hope that wherever they are now they are doing well.

Chapter 18

C hildren come into care for a lot of reasons. January, February, and March of 1991 brought us three very different children for three very different reasons. It is very easy to think that, once a child is placed with carers, he or she should be able to stay in that one place until either go home or reach the age when they leave care. But it doesn't always work out that way. One of the reasons children get moved around from foster carer to foster carer and even to residential homes is that, although parents can't cope for whatever reason, they sometimes have problems seeing their children settling down with other families.

One ten-year-old boy had been in numerous placements. As we'd had fourteen years of experience, we were asked if we would have him for a few days to see if we could get him to talk. We had him over a weekend. The havoc he wreaked was beyond anything that we had experienced before. It didn't help that we were in the middle of redecorating our living room. We did, however, manage to get him to talk to us about why he was so destructive. He told us that his mum and dad were telling him that they were redecorating his bedroom, and if he wasn't settled anywhere by the time it was ready, then he could go back home. They had been telling him this for about three years, and he was afraid that, if he let himself be happy somewhere else, then he would never be allowed to go home. What chance did he stand? We met him again six years later. He was still in care, living in a residential home because no carer could cope with his behaviour. He had made it very clear that he would never accept another family.

One of the saddest cases we ever had was an emergency placement of two brothers, a one-year-old and a three-year-old. Before they came to us, they had been put into private fostering by their parents who were students from another country living in our area but studying in London. They used to visit their children by appointment only and never realized the abuse that was going on in their little lives. There had been twelve children living in that house. The parents could visit only by prior arrangement, so when the parents arrived, their children were waiting downstairs to see them. What the parents didn't know was that there was someone upstairs with the other children keeping them quiet. After the visit ended, the little ones would be taken back upstairs and locked in the room with the others. Eventually a neighbour reported them to social services when they noticed a lot of children coming and going.

We had to take the boys to our local hospital for a medical check-up, and it was confirmed that the one-year-old had been sexually abused. These boys were with us for a week before their parents were traced and came to collect them. The parents weren't at fault; they thought they had placed them somewhere safe while they got on with their education. Social services advised them on how to look for safe carers. We could only hope they took that advice and acted on it.

The first week in March we had two more little boys that the police had found wandering around the local town. One was two years old, and his brother was three. When the police finally found their mum, it appeared that she hadn't been feeling well and fell asleep on the sofa. The boys had climbed out of the window and gone off for a big adventure. They were able to return home once social services were happy that Mum would take more care in future not to leave open windows anywhere in the house without safety locks on them.

Chapter 19

T he middle of March 1991 saw our next placement, which was supposed to be short term, but even today he is still driving us nuts. We were asked if we could take a two-and-a-half-month-old little boy, David, and also do some work with his parents as they lacked the confidence to cope with a new baby. They were having difficulty feeding him. He'd had to spend some time in hospital as he wasn't thriving, and the doctors would discharge him only if there was someone available to help his parents. We could see that they loved him very much and were prepared to work with everyone so they could eventually take him home and look after him themselves.

They were all taken to a day centre every day where they were shown how to mix David's feed, make sure it was the right temperature. They were also taught generally how to handle him with confidence. My days consisted of dropping him off every morning and picking him up every afternoon to bring him home for the night. There were no day centres open at the weekends, so that meant they didn't get to see him unless we could fit a visit in between doing things for the other children, which we did as best we could. Occasionally we would pick his parents up and bring them back to our house for Sunday lunch. During their time with us, they could take him for walks and get to know the people in the village. Almost always someone would recognize David and stop and have a chat with the family. Sometimes members of our family would be here at the same time so the family got to know most of the people involved in David's life. We seemed to spend most of our lives trying to work around other people, but if that was what it took to give the child any help, then that was what we did.

We had a really good relationship with David's parents and were really pleased and honoured when they asked us if we would help them to organize his christening and be his god-parents. We made arrangements with our local vicar. On the festive day, some of their friends and relatives were able to make it out to our village. Quite a few of our family members also joined in the celebration.

Around this time, we received an invitation from Don who had joined the army and was having his passing out parade. We readily accepted and were looking forward to seeing him. We thought we would turn it into a weekend break as we were going to be travelling to Dover. We planned to stay the night down there and go across to France for the day. We headed off very early on Saturday morning, allowing ourselves plenty of time. That was just as well because, when we arrived at the Dartford toll booth, the car just came to a full stop and wouldn't start again. With the help of their security people, we pushed the car to one side of the road and waited for the AA.

They turned up with a pick-up truck and towed us off the motorway. As it was so early, nowhere was open, so we had to wait around until the nearest garage finally opened.

We did get it fixed and managed to arrive only a few minutes late, so we didn't miss much of the event. But we used all our money mending the car, so we had none left over for our weekend. It was a lovely day; the weather was perfect. We were so proud of Don. We enjoyed a spectacular parade, and the celebration finished with a slap-up meal in their canteen. Given the standard of the food and the way it was cooked, we could understand Don's choice of being in the army. It was also the first time we met his dad and the rest of his family, which was great. We could see where Don got his personality from. We all hit it off straight away. We ended up having to make the return journey that night, which Dean and Marie understood. David was obviously too young to voice an opinion.

We arrived home shattered but safe. Everyone was too tired to do much on Sunday, but Robert had arranged to have Monday off, so we promised we would take the kids bowling in the next big town and have lunch out.

So, the next day we set off. We got about halfway there when the car started to judder. We thought we had better stop off at a friend's garage on the way. We signalled to turn right into his garage and were waiting for the traffic to clear from the opposite direction when I looked into rear-view mirror. I could see a car approaching that showed no signs of slowing down. I took my foot off the brake to give myself some control, and in seconds he had ploughed into the back of our car. We shot forward, but I had steered toward the kerb, and our car went onto the grass verge instead of the oncoming cars. He had hit us so hard that we couldn't open any of our doors to get out. Our friend had heard the bang. When he ran out, he recognized our car. He armed himself with the appropriate tools to get us out. The children were shaken, but luckily David had been strapped in tight and was safe. We went to hospital to get everyone checked over. Dean suffered from whip-lash and ended up having to wear a neck brace for a few weeks. The car suffered more damage than the rest of us; it ended up a write-off, so we had no transport for six weeks while the insurance was sorted. During this time, everyone in the village rallied around and took us anywhere we needed to go, including getting David to his contact.

In April of 1991, we had a nine-year-old girl who stayed for three months. In July she moved to live with her grandparents. Shortly after she left, we were asked to have a new-born pre-adoption boy. It was going to be a challenge because David was still only seven months old and needed lots of attention. But he was at the day centre every weekday, and that gave me time with our gorgeous little baby. I wanted to make the most of him because I knew he would probably be gone within a six-week period. We had been told that mum had already made a decision and had even signed the papers so social services could get straight on to finding the adoptive parents.

At the beginning of July, my sister Phyllis asked me if I would like to go on holiday with her and her husband to Hayling Island at the end of August as Robert would be working on the harvest. I had to get permission from David's parents and social services to take him with us because that would mean that his parents could have no contact with him for a week, but that was all approved. The timing seemed to work out for the pre-adoptive baby as social services found a couple very quickly, and he could be passed to them without too long an introduction. Because he was only a month old, he would adapt without any problems. We were told that the introductions could start the week before we were to leave on our holiday, and he would be gone by Thursday, which would give us a few days to pack and get to my sister's house. Will I never learn?

On the Friday before we were to leave, we received a call from our social worker. She told us that they had chosen a couple, but they were away on holiday and weren't due back until the same day we were due to leave. She did say they would try and track them down to tell them the news. My sister Phyllis said not to worry too much; we could manage the two babies between us. On Monday, social services rang to say the couple had rung to say they were cutting their holiday short and coming back early. Hopefully they would arrive home on Tuesday, but on Tuesday we received another call. They had missed the ferry and wouldn't be able to make it until Thursday. On Wednesday we received yet another call. They were on their way and would definitely arrive to meet us on Thursday. When they finally did arrive, we felt as if we were meeting family members—they were lovely. And, as this was their first child, they hadn't got a clue what they would need. They hadn't had time to think about anything except getting to us before Saturday. So on Friday we went shopping together. I made sure they had the important things for feeding and sterilizing, along with plenty of nappies and clothes, a pushchair, and bedding. Now they had enough to take care of a baby. All they needed was the baby to go with it! On Friday afternoon, they drove away with all their shopping and their new son. They still keep in touch, and every Christmas we get a wonderful newsletter telling us everything that has happened during the year so we can keep up to date with them.

We set off for our holiday. By now we had replaced our car with a second-hand Mondeo that had rear-facing seats in the boot, which were ideal for the smaller children. We arrived at the caravan at around lunch time, and we quickly unpacked and headed off to the beach. David loved the sea, but more than that he loved the treats from the ice cream van that came around the caravan site every day. As soon as the truck's jingly music started playing, his little arms and legs would go ten to the dozen until one of us brought him his cornet. Mind you, he wore more of it than he ate. Dean made his own friend there and was happy to go off with him and do his own thing. Marie stayed close to me. One day Phyllis offered to look after David while Marie and I went off to town on our own, which was nice as time on our own was becoming quite rare. More and more we were having placements that overlapped. The holiday went by in a flash, and soon it was time to return to the daily routine of school and contact visits.

Marie started at the local secondary school and loved it. She preferred it to the village school where, for the last year, she had been the only girl in her year. They were only back at school for a few days when our favourite twins, Veronica and Linda, along with their older sister, Patricia, arrived back with us. This time they had their pet dog with them. The family had been hoping to put him into a kennel, but it would have been very expensive. We thought, why not? We fostered a rat, so we might as well foster a dog for a change. Patricia stayed for only about a week, but Veronica and Linda stayed for five months.

In October, we attended a planning meeting for David. It was decided that, as the family were doing so well, they could have him home all day unsupervised. But he would be back to us at night and at weekends when there were no social workers available if anything went wrong. Things were going so well that it seemed that Christmas would be a good time for him to go home full time. Obviously, his parents wanted to see him over the Christmas holidays as it would be his first Christmas and his birthday a few days later. We arranged for them to come to us on Christmas Day for dinner. Robert planned to pick them up in the morning and take them home in the evening, but like so many of our plans, it didn't work out.

We had a wonderful day. Veronica and Linda were able to go home over the holiday, so we had only David along with Dean and Marie. Robert set off to take David's parents back to their flat, but when they got there, the communal front door was locked and they had no way of getting in because their neighbour was disabled and had settled down for the night. So back they had to come. We rearranged beds and found them somewhere to sleep. We often laughed about it later. When the holidays were over, it was agreed at the next planning meeting that David could return home full time by the end of January. We would still keep in touch and visit them to make sure that they were coping. They had our telephone number if they needed help at the weekends.

The first few weeks appeared to be going well, but then David's dad phoned to ask if we could have David back for a weekend as they were finding it difficult to cope with him, and it was getting very stressful. So we agreed. Social services were aware of it, and as we were his godparents, we were more than happy to do it without any payment. We carried on doing a weekend once a month for several months, but as he got more mobile, they found it even more difficult, and we ended up having him every other weekend. He was like a little whirlwind. It took four or five of us full time running around after him to keep up with him. One Sunday he kept trying to get into my kitchen cupboards. He had a habit of trying to empty them out. I kept lifting him away from them. He ran into our living room, got hold of a box of toys, just scattered them, and then called me. I went in and started to pick them up. Before I knew it, he shot through to the kitchen, opened one of the cupboard doors, and proceeded to pull everything out. What chance did two of his parents have?

On another Sunday, we went to visit my sister Phyllis. The children were all outside playing while we were chatting in the front room. In walked David eating a great big lump of cheese that he had helped himself to out of her fridge. But it didn't seem to matter what he did; we couldn't get angry with him. Everyone loved him and accepted him the way he was. There was no such thing as disciplining him as stern words bounced off him like water off a duck's back. He had no fear of being told off and would just look at us and laugh. And this hasn't changed much over the years.

Chapter 20

In February 1992, after David had officially returned home, we were asked to have a two-year-old boy. He had been placed in a residential home along with his older brother and sister with the hope of keeping them together, but there wasn't enough staff to cope with this little one who he was obviously going through the terrible twos.

When the doorbell rang, I went to answer it. In walked a social worker with a child under one arm. She apologized and said that was the only way she could get him from the car to the door safely as he had a tendency to run off. This was our first sight of Logan, a figure who was going to loom large in our lives.

She set him down on the floor, and he looked up and beamed at me. It was very difficult to recognize if it was a boy or a girl. His hair was shoulder length, and he had a really pretty face. Marie and her friend took him off to play while I spoke to the social worker, who didn't have a clue as to how long this placement was going to last. They were trying to get a care order on all the children. It could be months before that got to court, and there was no way residential care could cope indefinitely with such a young child; they are set up for teenagers. I could understand the problem; residential care wouldn't have been the right environment for him as sometimes the young people there can display very violent behaviour.

The social worker went through his background with me, which is normal procedure. We set up a date for a placement agreement meeting, which has to be within a certain amount of time after a young person comes into a foster carer's care. That meeting usually involves discussion about the day-to-day routine for the child, contact arrangements, and any extra help that may be required. The social worker then went off leaving us with this pure bundle of mischief.

From here on in we were in for a very lively time. Thankfully we were not aware of it; otherwise, we might have called her back.

He settled in well and loved playing outdoors. In fact, we had a job to keep him inside the house, he was so full of energy. I used to watch him from the kitchen window with my heart in my mouth. He would run from one toy to another, play with a football, then climb onto the slide. But he didn't use the slide in the normal way that other kids played on it. He'd climb up the slide and jumped off the top doing a somersault. I was also childminding another little boy who was a year older than Logan. They got on really well. When they played football, the ball would often go over the wire fence that separated the garden from the vegetable patch. Most kids would go through the gate to retrieve the ball, but not Logan. He would climb up the wire netting and throw himself over, yet again doing a perfect somersault landing, and coming back the same way. For the sake of my nerves, I gave up watching him for the most part. I did happen to watch him actually climb up the ladder of the slide, but, oh, he had not done that so he could slide down. He did a somersault down the slide, got up, looked around to see if anyone was watching, rubbed his bottom, and ran off to play something else.

David was still coming to us at weekends. He and Logan became very close. It seemed that we were doing everything in duplicate because what Logan did David tried to copy, even though he didn't necessarily get it right each time.

At the end of February, Veronica and Linda were due to go home. We waited with bated breath, but it went okay. They were happy to get back to their mum. After they left and before the next placement, my mum and dad came to stay for a few days. They loved our village as it reminded them of Ireland where they could go for walks down the lane or up to the village where they would meet people and have a chat. This time my dad found the visit a bit more difficult with Logan because he never knew where he was, and he was concerned that, with his declining eyesight, he might trip over him! But it never happened, and as usual, they had a good time.

Contacts were set up for Logan to see his mum. A social worker would come and collect him, but unfortunately, more often than not, his mum would not be where she was supposed to be, and he would be brought home fast asleep because he had cried so much he exhausted himself. In the end, we had to tell him that he was going for a drive with the social worker so that, when his mum did make the meeting, it was a nice surprise.

We were limited as to what we could do at the weekends when we had both Logan and David, but a few carers from our support group got together and decided to organize a car boot sale to help each other have a good clear out. Fortunately, it was organized for a weekend when we didn't have David. We went along to a local football ground. We were to take it in turns to look after the stand so that everyone got a chance to have a look round the other stands. We all duly arrived with our belongings and kids. Everything was going well, and we were quite busy. Robert was keeping an eye on Logan. He took him off and bought him a lovely large yellow truck to keep him occupied. I had finished one of my stints on the stall. While Logan was playing nicely with his new truck, I went to get my bag from the car. When I turned around, Logan and his truck were nowhere to be seen. With my heart in my mouth, I asked everyone if they had seen him. They all said he had been there a minute ago, but no one had seen him go. We searched up and down the rows without any luck. By now Robert and I were having quiet panic attacks, but then someone called us to go up a bank to look at the football pitch where there was a game in progress. There, in the middle of the field of players, was Logan playing quite happily with his truck oblivious to the game going on around him. He had managed to find a small hole in the wire fence and thought the field would be a good place to play. It was with very red faces that we ran out and got him off the field. After that we kept a much closer eye on him.

At the beginning of April, we were asked to have a ten-year-old boy. We actually went to the children's home to meet him. Then he came to us for tea and an overnight stay before finally moving in just before Easter, which worked out as we were able to take him out along with everyone else over the holiday. During the weeks, my days now consisted of getting Logan ready for contact, taking David to hospital appointments with his mum and dad, having Dean and Marie's friends over, dealing with social workers who were popping in to see the children, and attending training sessions. We certainly were busy.

In June, I went to see the doctor as I was suffering from a severe pain in my stomach. The doctor was very concerned because of my history of Crohn's. He rang the hospital straight away to get me admitted. He then told Robert to take me home so I could pack some overnight things. Then he was to take me to the hospital. He was worried that I might have septicaemia, and he didn't want to waste time. We got back home and organized a friend to look after the children while Robert took me to the hospital. The following day he contacted social services to let them know what had happened, but we were okay as friends had rallied around to help out with the children so they wouldn't have to be moved. Robert could start work later in the mornings. He brought all the children to see me the next evening. They didn't stop long as Logan spent more time under the bed than next to it, bless him. I had to stay in for the week wired up to a drip, having nothing but liquids. I lost a stone in weight, which I didn't mind. They did numerous tests and X-rays. For some reason, they said, a few dead Crohn cells had become inflamed, which was the cause of the pains. I was discharged with instructions to take things easy (ha ha). Robert had managed really well. The house was still standing, and all the children were still alive and well fed.

During the summer months, we also had some youngsters for respite while other carers went on their holidays or just had weekend breaks. In September, David's parents were allocated a house. Robert helped them to decorate it before they moved in. When it was ready, David's dad suggested we have a night out together. We organized a baby sitter, and I had my first taste of dog racing, which I thoroughly enjoyed.

At this time, Logan started going to our village playgroup several times a week, which he really enjoyed. He would watch at the window in the morning waiting for the other children to turn up, and then he would jump up and down trying to get me to hurry up and take him.

In November, we were asked to have a twelve-year-old boy Steve. He made little difference to Dean or Marie as he was going to school in another town and had his own friends, although they did hang around together sometimes at the weekends. Marie had a boyfriend who lived in the next village. He had three siblings, and all of them were around the same ages as Marie and Steve our foster child. We all used to go out together at the weekends to places like Mountfitchet Castle or anywhere that had a play area. All the kids got on well with each other, so it made for some very pleasant outings, which included both Logan and David. Don had been back from serving overseas and came to visit. Chris, Vicky, and Nicole were still coming for the odd Sunday lunch. Another year was coming to an end, and in December, Steve went to a friend's house for a weekend sleepover. Logan had an extra-long contact visit with his mum, and I managed to take Marie and one of her friends to a Jason Donovan concert in Wembley, which we all thoroughly enjoyed. At Christmas we had the usual ten or twelve sitting down at the table. On Boxing Day, I had my birthday treat of going out for a meal instead of having to cook for everyone.

Chapter 21

Before we knew it, 1993 was upon us. January was very quiet no extra placements. By February, everyone realized that Logan had been with us for a year and no work had been done by his social worker to get his freeing order so that he could be placed for adoption before he got much older. So work had to be started. There was a change of social workers, and the new person started getting his background information together so that it could go to court. In the meantime, the boy I childminded started going to a nursery in the next-door village for full days, and Logan missed him. He asked if he could go with him. We asked his social worker, and she was agreeable providing it wasn't too tiring for him (perish the thought!). We started sending him three days a week as he still wanted to carry on going to the village play group in the mornings of the other days. My days were now taken up with taking him to nursery in the mornings and picking him up in the evenings, but it did free me up a bit during the day, although I still had plenty of meetings, training sessions, dental appointments, hospital appointments, and general housework to keep me from getting bored.

Marie had turned thirteen and was doing well at school and making lots of friends. The only problem was that she kept bringing them home, and they didn't want to leave. Most stayed overnight at the weekends. Dean was in his last year at school and was looking forward to leaving. He didn't like school at all, so we had plenty of phone calls from his school complaining about his behaviour. His attitude around the house began to deteriorate and cause us lots of problems. I never knew when the school was going to ring. Many of his problems centred around the fact that he was adopted. He was trying to find out more about his background. It didn't help the situation that Marie had been writing to her birth mother for a few months. I had met her by accident in Stevenage. At first I thought she was Marie and wondered what she was doing there rather than school. Then I realized who it was. We spoke for a while. I explained to her that Marie was asking all sorts of questions that we were finding it difficult to answer, not because we were worried that she was asking, but because we didn't know the answers. So we agreed that Marie could write directly to her to see if she could answer them. Marie and I sat down together to write the first letter. After that she was happy to carry on by herself.

We organized for Dean's old social worker to come and have a word with him to answer any questions he had. I think it made matters worse because his sister was living just across the road, and she wanted more information. She wanted Dean to be as eager as she was to find out more about their family history. As we had no idea where his birth parents were living or even if they were alive, we put him in touch with Family Finders, a division of the World Association for Children and Parents (WACAP) that works to match children with adoptive parents. Unlike Marie, he had to be interviewed to see if counselling would be advisable before any information was given. It must have seemed so easy for Marie given what he had to go through. He was told that his sister and he could go on the register of people who wanted to trace their families to see if any of his family members wanted contact. They did, however, find that he had some younger brothers who were still in care. Contact could be organized through social services. It might be in the interest of the other youngsters for them all to meet. It was all set up; his two brothers were brought by their carers to his sister's house so they could meet. Dean was pleased to see them, but they had suffered so much emotional damage, he felt they wouldn't be able to cope with too much contact. Although another visit could have been organized at a later date, he never really followed it through. But someone did find out where his father lived and offered to write to him to see if he would like to have contact, as Dean was eager to find out as much as he could. The answer came back that he would, and his present partner would also like to come and meet Dean. It was arranged that we would meet with them at Victoria Station as that was halfway between where they lived and where we lived. Marie offered to stay at home as she felt this was special for Dean.

We arrived at Victoria Station not knowing what way this meeting would go. Dean was nervous, which was to be expected. I don't remember how we recognized each other, but we did. Rather than risk the two of them being nervous while asking questions in front of us, we left the two of them together while his partner came with us to look around the shops for an hour. We felt that would be long enough for them to size each other up. When we met back up again and had a cup of coffee, they both seemed happy to carry on with future meetings. Because of the distance involved, we suggested another meeting in Victoria Station, and if that went well, then perhaps Dean could go to them for a weekend as they had three other children they would like him to meet. Dean's dad's partner made a comment that threw Dean and Robert and me. She told Dean that he should now think himself lucky as he had his mum and dad there for him at the same time as having Robert and Marie. Dean and I looked at each other but decided not to say anything. We spoke later and decided that she probably didn't understand the difference between fostering and adoption. We both knew that Robert and I were his mum and dad. A second meeting was organized, and that went well, so we made arrangements for Dean to spend a weekend with his dad and his dad's partner during the summer holidays.

In the meantime, we had several very short-term placements. One was a girl for a two-week respite break, and the other was a young lad who needed regular respite once a month for the weekend. That started off okay, but after four or five weekends he and Logan had a few problems, which we tried to keep on top of. But it came to a head when Logan was eating at our dining room table and this other boy went in and banged Logan's head so hard against the table that he split his lip. Given that he was six years older than Logan, it wasn't a fair match, so we had to say that he wouldn't be able to come to us for any more weekends as it was too dangerous for Logan.

Dean's weekend went okay. He was pleased and it was agreed that he could go and spend a week there before he started college in September. We took him down there so we could meet the rest of the family; that way it was easier for Dean to be able to talk about them as we would know who he was talking about. Around the same time his sister, who lived across the road, also started having contact with them, but they kept their visits separate so they each had the proper space to get to know everyone.

Dean started at the local college on a car mechanics course and got an apprenticeship at a local garage one day a week and at weekends. This meant he couldn't get down to see his birth family quite so easily, but they kept in touch by phone, and his sister kept him up to date.

Time carried on. Logan started back at playgroup and the nursery although this term he wasn't enjoying nursery as much, but still he carried on going to be with his friends.

Earlier in the year, Logan's social worker had started work on his life story and had been taking him back to places he had lived with his mum so that photographs could be taken to go in his folder. He enjoyed the days out even though he had no recollections of any of the locations. But the procedure did get information recorded for at a later date in case he needed to do any follow-ups.

The rest of the year went by without much fuss. Steve was reasonably settled with us now and was attending the Sea Cadets regularly twice a week, which he enjoyed.

We did go to one open evening to raise funds. They had turned it into a fun night. Steve dressed up in one of my dresses and a pair of my high heels, which he walked in better than I could. We borrowed a wig. Marie applied make-up. He should have gone to stage school. People who didn't know him were amazed at the end of the evening when he took his wig off. They had been buying raffle tickets from him all night and had no idea that he was a boy. He was that good an actor.

Logan and Steve got on well together as did the whole household really. We still had David coming along every weekend and most days during the summer holidays. We didn't go away that year as there was so much going on with individuals, but we did have a lot of days out to the coast or on picnics to places that the children suggested. All in all, we had a very busy year, but soon Christmas was upon us again. It wasn't such a busy one this year, except visits from family and friends during the Christmas week. Soon we were wondering what the next year would bring.

Chapter 22

We saw 1994 in with some friends and spent New Year's Day at my sister's in High Wycombe. They were now settled there with no more thoughts of going back to Cornwall. It was so much nicer having them living closer.

The children all started back to school. Logan was the only reluctant one; he still wasn't happy going to the nursery, but he still went.

During the previous year, social services had decided that, if we wanted to carry on fostering children in the age range of eleven and older, we must officially become teen carers at the same time as being foster carers for children from birth to ten years. We weren't too happy as this system was being pushed to be more business like. Rather than the children being part of the family, everyone had to sign a contract when the children came in. Part of the contract stipulated that we now had to go to fortnightly support groups for teen care while still attending our once-a-month support group for fostering. Also part of the deal was that teen carers were to be allowed one weekend off a month; there were carers who did only teen care respite.

If respite carers were not available, other carers helped out by having an extra child for a weekend. It all sounded fine, but we still had under tens and were not entitled to a break from them, so when did we actually get a break? We felt it wasn't fair on the children who had to keep going away once a month. They were being pushed out of our home, and they sometimes feeling left out of the things we were doing with the younger ones. The only positive thing was that it was now recognized that we were doing a difficult job, and as such we should be paid a fee that was ours for the teen care child on top of the allowance. But we would be paid only the allowance for the younger fostered children because they were considered less difficult than teenagers. They should have tried looking after Logan and David for a while.

We now only had one week a month when we didn't have to attend a support group. Once a month, on a Friday, we had to take our youngster to respite placement, which more often than not was twenty miles away, so that took care of Friday night. Then we had to collect him or her by four o'clock on Sunday, so we were limited in what we could actually do in our weekend break, but we kept to the deal.

Late one evening in February, we were asked to have an emergency placement of a fifteen-year-old boy. When Tel arrived with his social worker, he looked quite scared. Luckily, Dean was babysitting next door, so I took Tel around to meet him. I thought it might make him feel more relaxed, and he told me later that it had. He said he was feeling nervous, but as soon as he met Dean and saw his long hair and leather jacket, he felt a bit more relaxed to know there was someone near his own age. Tel fitted in like a glove. He got on with Dean, Steve, and Logan, but the one that he got on best with was Marie. They were more like brother and sister than Dean and Marie.

His dad gave him a scooter for his sixteenth birthday, and he would go off all over the place on it. One day he said he was going to go visit his aunt who lived in Milton Keynes. He got a bit lost on his way home and ended up coming back on the motorway until he got stopped by the police near Watford. We asked why he'd gone down as far as that instead of getting off at a nearer exit, and he said he recognized Watford and knew his way from there to Hertford, and from Hertford he was confident about finding the rest of the way home. I dread to think how many extra miles he did that night. He had a terrific sense of humour, and we had lots of fun with him. We told him one story that got everyone laughing. We told him that I used to make lunches for the soldiers during the war, and the only time it got a bit difficult was when they were fighting in France. Because they couldn't get back at lunch time, I had to take sandwiches to them. He asked all sorts of sensible questions about how I would get there and back. We told him one of my friends owned a plane and would take me there and wait to bring me back home again. We felt we very nearly had him believing it. I didn't know if I should be insulted or not to think he must have thought me old enough to have been around during the war. At least it was the Second World War and not the first!

When Tel first came to us, one of my jobs was to teach him how to cook for himself. He said he was very worried because he couldn't even make a sandwich and a cup of tea. I told him not to worry. He wouldn't even know that he was learning because we would have lessons at his own pace. The first thing he learned was how to make a sandwich because sometimes I didn't have time to do lunch. Then we progressed to toast. From there it was on to baked potatoes. Quietly, he helped me when I was cooking for everyone. Before he knew it, he was able to cook himself a reasonable meal if I wasn't around.

Mostly all the kids would help each other so that no one was left alone to do anything. Marie and Tel would often go to town and spend time with her friends or go for walks. He tried to help Robert with the gardening but gave that up as a bad job when he started pulling plants up instead of weeds. But it was all good fun.

Logan's freeing order had come through, which meant that social services could now start looking for a long-term family. It also meant that he had to have a last goodbye visit to his mum and siblings, which we knew was going to be tough on him. It would be a very emotional meeting. He may not realize it was his last visit, but they would, and their emotions would be running high; Logan would feel it from them. The meeting went ahead more successfully than I anticipated. He came home in a happy mood loaded down with a pile of presents from them, which we looked after until he was old enough to look after them himself.

At about this time, Logan was getting very unsettled at the nursery. It was getting harder and harder to get him to go. He was coming home in tears more often saying that the others were hitting him and calling him a naughty boy. When I tried to talk to the person who ran the nursery, she wasn't at all interested. I even stayed there one day to help out and saw for myself how she ignored him when he asked a question. They were playing a memory game. She would put a collection of toys on the floor. After the children had studied it for a while, she would cover it up with a cloth. One time, when she turned around to talk to someone, one of the other children pulled the cover off. Logan started to put it back on. The teacher caught him doing it and told him off for touching it. When I explained to her that he was actually putting it back, she told Logan that he shouldn't be touching it for whatever reason. She totally ignored the child who had pulled the cloth off. So I could see why Logan was constantly getting upset. I decided that it was time he cut down on his hours there. A little time would be enough for him to mix with other children.

Logan was getting more and more energetic and taking up most of my time. Social services agreed that, because we were having monthly breaks from the older boys, we could have the odd break from Logan. He went to one carer in a local town, but when we went to collect him, she said that, although he was lovely, she'd had a job to cope with him and would rather not have him again. Social services found another carer willing to give him a go. This particular carer and her family really took to him. Like us, they had a large garden for him to play in, so it was lovely when we went to collect him to be told that he was wonderful and they were prepared to have him again.

We did keep them to that, as that year was exceptionally busy. Steve was having contact with his older sister, so that meant trips back and forth to where she lived. Tel had meetings with his solicitor and a court hearing to attend. I was attending meetings for all the children for various reasons. Steve was attending counselling sessions, and we still had to take him to Cadets twice a week. And we still had to attend parents' evenings for all the children, Marie included. Any school plays, fêtes, sports days, and the like had to be supported. Bear in mind we now were associated with four different establishments. Tel was able to keep up his own contact with his parents as he had his scooter. In between, we made time for Marie to see her friends either in town or at their homes, and sometimes they came to us. There was no public transport to or from our village, and I dreaded to think of the amount of miles we were knocking up. It's no wonder we got through cars rather quickly.

Logan was still taking up most of our time as he needed constant watching. He had no fear of anything or anyone. When Robert and I took him out shopping, we couldn't each hold one of his hands because he would start doing somersaults between us while we were walking along, which could be very awkward in a crowded place. But we did have to be aware that at least one of us was holding him. And if I stopped to talk to anyone, I had to make sure it wasn't near a lamp post or any kind of pole because he would shimmy up before I realized what he was doing. When we had David at the same time, we really had to be on our toes.

One of my brothers lived in Lincolnshire. When he and his partner went to Tenerife every year, they would leave their car at our house, and we would drive them to the airport. They would also leave us their house keys so that we could use their place for a few days while they were away. Logan loved it there. We would take him to the mud flats where he could run free. He always said this was his special place with us.

As it got nearer to the summer holidays, I thought I had better start making arrangements to end Logan's attendance at nursery. I knew he wasn't happy there as quite often I would get a phone call to go and pick him up because he was having a temper tantrum. I would go down there, and as soon as he saw me, he would cheer up.

One day when I asked the teacher what the problem was, she said that the children were told to get ready to go outside to play, and when Logan was ordered to put his shoes and socks on, he refused. I asked her if she had asked him or just ordered him, and she said she had ordered him. I told her that Logan liked to be asked to do things, and as soon as he was ordered, he would refuse. I always got him to do as I asked. She then reported me to social services and told them that I had trained Logan to do what I wanted him to do. I responded that I treated him like a human being. The teacher told me that people like him and his family were of such a low class that they had to be treated as such. I informed the person in charge that Logan would be leaving the same day the older children broke up for the summer. I was told that I couldn't do that without the permission of social services. The teacher had already spoken to his social worker, and they had agreed that he would stay there until a few days before he started the village primary school. (*I think not!* I thought to myself.) I asked the teacher if she or the social worker would be picking him up in the morning and then holding on to him until I got home after a day out with the other children. Well, neither of them was going to do that! It was my job to deliver him and collect him. I explained to her very nicely that I would be doing no such thing as we were not going to spend the holidays making arrangements around Logan attending nursery. It wasn't essential for him to go. Also he was as entitled to a summer break as much as the rest of the family. So unless either she or the social worker was prepared to do the running around, then as far as I was concerned, Logan would be leaving. I also spoke to the head mistress of our primary school and the educational psychologist, and they both agreed that it would be better for Logan to have a natural break over the summer before starting proper school because, at the moment, he was being made to have a sleep at midday, and no one wanted him falling asleep in class. Therefore, he must have time to adjust his time clock to working a full day. Even that didn't make a lot of difference to the teacher, but she still had me to convince.

When the day came for him to say goodbye to his little friends, he was excited to be leaving. Off he went that morning with his bag of sweets to hand out as goodbye presents. But when I went to collect him, he was very upset because the teacher hadn't allowed him to hand out the sweets or to say goodbye to anyone. When I asked her why, she said it was because he wouldn't be leaving and would see them all on Monday. I was beginning to think she had a mental deficiency. I then asked her who would be picking him up at eight o'clock on Monday. Same story ... So I took Logan by the hand and said loud enough for everyone to hear, "Logan, say goodbye to all your friends because you won't be back here ever again." He beamed, said his goodbyes, and walked out of there with the biggest smile I had ever seen. I have never seen that teacher since that day; neither would I ever put another of my foster children into that nursery again. I would rather travel twenty miles in another direction.

Earlier in the year my sister Phyllis had been diagnosed with multiple myloma, so we all spent a lot of time going to see her as much as we could. When she was finally admitted to the Royal Marsden Hospital, as many of the family members as could tried to go and see her. One Sunday there were about twenty of us around her bed. The staff members were very understanding and were intrigued at seeing so many family members turn up together. As Phyllis was in her own little room, we managed not to disturb anyone else. It meant so much more to her to have all of us there at the same time instead of visiting separately because we all enjoyed each other's company. It was a really emotional day; we were all able to tell her how we felt about her as we acknowledged that she wasn't going to be around for much longer. She was going to be missed so much, but she would never be forgotten.

Sadly, Phyllis died on 4 July. The only member of the family who didn't make it to her funeral was my brother Jim who lives in Australia. But our thoughts were with him.

Both Logan and David had known her quite well, so they were upset that they wouldn't be able to see her again. We felt they should know why she was gone out of their lives. We didn't want them to think she had just disappeared, especially as too many people just vanished from their lives without explanations.

Dean went off to Cornwall in August to spend a week with the twins and their mum. They came back with him and spent a week with us. Although older than Logan and David, they all got on with each other and played well together.

We started Logan on swimming lessons, but after a few weeks, the instructor said she was sorry, but she couldn't manage him. He had absolutely no fear, and she felt he was in danger. She said that, when she asked the children to drop feet first into the pool from where they were standing at the edge, all the others did it correctly. But not so Logan. He just stood at the edge of the pool and leaned over, flopping into the pool at an angle rather than feet first. So, for me, it was back to the drawing board to find him something constructive to do. Social services decided it was time to do some life story work for him, and a professional assistant spent a lot of time with him sorting through photographs and taking him to places where he had lived with his mum and siblings. They made a scrap book for him to keep.

We had just got over my sister's death when my mum had a stroke. She had been living in Ireland with my sister Nuala, Bab's mum, for a while, so it wasn't so easy to go and see her. My sister Elizabeth and I went over to spend a few days with her while Robert looked after the children. Robert brought Logan to the airport so that he could wave to us as we were going out to the runway. Logan understood where I was going and that I would be back. I managed to get over a few weeks later with my brother Willie; this time it looked as though our mum might not have much longer, and I was torn between staying there until the end or coming back because of the children. It wasn't fair that Robert had to cope while going to work at the same time, although Dean and Marie did their fair share along with some of the neighbours. We decided that it would be better if I came home as mum could last for a few more weeks. It was one time when we wished we weren't fostering because I would like to have stayed with her until the end. I was back home for only a few days when Nuala phoned at 4.30 in the morning on 12 October to say that had mum had passed away.

In Ireland, when people die, they are buried within three days, so I didn't have much time to get my act together and get there. We already had plans made so that, when the phone call came, I would phone two of my siblings, and they in turn would phone others and so on. (Remember, there were sixteen of us!) That way, no one had to spend time on the phone. Instead, we could all focus on starting our various journeys. Again, we had it all sorted. My brother Nick, who lived in the next village, picked up Dean and me. Then we went on to collect my sister Terry from High Wycombe. From there we headed to the ferry. We all arrived within hours of each other; even my brother Tony from America managed to get there the night before the service. My dad was so pleased to see us all there apart from Jim, who remained in Australia. There was no way he was going to make it with such short notice. We were spread out all over the village where Nuala lived; friends and relatives gave us somewhere to sleep. Most of us stayed at Nuala's. There were bodies everywhere, but we didn't mind. We enjoyed being together; it was such a shame that Robert couldn't make it. We had not had time to organize somewhere for the children to go at such short notice. Dean came with me, but Marie offered to stay at home and help Robert.

Most of us stayed for about three days. If it hadn't been for the fact that we were there for Mum's funeral, we all agreed that it was a fantastic time and enjoyed just being together. We all said how much Mum would have loved to have seen us like that.

Logan had started the village school in September and was loving it. Social services paid additional fees so he could have a classroom assistant there to keep an eye on him in case he had any problems settling down. His concentration span was limited, and we were trying to stop him from disrupting the rest of the children. In the meantime, his educational needs would be assessed. Social services had found potential adopters for him and had scheduled a blind viewing for the prospective adoptive parents so that they could see him. Based on their gut reaction, they could decide if they wanted to go ahead. Unfortunately, due to unforeseen circumstances, nothing came of it, so it was back to square one to find him special parents. All the time he was getting older, and fewer people want to adopt a child five years old or older; most people would prefer to adopt babies. Logan missed me while I was away, and he had a few bad days at school. I did talk to him on the phone, but it wasn't quite the same. He settled down once I was back home. He was very popular with the other children at school; they all loved him, and he had many friends.

Steve was getting ready to move on to long-term carers. He had been with us for two years, and we felt that, as he was getting older, he needed to be nearer to Stevenage. Then he wouldn't be able to use the village as a place to hide away, and he would be in a better position to see his friends outside school. He was always very quick to find excuses for not socializing. He was introduced to his new carers and spent several weekends with them to get to know them. When he had time to think about how he felt about moving, he agreed that it would be in his own interest to move closer to town, so he finally moved in November after we had a little goodbye party.

Logan asked if he could move into the downstairs bedroom, to which we agreed with hearts in mouths. He loved being in there. He told Robert that he wasn't going to like his new mummy and daddy as he wanted to stay with us. Robert explained to him that his new mummy and daddy would be special people who were specially picked for him, and after he met them he would grow to love them.

Tel was still with us and getting about on his bike. He now had a small part-time job working at Martin's, the news agents, either after his college classes or at the weekends.

Shortly after Steve left, we were asked if we could take a young girl just coming up to sixteen years old. Julie arrived with her social worker. Marie and Julie decided that they would be happy to share a room, and that worked okay.

Dean and Tel went to the same college together doing the same mechanics course. One day early in December, Dean phoned to say that Tel was in trouble for smashing a car at college, and he had walked out of the school. Then his dad phoned to say that he had turned up there, but so had the police. They had arrested him, but they let him go after several hours.

Near the end of term, Logan was getting a bit tetchy at school as they were no longer doing the normal routine; some lessons had been put on hold because they were practising the Christmas play, and he had difficulty coping with changes in his routine.

We were still having David at weekends, and one particular weekend we took both him and Logan to see Father Christmas, which got them excited. As a result, David fell over and had to be taken to the hospital to have stitches. The hospital staff members were very good, and they even put a plaster on his teddy bear in the same place that he had his stitches. When we took him home, Logan was really concerned about him and wanted to keep him with us so that he could look after him, but obviously we told him that David had to go home to his mum and dad.

Now it was finally time for all the play performances. I went to Marie's first talent competition in the afternoon to watch her perform, and I was so proud when she won! Her boyfriend lifted her up on his shoulders in the hall. We then went to see Logan's play that same evening. He was to play the part of a big brave mouse. He had come home from school with his face ready painted, and somehow, he managed not to rub it off before returning in time for the play.

A social worker who had worked with some of our previous children called around to see us as he was trying to invent a new game and thought our house would be a good place to try it out. I don't know what ever happened to it, but all our kids enjoyed playing it that evening.

Another year was nearly over. As I look back, I try to work out what time we had for ourselves because there were also so many doctor, optician, dental, and hospital appointments. Then there were parents' evenings, review meetings, planning meetings, and social worker visits for all the children individually. We attended three support groups every month. And we kept "our kids" in contact with their friends, including Dean and Marie, but somehow, we managed to have a bit of a social life. Because of the loss of my sister and my mum, we weren't able to have a holiday that year, but nobody seemed to notice as I did manage to take them out quite a bit during the summer holidays. That Christmas we felt we needed to be near family, so we spent Christmas day with my sister Elizabeth and her husband, George, in Wembley. On New Year's Day we went to John and Terry's in High Wycombe. Another year over, and we were still alive.

Chapter 23

We all went into 1995 still missing mum and Phyllis, but we had to concentrate on the children. Julie was settling in nicely, but as she was sixteen, we were told that she couldn't stay long and would have to move into supportive lodgings even though she was still going to school doing exams. We tried to get them to leave her with us at least until she had finished her exams, as she was doing so well with her studies. Teachers and administrators at her school were pleased with how she was coping given her circumstances, but this made no difference. She was given a moving date near the end of January. She packed her belongings and was sitting in our living room in tears when the social worker came to collect her. She grabbed me and didn't want to let go. I had to walk her out to the car, and we both had tears in our eyes. It was so upsetting to see her go in that state, but there was nothing we could do but give her our love and wish her all the best.

Soon it was Tel's time to move on. This was a little easier as he was ready and feeling confident about his move. He was happy now that he could actually cook his own meals without panicking. And he learned to budget his money. Even so, we knew we would miss him, especially Marie as they'd had a really strong friendship. We were happy for him, and it was nice to have a positive ending to our relationship. He did keep in touch for a while after he left. The only news we had regarding Julie was that she was finding it very hard to cope and had got in touch with social services asking for some help. She was especially finding it hard to cope financially. But as she was sixteen and no longer in care, there was nothing they could do to help her, and she had to manage on her own. Life was very unfair for sixteen-year-olds back then; at least now they can be looked after until they finish their education, so we have come forward in that respect.

Julie had only been gone a few days when we received a call asking us to have a fourteen-year-old girl. She arrived about two days before Tel moved out, and they just about managed to say hello to one another.

Heather settled in very quickly, especially as she was with us less than three weeks when we were asked to have a new-born boy. We had to go to the hospital to collect him. When we got home, I had to fight with Heather for a chance to feed him, but there was no competition when it came to changing his nappy—the honours were all mine.

This baby's time with us had a completely different ending. He came as a pre-adoption, but his mum came to visit a few times, and within six weeks, she decided that she couldn't part with him. She ended up taking him back home with her. In some ways it was a shame that she had to miss his first six weeks, but at least she did have some breathing space to make a rational decision. It was lovely to see them go off together.

When he had gone Heather, was at a loss for a few days. I knew what she was going through as we all felt that way when the babies move on. But it didn't take long to get back to normal. She settled in at her new school and started making friends. We started taking Dean, Marie, and Heather to riding lessons on Saturday mornings. It was something they all enjoyed and could do together. It wasn't long before Dean and Marie wanted to give it up, but Heather continued on her own for a few more months until she decided that she would rather spend Saturdays seeing her friends in town. She still managed to keep in contact with her friend who lived locally, and we had her to come and stay at the weekends to save us running back and forth if they wanted to see each other for both days. It worked well because on some weekends, Heather would go and stay at her friend's house, of course after her parents secured permission from social services. In order for Heather to stay overnight with her friend, their family had to agree to be police checked. After that, they could come and go as they wanted.

Marie went to Belgium on a school trip. She came back full of having been in the trenches, and she'd had a thoroughly great time.

Logan was still enjoying school. He settled down again after Christmas when everything got back to a normal routine, but there was still no news on finding him an adoptive family.

Everything seemed reasonably peaceful in the house as Heather was causing no problems. She was getting on well at school and was good about the house. She fitted in with everyone. Logan was his normal self, driving us up the wall, but it was what we were used to with him. On the weekends when David was with us, things were still a bit manic, but again we didn't expect anything else. Because Heather was allowed to stay at her friends some weekends, we asked social services not to schedule her for weekend respite. It felt more normal for her to be staying with her friend. We were still being given the odd weekend break from Logan, which Robert and I appreciated. Dean and Marie benefitted from those quieter weekends too.

That year we had decided that we would take a trip to Cornwall to see Toni and her twins, who had been with us for a while. Heather asked if she could stay with her friend. Dean and Marie wanted to do their own thing. And we thought Logan would benefit with some time on his own with us. We set off on a Saturday morning. The journey took most of the day as we travelled at a comfortable pace and made several stops. By the time we got there, we weren't too tired, which was just as well because, by the time their dog stopped jumping all over us (he recognized us from having stayed with us) and the twins had shown us around, it was getting late. Then we had something to eat and decided on an early night.

The next morning, the girls showed us around the town and told us how to get to the beach, which Logan thoroughly enjoyed. After lunch, we went to the local leisure centre where all three of the children spent most of the afternoon in the pool going down the snake slide. By dinner time, they'd had enough, so we all went to get something to eat. The next day we all went to a lovely beach that was a bit further away; we sat and sunbathed while the youngsters went off trying to catch crabs, or in Logan's case, anything that crawled. The twins had to go to school during the day for the rest of the week as it wasn't their half term until the following week, but that gave us time to spend with Logan. We took him to the beach every day, and when the girls got home from school, we took them all to the leisure centre. Too soon the week was over, and we were due to go home on Friday. Before we left, we had a walk around the local market and eventually set off at lunchtime having said goodbye to the girls in the morning before they went to school.

We hadn't been on the road long before Logan fell asleep. We woke him up to take a toilet stop and grab a drink, but he no sooner sat down than he started to fall asleep on the table. We set off once more not bothering to stop again as he was fast asleep. We eventually arrived home at about eight o'clock. Robert had to carry him from the car and put him straight up to bed. He just about woke up for his breakfast the next morning. Then, laying himself down on the settee, he promptly fell asleep again. He did manage to wake up for his dinner but was back up in bed by seven and stayed asleep until the next morning. He was a bit livelier but not much. He sat and watched television for most of the day. I was getting a bit concerned about how he would be at school the next day, but he managed to get up in time and went off, quite happy to tell everyone about the wonderful time he'd had and to show them the bucket full of seashells he had collected for the nature table. That must have been the best week ever at school. They had no problems with him. He sat in his place all the time without wanting to get up and run around as he normally did. We asked social services if they could send us off on a holiday like that at least once a month as it had tired him out so much he didn't have any energy left to mess about at school, but they declined. Well, you can but ask.

In May we were asked to take a teenage girl, which upset the apple cart a bit as we now had three teenage girls. There were the usual girly arguments and fall outs. One centred on clothes being borrowed without permission and being given away to school mates. Although denials were strong, it was obvious who the culprit was as it hadn't happened before Kate arrived, and one of her friends was seen wearing Heather's jumper. These things had to be dealt with, which caused a lot of friction in the house. But it was no more than any household with more than one teenage girl. We did have a break from this when we were asked to have a boy for a few weekends to give his carers their respite. The girls seemed to calm down during the weekends when he was with us.

Not long after Kate arrived, we were asked to have a two-month-old boy who had fallen off his parents' sofa during one of their arguments and had been injured enough to cause concern. We had to pick him up from the hospital. The pickup was a bit sinister as we had to sneak in and collect him through some back doors because both parents were in the hospital creating a fuss, and the doctors wanted Anthony moved to somewhere safe until the case could be fully looked into. He was wonderful. The girls now had something else to fight over. He was a bit more breakable than their belongings, but nevertheless, they did love seeing to him. Marie stayed out of most of the arguments as it wasn't her things that were being borrowed. The friction was mostly between Heather and Kate.

Logan adored Anthony, and the baby started to thrive and gain. In the end, we were calling him our sumo wrestler. He was just so cuddly. The extra weight soon came off him when he started to move around on his own. I realized that I had been having it easy because now that we had Anthony, my days were organized around his needs.

The social workers and doctors had finally come to an agreement that it would not be in Anthony's best interest to return home unless an assessment was carried out. That meant his parents would be allowed supervised contact most days. The mum and dad didn't want to be together, so that meant that contact had to be at separate times. So, two days I had to take him to see his mum in her flat and spend about one hour with her, then another two days I had to take him to his grandmother's house where he could have contact with his dad. I got to know grandma quite well because often Dad wouldn't turn up, and I would end up having coffee and a chat with Grandma. Luckily, she was only too pleased to be able to see Anthony. Sometimes it would have been nice if the dad had phoned to say he wasn't going to be able to make it. Then I could have spent some time at home catching up on mundane things like ironing and housework. Sometimes we felt as if our lives were on hold when we had to take some of the children for their contact visits because no one takes the lives of the carers into consideration when making these arrangements. Quite often we had to remind social workers that we did have more children to look after than the one they represented. They made all the dates and times for meetings and contact visits without asking us if it was convenient. It was especially when they made an appointment for around 3.30 in the afternoon and I had two or three others coming home from school, but we did seem to manage.

Dean had his eighteenth birthday that year, and he started to think about spending some time getting to know his birth father, so we made arrangements for him to go and see them for about five to six weeks when he broke up from college. He came back a bit confused as the history they were telling him was slightly different from the history that social services had on record, but he needed time to think about it. We were there for him when he wanted to talk.

Logan's educational statement had come through and it was decided that his needs were too great for him to be able to cope in mainstream school; he should be found a place at a special needs school or a special unit. I would be informed at the appropriate time. All we could do now was wait. His social worker went off on maternity leave. I heard nothing for weeks, and it was getting closer to the end of school year. Logan was talking about going back to see his friends in September. I felt that he should be told that he would be leaving the village school, and he should know where he would be going in September. I tried getting hold of his social worker but to no avail. I spoke to her manager, and she explained that she had gone on maternity leave and didn't want anyone else taking the case over. I explained the situation and said I felt someone should be working for Logan as things needed to be sorted out now and not in September when she was due back. She said they had no one who was free enough to take the case on, so I asked if I could have her permission to ring the education department to find out what school he would be going to as there were only three weeks left before the end of term. She told me it would be okay for me to do that. I phoned the education dept only to be told they hadn't allocated him anywhere yet and would be in touch when they had found somewhere. I phoned them again the next day, the day after that, and the day after that. I told them I would keep phoning until they gave me the name of a school as we were talking about a child who had feelings and not just a name on a piece of paper. I told them that this particular child needed to be able to say goodbye to his friends and know where he would be going. On a particular Friday, they still said they would get back to me. So, on Monday morning I phoned again. Again on Tuesday. By now I think they were getting the message because, on Wednesday afternoon, they gave me the name and telephone number of a school.

I hadn't long put the telephone down when Logan's social worker rang and wanted to know what I thought I was doing. I told her that, as Logan now had only just over a week to go before the end of term, we needed to let him know what was going to happen to him and give him time to say his goodbyes. I didn't want his departure to be like his departure from nursery. She told me in no uncertain terms that I was not to contact the school. I was to let it rest until she came back from leave; it was her job to do that and not mine. I politely told her that, if it was her job, then she had better get off her bum and do it because, if I hadn't heard back from her by Friday morning, then I would be getting in touch with the new school so that I could organize a day to take Logan to see it and meet his new teachers. Logan was the one that I was worried about and not her, I assured her.

I heard nothing by Friday, so I contacted the head teacher of the new school who readily agreed with me that he needed to have a visit as she needed to see him and me as well. So we made arrangements for me to take him over the following Tuesday. That would give him Wednesday and Thursday to go back and tell his friends all about his new school and be able to say goodbye before leaving on Thursday. When I told the head teacher at the village school, she was pleased that this time he would have time to get used to not going back there.

When we arrived at the school on Tuesday morning, the headmistress came out to meet him. She was really nice and spent a lot of time with him. Then we took him to meet the teacher who was going to be assigned to him and to see the classroom where he would be having his lessons every day. There were also several of the children he would be working with for him to meet. He was so pleased to be able to go back to school the next day and tell his friends his news about leaving. He told them where he was going and how much he liked his new teacher. The only sad part was not only leaving his friends at the village school but also leaving his classroom assistant. He had grown to love her very much and was really sad at the thought of not seeing her every day. But I did take him shopping after he had been to see his new school, and he bought her a lovely butterfly brooch to remind her of the times that she used to take him out into the wild garden whenever he got upset in his lessons and needed time out. He was now ready to move on and was able to talk positively about where he would be going.

It seemed as though we were just coming to terms with having lost my mum and Phyllis the year before year when my dad died. Again we received a phone call early one morning, and there was no time to get the children sent anywhere. Robert once again had to stay behind and hold the fort while I went with the rest of my brothers and sisters. This time the parish priest did give them one extra day to allow time for Jim to get over from Australia, which he managed with only hours to spare. This time, all fifteen of us gathered together; only the sixteenth sibling, Phyllis, was missing. As much as I wanted to stay longer, I could manage to stay only for a few days, but we did say that we would organize a family reunion so that we could spend more time together under happier circumstances. It was left to Jim to let us know when he would be able to get back over from Australia next time, and he would bring his wife.

Logan's life seemed to be at a standstill. No suitable prospective adoptive parents had come forward, and his social worker was beginning to get worried. She started suggesting that we consider taking him on long term. Robert and I did think about it whenever we had a spare minute, which wasn't often. We both agreed that it was tempting to go for it so he could get settled, especially as he'd been was going around asking members of our family if they were going to be his new mummy and daddy. In fact, several of them had been very tempted. It was only when they saw him in action that they had second thoughts. It was one thing coping with him for a few hours when either we were visiting them or they came to us, but to manage his behaviour twenty-four hours a day was something else. We loved him to bits but were beginning to sag a bit at the edges. But his social worker kept chipping away at us; in the end, we felt very pressured and didn't know what to do.

Family Finders were now involved in trying to advertise for adopters. A social worker came to meet Logan. She took loads of photographs, one of which would be published in their magazine. I had to take him to her office so she could get to know him because she had to write his profile. That trip had to be fitted in between Anthony's contact arrangements and arguments between Heather and Kate.

Marie was getting on with her life. She was now fifteen and becoming very independent, but still bringing her friends home at weekends and some evenings. She was also taking singing lessons. She quite impressed the neighbours when she used her karaoke machine in her bedroom with the window open—until one of them complimented her on her voice. Suddenly she began to keep her window shut and the volume turned down.

Dean was still agonizing over what to do about getting to know his family. We told him we couldn't make any decisions for him, but if he felt that he wanted to go down again for a holiday, then that would be fine with us. His sister, who lived across the road, was getting involved and wanted to get to know them. We couldn't get involved in her side of it as we weren't her adoptive parents. She needed to talk it over with them, but there was nothing wrong with she and Dean talking things over together.

Life carried on in much the same vein, only now we could go out a little bit more in the evenings. As Dean was eighteen, he volunteered—for a fee of course—to babysit. We always made sure that Logan was asleep before we went anywhere; we knew that, once he was asleep, he was out for the count. We had experienced how heavy a sleeper he was when, one evening, he asked if he could play in Marie's room. We didn't bargain that he would lock the door, so when Marie went up, she couldn't get in. She knocked and called for him, but there wasn't a sound from him. Robert had to get a ladder, climb up to the window, and break a small plane of glass. The shards went all over the bed on which Logan had fallen asleep. Robert climbed in through the window and opened the door so Marie could go in. He then lifted Logan off the bed so that Marie could clean up the broken glass and change the sheets. Robert settled Logan into his own bed, and he never woke up until the next morning. So we felt quite happy going out after he was asleep. We normally only went to our local pub which wasn't far away.

Anthony's contact had increased. He was going to a family centre so that staff there could assess how his mum was interacting with him. This meant longer days for me because I now had to take him in the mornings, leave him there all day, and pick him up late in the afternoon just before Logan was due home from school.

David started school and loved it. He managed to get accepted for a school in his home town, which was a school for special needs. I used to go along to any meetings with his mum and dad as they were concerned that they wouldn't understand what was being said; they wanted to do their best for David. So the school knew me as well as they knew his mum and dad.

Because Anthony's contact was getting more and more involved at the same time as Logan's life story work and Family Finders profiles was taking up more time, it was felt that perhaps it might be a good idea if Anthony was moved to new carers who could give him the time he needed. That also might make it easier for him to be weaned away from our family before moving back home, as things looked to be going well. That would free us up and give us more time to spend on Logan.

We were pleased that Anthony would be moving to carers whom we already knew really well. We were used to socializing with them, which meant that Anthony already knew them, and this made it easier to build up his introductions to moving there. But it still didn't stop us feeling sad to see him go. Robert had grown quite attached to him and used to love taking him for walks down the lane in the good weather along with the dog. It did mean we couldn't see our friends for a while until we felt that he had settled with them.

Logan started his new school and loved it. He really liked his teacher and made new friends, but like all Logan's efforts, they could only last as long as his concentration, and it wasn't long before we were having complaints about his ability to sit still in class. He now had to go to school in a taxi, which added more problems because he needed to be supervised in the car, to which he took umbrage. But he soon came around to the idea. Quite often the driver would tell me that he'd had to go into the classroom at the end of the day and carry him out to the cab as he'd had a bad day and was refusing to walk out. Logan again had problems as Christmas approached and the routine changed yet again. It was the same old story—he couldn't understand why they weren't doing normal lessons. He thought that was why he was going to school. The taxi driver used to laugh because sometimes when he had to carry Logan out of the classroom, just to get the last action in, Logan would swipe at something on the way out of the classroom and leave a trail of destruction. He was certainly proving to be a challenge.

Another Christmas was soon looming. It was decided that Kate could go home just before the Christmas holidays as things were going well when she had contact weekends at home. We thought we might have a quiet Christmas with just Dean, Marie, Heather, and Logan, but the week before they broke up for school, we were asked to have a fifteen-year-old boy who was misunderstood. His dad had accused him of stealing his stepmum's jewellery and selling it. I was assured that there was no way this kid would have done it, but they did want him kept away from his friends in town as he was mixing with the wrong crowd; it would be better if he was not able to see them. We agreed to have him.

He was a fairly nice boy and very polite, but he wasn't too happy about not being able to get to town. When his social worker came to visit him, he would complain to her. She would sympathize with him and tell him that she would supply him with a taxi whenever he wanted to go and see his friends. Because he was excluded from school, a person had been appointed to collect him and take him to town so that they could go to the pictures or bowling or any leisure activity that he wished to do. This particular worker would come back with him and occasionally would have a cup of coffee and fill us in on what they had been doing that day. Quite often he said that the boy had asked him to let him wander around unsupervised. If the worker would do that, the boy promised that, while he was with his friends, he could get the worker anything he wanted from any shop in the town. So much for this misunderstood boy who wouldn't dream of stealing from his family! I believe that he didn't dream of it; I believe he actually did it. I gave up trying to understand the logic of his social worker who wanted him removed from town and who allocated a worker to entertain and supervise him during the week, and then supply him with a taxi so he could meet these bad, influential friends at the weekend. Apart from the moaning about being so far away from town, he wasn't too bad around the house and got on well with all the others.

Heather had made her Christmas wish list by sitting down with an Argos catalogue and ticking off the things that she would like. Marie and Dean had already given us their lists, and we knew what Logan wanted, so we were organized as far as the presents went. It was just the food shopping left to do. I thought I would do that the day before Christmas Eve. Dean offered to look after Logan so that we could get around the supermarket a bit faster. I'd had a phone call from Logan's social worker the day before; she'd asked if she could come and see him to give him his present. I'd explained that we would be going shopping but she was more than welcome to see Logan. Dean would be looking after him. She immediately jumped down my throat saying that I was not to go shopping and leave him at home. She would come and see him on Christmas Eve. I answered that she could leave it until then, but I still wouldn't have much time for her as I would be getting my vegetables and other things ready for Christmas day. She said she would come in the afternoon. That was okay with me.

I managed to do my shopping by leaving Logan with Dean, who was over eighteen and quite capable. There were also neighbours living close by who could be called on if necessary. On Christmas Eve, Logan's social worker called in. I told her she could talk to Logan in private in the dining room while I got on with my jobs, but she followed me into the kitchen. She told Logan to go into the dining room as she wanted a word with me first. I said she would have to excuse me, but I wasn't going to stop working. That was fine as far as she was concerned. The first thing she asked me was had we given any more thought to going long-term with Logan. I explained that we had given it a lot of thought, but we were feeling under pressure because of the way she kept on asking us. We'd already had a stressful eighteen months with first my sister dying, then my mum, and not so long ago my dad. Plus, Logan himself was wearing us out, and we just wanted to get Christmas out of the way and sit down next year and have a really long and hard think about it. It wasn't something that we could enter into without taking into consideration all the facts, like our age for a start, because as much as we loved him, we felt that he should be given the chance to have a younger set of parents who would have more energy to cope with him. She then went on to say that, if we didn't agree to go long-term with him, she would then make it her business to make sure that, by this time next year, he was in a residential home at the bottom of the pile.

Well, I just saw red! I told her that, if that was what it took to get her to leave us alone, then she had better leave our home and go away and start doing it, because there was no way that we were going to make such an important decision under those circumstances. I showed her to the door, hoping to catch her heels on the way out, but I don't think I was that lucky. I was furious, but I had to calm down and concentrate on giving the kids a good Christmas,

The children all got up bright and cheery and loved their presents. It would have been a wonderful day if it hadn't been for the fact that, every time we looked at Logan, all I could think of was that this time next year he could be in a residential home, and this kid didn't need that hanging over his head. But I still didn't feel happy about making a decision because it would affect the next fourteen or fifteen years.

We got over the Christmas holiday, and on the first day the social workers went back to work, I got a phone call from my support worker, who told me that Logan's social worker had put in a complaint against me saying that we were going out and leaving Logan in the care of the other foster children. I was amazed and wondered how she managed to come up with that one. She must have spent the whole of Christmas trying to think of something to complain about. I think I must have upset her slightly over the year. I explained to my worker exactly what had happened. They all knew that Dean was eighteen anyway. Also, she wasn't too happy about the pressure that was being put upon us, and said she would deal with it. We never heard any more about taking Logan on long term, which in a way annoyed me as they are very good at sweeping things under the carpet in their favour. It seemed that we now had to watch our backs with the social workers at the same time as we covered ourselves against allegations from the children. Well, we survived it, and each of us with clear conscience. I wonder if she could say the same.

All too soon, another year was coming to an end. We were wondering how much longer we were going to be able to cope as there was no end in sight for Logan's stay with us, and he was getting harder to work with as time went by. The only saving grace was the fact that the people who were having him for respite were still prepared to have him, so we did get occasional breaks. But we did now have to try to work with someone who was determined to make life as difficult as possible. All we could do was look forward to the New Year hoping it was going to be better than the last two.

Chapter 24

There was nothing new to start the year with—no emergencies over the holidays. Everyone managed to get through without being had up for murder regarding Logan. We even had David for a few days, which was nice. So 1996 came in quietly.

With Kate gone, things calmed down with Heather and Marie. Now, with only the two of them, no more clothes went missing. Daniel was still here he was now provided with a taxi to take him in to town on specific days and a home tutor was supposed to come and do work with him here.

We took Marie to an open evening at college as she had a Saturday job working in a health and beauty shop in town, which she thoroughly enjoyed, so much so that realized that was what she wanted to do as a full-time career.

At the end of January, my brother Dermot was coming over from Ireland, and I needed to go to Stansted Airport to collect him. I explained to Daniel's tutor that I would be taking Daniel with me as I didn't know how long it was going to take me and I didn't want to leave him on his own in the house. She said that she would stay with him until I got back. Reluctantly I agreed and set off when she arrived. However, when I got back there was no one in the house, and one of my cupboards had been ransacked. It happened to be the one in which I had kept a tin full of £1 coins, because with five teenagers needing £I every day for dinner money, I liked to keep some coins to one side; otherwise, it would have been impossible to find five £1 coins every day in my purse. I couldn't say exactly how much was in there, but there was quite a lot as I had been saving them for a while. I immediately rang the tutor to ask why they hadn't been there when I got back, and she said they had finished what work they had been doing, and she felt no need to stay with him as he was old enough to look after himself. I said he certainly was, and thanks to her he looked after himself very well by stealing from us. I also told her that I didn't usually leave them unattended until I was pretty sure they could be trusted, so I thanked her very much for what she had done. I then phoned his social worker, who said he wouldn't have done such a thing. I told her to take her blinkers off and see him for what he was because they would have the same problem in his next placement if she wasn't careful. He certainly wasn't coming back to us. I told her that, if they found him, they could place him somewhere else. She phoned me later to say he had turned up at the offices to say he didn't want to come back to us (surprise, surprise). She would be placing him somewhere else. I told her I would be reporting the theft to the police, which she tried to talk me out of. Then I had a phone call from his new carer to ask if she could bring him back to collect his belongings.

I said they could, but not until I got back from a meeting I had to attend as I didn't want him in the house while I wasn't there. Well, guess what? When I came home they had already arrived. Luckily, Dean had gone upstairs with him to get his things, so he didn't have a chance to steal anything else.

A few weeks later, I got a call from his new carer saying he had absconded from her taking about £200. She expected my sympathy, but there was no way I could offer it. I told her that it was no more than I expected and that was why I had asked her not to bring him here to collect his things while I was out. I told her she should complain to his social worker as they hadn't believed me when I had told them what happened while he was with us. I told her to also be aware that there wasn't much the police could do as he was living in the house and hadn't broken in. We never heard much more about him after that.

Life carried on here with Heather and Logan much the same. Logan was still having problems at school. We were still under pressure from his social worker; she never let up. Heather was now having contact with her birth family, but there was never a chance of her going back home to live even though contact went well.

Dean had decided he would move in with his birth family to get to know them. We supported him in this and helped to move him down. We promised that we would visit as often as we could, and he could come back to see us whenever he wanted because, as far as we were concerned, our home was his home and always would be. We understood why he had to go as it was the only sure way he had of getting to know his background and come to terms with it before he could get on with his future. He also had a very good friend who lived locally, and he used to go up and down to visit him, which was lovely as it kept more than one door open for him at our end.

Family Finders were still looking for a long-term family for Logan, but the older he was getting the more difficult it was going to get. We were still getting the odd weekend respite, which was a help. Mostly Logan who was now seven years of age was happy if things were going in a routine. Every morning he would come downstairs as soon as he heard Robert getting up for work. Then he would sit in the dining room watching a Disney film. Robert would make him a cup of tea and give him some biscuits. Robert would then get his own breakfast, and they would watch telly together until I came down. At the beginning or end of a video, there was always an advert for Disney World, and Logan would always ask Robert if we would take him there. We promised him that, if we ever got the chance, we would.

In April, we received a call in the early hours of the morning. We were asked if we could take a three-year-old who had been found wandering the streets. The police brought him to us, and he settled well considering how many strange people he must have had dealing with him. He stayed with us for four days while social services looked into why he had been allowed to wander at that time of the day, and why he had been able to get out of his home. It was eventually sorted, and off he went. Heather missed him as she had done most of the looking after him. I didn't get much of a look in.

A few days later, another call came, and we were asked if we could take two brothers as an emergency placement. Both had been beaten by their dad. But that lasted only for about twenty-four hours as the allegations were found not to be true. While they were with us, a fourteen-year-old girl was placed with us for a two-week period. She'd had a falling out with her mum and had asked to be taken into care as she didn't feel safe, but that was another case of a difference of opinion between a mum and a daughter. This used to happen quite often, but these situations always had to be taken seriously and investigated, although when these children came here, we had the best of them because they made the most of it, turned it into a holiday of sorts, and were never any trouble to us. We even enjoyed having them.

My sister's daughter, Babs, was getting married, and we had received an invitation to the wedding, which would be taking place in Ireland. Marie was asked to be a bridesmaid, and we were all looking forward to it. Heather and Logan had been invited, but we felt that we could use the time out to have a really good think about what we wanted to do about him as we were still being pressured by his social worker to take him long term. We asked if some respite could be organized for him while we went away for two weeks. The people who usually had him for weekend breaks couldn't have him that particular fortnight, but another couple of carers said they would have him, so introductions were made. We took Logan to visit them for tea. Then he went to them for a weekend for him to get used to them. By the time we were ready to go, we felt he was happy to go to these carers.

We hired a log cabin in County Cavan for the first week so we would feel rested when we went down to Kilkenny for the wedding. It was glorious. Marie's boyfriend came with us. He spent most of his time fishing while Marie and Heather went horse riding. Robert and I hired bikes and took a tour around the area during the days looking for places where we could eat in the evenings. We then went to my sister's in time for the big day. The weather was glorious. Most of my brothers and sisters were there. Only one thing didn't feel right—we were missing Logan. I kept looking around to see where he was. Then I'd suddenly realize that he wasn't there. We felt as though a part us was missing.

We finished our holiday and returned refreshed and ready to seriously have a good think about asking to keep Logan long term. We spoke to Dean and Marie. Although Dean was no longer living with us, it still mattered to us what he thought, and Marie would soon be moving as she was planning to attend college and would need to move as we had no way of getting her there every day. Both of them understood what we wanted to do and why. They said they didn't have a problem with it as they already thought of him as their little brother anyway.

In the meantime, we had several new placements who had come and gone. One had been for weekend respite only, which had tied us up from having a full-time placement, but it did mean we didn't have to ask another child to go somewhere else while we went away as we would not have had room in the car for anyone else, so that worked out okay.

A new support worker was assigned to us shortly after we came back from holiday, so we thought we would give us all time to get used to each other before we mentioned how we were feeling about Logan. It was early July before we sat and had a serious talk with her. She had a word with his social worker and came back to us with the message that we had left it too late and she was in the process of finding new carers for him because the residential home that she had applied to would not take him. That particular home was for very seriously damaged children; it would not have been the right place for him. We explained to our support worker what had happened, and although she thought it wasn't a very appropriate thing to have happened, she had no control over his social worker's actions. A planning meeting was organized, but again she had it all sewn up— even new carers identified. Introduction tea and weekend contacts with the new carers were organized. She had approached the couple who had taken him while we were at Babs' wedding, so the transfer could go through more quickly than if he had not known them at all.

Everyone in the family was disgusted at the way this transfer was done. As much as they all found him hard work, that didn't stop them from thinking a lot of him and liking him very much. We just about had time to put in a trip to the zoo with his school and attend his sports day.

David now 6 had settled at his school and was loving it. We had to attend his first sports day. Robert had a day off work so he could cheer him on. We sat at the side and got the camera ready for when he was close to us. Just as he got within the right distance and I stepped forward to take a photo, he saw me and stopped in his tracks and posed for the camera, which made everyone laugh, especially as he was winning until then. Apart from that, he did really well in the other races.

We had also received an invitation to Patricia's eighteenth birthday party, so it was nice to catch up with the family. The twins were still causing their mum aggro but everyone had come together for Patricia's party and kept a low profile so as not to spoil her day.

Heather was planning to spend some time with her family during the holidays. Her social worker made all the arrangements for that so all we had to do was take her and collect her the following week.

Logan's introductions to his new carers were now complete, and all we had to do was give him a good send off. On 11 August we organized a drop-in day at our house for everyone who would like to come and say goodbye to him. Most of my family turned up along with the majority of the village, loads of our friends, and all the friends that he had made at the village playgroup and school. Even some of Dean and Marie's friends came to say goodbye to him. We still have all the photos that were taken. He may have been hard work, but everyone who knew him liked him very much as he had a wonderful personality, and he would be missed in lots of ways.

The big day arrived. We had helped him pack over the previous weeks and had taken some of his belongings each time he had gone to visit, but there were still some bits that had to be taken with him. It was amazing how much he had accumulated over the time he was with us. And of course, he had received lots of going-away presents. One gift was a book. He was in it because it was part of his life story. He thought that was fantastic. People had had his name especially printed on some of the other gifts. He was over the moon with all of them, so we made sure they were all packed carefully. He even had some artwork he'd created when he was at playgroup. These were all very important to him, and he had looked after them. Some of the things that he had kept until last were the very last presents that his mum had given to him during their last contact.

Robert went to work as he was only going to be across the road. We agreed that I would call him when the social worker arrived so that we could wave him off together. She arrived at about noon and got Logan to put his things in the car. I told her I was just going to get Robert, but she said there was no time. I said he was only across the road, but to no avail. Logan had a handful of his favourite dinosaurs on the armchair and asked if he could have a bag to put them in. When I went into the kitchen to get him one, I heard her telling him not to bother with them. She made him just throw them back on the chair. When I came back into the room, she had him running out to the car. She shoved him in just as Robert was coming down the farm entrance. The next thing we knew she was driving up the road. We never got to say goodbye to him. I looked at my watch. It was four minutes past twelve. When I told my support worker what had happened, I was told that there wasn't much that could be done now that he was gone. It took us a few days for the shock to wear off. If that was the effect the experience had on us, what effect must it have had on Logan? He must have been devastated.

Within a day or two, we had a phone call from the father of the little baby that nearly came to Hayling Island with us. He and his family were moving quite a long way off and wanted to come and see us before they left so that we could see the little one before their journey. I couldn't believe how much he had grown. He was now five years old and even had a new baby brother. It was lovely to see how happy they were. They had their whole future in front of them. They moved shortly after that visit, but it wasn't the end of our contact because every year at Christmas we receive a card and a lovely long newsletter keeping us up to date on how things are going and how fast the boys are growing up.

Marie had by now moved, and suddenly the house seemed to feel empty. But not for long. We had a call and were asked to have a girl for a two-week respite while her carers had a holiday. She arrived the Friday after Logan had been taken, so the bed hadn't been empty for long. She asked if her friend could come over on Saturday, and we agreed; in fact, she ended up staying for the whole two weeks. This particular girl had a history of either running away or staying out overnight, so we expected a bumpy ride of late-night calls to the police and the emergency duty team; however, the first week went without any problems, at least for us. It was a different matter for the organizers of a youth club that they attended. They had organized a trip to Alton Towers. We dropped both girls off early on a Saturday morning at the train station to catch the coach. We asked what time we had to pick them up, and we were told ten that night. We actually had a peaceful day as Heather was spending the weekend at a friend's, so we had a quiet day to ourselves.

We arrived at the station at about 9.45 p.m. We like to arrive early when we pick up our kids so that we are waiting for them and not the other way around. When the coach arrived, we waited for the girls to get off. Lynda's friend jumped off, saw us, and came over to say that Lynda had been kicked off the coach at the last stop for arguing with the driver. One of the helpers had had to get off with her and phone her husband to collect them. They would bring her to us if we would hang on and wait for them. They finally arrived at 11.30. We got them home safe and sound, with a few choice words from the back seat regarding the driver. But never mind; we were used to that. At least she was going to be sleeping under our roof. Several days later her social worker came to see her. He told her that he had half expected her not to be there, and when she asked why, he told her that she hadn't stayed out or tried to run off. He was interested to know why. She looked at him and shrugged and said she hadn't realized. Well, the next day I had to ring him and thank him for that because Lynda and her friend hadn't turned up at the place where we had arranged to meet them. The police were amazed they hadn't heard anything about her for over a week. They actually figured she had left the area. The girls did come back two nights later, but then it was nearly time for Lynda to go back to her carers. These adventures did take our minds of Logan for a while.

We had a very short placement for a week while another carer had a break, but that was uneventful.

The next placement, however, made up for it. A twelve-year-old girl, Melinda, arrived. Social services were trying to get her back to her mum's, but every time something was set up it kept going wrong, so Melinda was getting very angry and just wanted to go home. She didn't want to be in care and wasn't going to work with anyone in case they tried to keep her. It was another Friday night arrival. We liked to make moves on Fridays because it gave the children time to settle in before they had to go to school on Monday.

The weekend went fine; we had no problems. When the taxi arrived on Monday morning, Melinda went off quite happily. She arrived home before Heather in the evening, and as she came around the back door, our front door bell rang. When I went to answer it, the taxi driver was standing there. He asked me if his cigarette lighter had accidently dropped into my little girl's school bag. I shot back to the kitchen with my hand out and asked her for the lighter. She took it out of her bag saying, "I wonder how that got there?" I spent the next few weeks checking everything around the house. If we missed something, straight away we would get it back; but if there was a delay and the item had left the house, we could say goodbye to whatever it was. We found ourselves constantly going around the house counting ornaments, looking for empty spaces, even counting cutlery. Among the missing were a Mickey Mouse spoon that had belonged to a set David used, a tiny chicken belonging to a set of three that Robert had bought me, and a few bits of cheap jewellery—not bad, considering.

It was around this time we realized how the taxi drivers were affected by our children. Normally social services used the same company. We were often told by them that Logan was missing us. When they picked him up from school, he would ask where they were taking him, and they would say they were taking him home. He would smile and ask if that would be to our village. But when they said no, they were going to his new carers', he would sit very quietly and say nothing.

We were allowed to see him for one visit when everyone felt he had settled. But he was very upset when it was time for our visit to end, so it was felt that we had better wait a bit longer until he settled down even more. We waited for months before we heard any news of him from social services,

In the meantime, Melinda was settling in reasonably well under the circumstances. She was having regular contact with her mum, the household had settled down, and half term was looming. The inevitable phone call came. Could we take two brothers who were 11 and 12 and already on respite with another carer. Respite had broken down, but their normal carers weren't due back for another week. So why not? It wouldn't affect Heather as she had her own circle of friends, and they would be company for Melinda. David would be there, and it would be nice for him to have two more boys as he was missing Logan so much.

They arrived on a Monday. They hit it off straight away with Melinda. Initially we thought it was a good thing, but as it turned out, I ended up having a complete week without sleep as they asked to go into Hitchin together on

Tuesday. We agreed, and they were very good. They came back to meet us as we had asked. But on the way home, they asked how long it might take them to walk from our village to town. We told them it wouldn't be a good idea as it was a very busy road and it was very dangerous. They agreed with us, but they also decided that it would be safer during the night as there wouldn't be any traffic. The first night I caught them trying to creep out twice. On Wednesday night, I caught them three times. On Thursday night, they tried only it once. On Friday during the day, they asked if they could go for a walk around the block. I said that would be okay, hoping it would tire them out and give me a night's sleep. They were gone for ages, but then all the others used to take their time as they would stop off at various places. They had even taken a picnic so I wasn't too worried—until I got a phone call from their social worker saying he'd had a call from the police saying that they had found three children playing around on the crossroads just outside of town. The police had taken them to the station, so I should go and collect them. They were very apologetic for having put me out, and they said they would have walked home if the police had let them. I really needed to hear that. Luckily, we had to take the two boys home on Saturday, so I could catch up on some much-needed sleep.

The following week, we were asked to have a teenage Sikh girl, Sab. She arrived after school on a Wednesday. She was lovely, and we hit it off straight away. Sab was seventeen and a half, which was probably why she seemed to be more sensible than most of the others. Again we had to adjust our shopping, but this time she came with me to choose the things she was allowed to eat. She even cooked some Asian food for us, which we thoroughly enjoyed. I felt I was being spoilt.

Melinda was beginning to become very unsettled as she realized that she had been with us for a month and there was still no sign that she would be going home. She kept asking to go, but it obviously wasn't an option. She decided that, if she broke the placement with us, then social services would have no choice but to send her home. She played up at school and got herself excluded, which meant that she would have to be at home all day. She asked me to call her social worker to come and take her home. I explained that they couldn't do that without her mum's permission, but she was determined and said she was going to run away. I told her that I couldn't stop her, but I advised against it as she now knew how long it would take her to get to town. But her mum lived a bit further away. She walked out but came back after half an hour saying she couldn't be bothered. She said she wanted her social worker to collect her. I phoned the social worker and told her what was going on, but there was no way she could take Melinda home without her mum's permission. She explained the situation to Melinda over the phone, but it didn't make any difference. She was still determined to go as she had been with us too long and didn't want to settle because, if she did, then her mum wouldn't want her home anyway.

It was the start of a very long revolt. First of all she turned our music centre up to full volume. Then she went into the bathroom and turned on the hot taps and left them running. After I turned off the music, I went in and turned the water off. On came the music again, then she was back in the bathroom. This went on for about a good hour, and no one was getting anywhere I kept trying to calm her down, but she wasn't having any of it. Then, as a final act, she went into her bedroom with her cigarette lighter, turned it on, and held it next to the wooden posts on the bunk beds. She said that, if she wasn't allowed to go home, she would set it alight. I told her that I would call her social worker again. When I did, I told her that she had better come and get Melinda as I wasn't prepared to keep her any longer. She was too big a threat to everyone else in the house. The social worker duly arrived within the next half hour and escorted Melinda off the premises. By the time Heather got home from school, Melinda was long gone. We heard they had taken her to a residential home, and that night she had set off the fire alarms there.

It wasn't long before another teenage girl called Verity was placed with us; in fact, it was less than twenty-four hours. So it was a mad rush to get her room ready as I like to give the rooms a good cleaning between each placement so they all get a fresh start.

Luckily all three girls got on well together. This time there was no room sharing, which made things a lot easier as they each had her own space. There were still a lot of visits to solicitors, school functions, placement planning meetings, the children's reviews, contacts with siblings and families, so even though the girls got along, it was still a busy household, and with various eating habits and food requirements, there was still a lot to do. In fact, during the previous years, I had found that everyone had such a variety of likes and dislikes that we started doing a menu at the beginning of the week so that each child could put his or her name under a choice of two possible dishes. I then knew each day what I was cooking. Sometimes I would write "DYO", which meant they had to do their own. This gave them a chance to practise cooking. Often I would be left messages like, "lazy devil" or "I'd rather starve". It was all taken in good fun, and everyone would rush to see what they were going to have. The menu plan saved me having to work out each day what to do that everyone would like. I didn't believe in making them eat anything that they really didn't like. As I wouldn't eat certain things myself, I didn't mind doing a couple of different dishes each day so long as I knew they were going to be eaten.

The rest of the year was lovely. There was no arguments. Marie often came back home for meals and at weekends. She had usually been the one who left me the most messages. Sometimes in the evening we would go to the local airport, watch the aeroplanes for a while, and then go across and have a Kentucky for dinner. One evening, we were having our meal when Marie made a remark that had us in stitches. She said, "Look around this table, Mum, at all the different hair colourings and nationalities. Not one of us looks like Dad. Everyone must think you are a right tart!" Well, what could I do but laugh? Times like that helped us to realize how much fun fostering could be. Those are the scenes we remember when we get a particularly tough placement.

Christmas was fast approaching so it was time for the girls to sort out what they would like as gifts. They all gave me their lists, and we managed to get them most of what they asked for so everyone had a happy Christmas, although Robert and I did think back to the previous year when we spent most of the time worrying about Logan. Although this year we still missed him and hoped that he was happy, we were still not allowed to see him or get in touch. All we could do was carry on with our lives and hope that one day his social worker would listen to our support worker and her manager, who had been asking her to get in touch with us to let us know how he was and to try to let us see him. But it was a waste of their time as she wasn't taking any notice of what anyone was saying. She obviously wasn't worried about what was in Logan's best interest. We all felt we were banging our heads against a brick wall with her, so all we could do was keep on trying. Before we knew it, another year was gone.

Chapter 25

Soon 1997 arrived peacefully. There had been no emergencies over the holiday period. Everyone soon got into a normal routine. January passed without any major incidents. At the beginning of February, Sab came home with the exciting news that, as part of her business studies, she had to organize an Asian evening at school. She was going to organize it around a fashion show, and she spent hours working it out to the last detail. She went around town and managed to get shop owners to donate raffle prizes in exchange for complimentary tickets. She then needed to get new saris for herself and for both her sisters. We made arrangements during the half-term week to go to Wembley to my sister Elizabeth's house. From there we could walk down the Ealing Road to do some shopping. It was an experience that my sister and I thoroughly enjoyed. There were so many beautiful outfits, the girls had difficulty choosing, but in the end, they all came away very happy with what they had picked, and we had our own fashion show that evening while they tried them on to show Robert and the others.

After all her hard work, the event went ahead on 28 February. We had sold some tickets to our friends who wanted to support her hard work. All I can say is that I don't think we ever enjoyed an evening at a school production as much as we enjoyed that night. Her uncle had been busy with the catering, and her friends and some of her cousins had taken part as models and dancers. The show began with basic, every-day Asian wear and finished with bridal outfits. The festivities were finished off with a wonderful supper of Asian food.

Although the three girls got on well together, Heather and Sab gave us no problems. Verity was a bit erratic. She could be wonderful or completely the opposite if she got in a mood.

One evening, Verity was late coming home from her dance classes. Dinner was ten minutes away. When she asked for her dinner, I told her that I would be serving up in a few minutes. I asked her if she would like to sit at the table with the other girls. No, she wanted hers right away. I told her it was practically ready; all I had to do was drain the potatoes and mash them. "Well, I want it now!" she said. I explained again that it was nearly ready, but she was having none of it. The others couldn't believe what they were hearing. They even told her to sit and wait with them and to let me get on with it. But no. Verity said she'd had enough and was going to run away. With that, she went out the door, banging it behind her. We all laughed and wondered what had upset her, but we sat down and had our meal as there was no point in going after her as normally, when kids did something like that, they'd cool down after a few minutes and come back in. We had just started the washing-up when there was a knock at the door. One of the girls went to answer it and came back in saying that Verity was at the door with our local policeman. When I went to talk to him, he said that he had received a call from a very distraught girl who was claiming that I had refused to feed her. I laughed and explained what had happened. I told him that, if she hadn't walked off, she would have had her dinner by now. He smiled and told me to just make sure she got something to eat before she collapsed with hunger. When he had gone, I gave her the dinner that was waiting for her. The other two laughed so much at her that, in the end, she ended up bursting into fits of laughter. So ended another tragedy.

It wasn't too long before Verity had another episode. This time she said she'd had enough of being in care and wanted to go home to her mum. Obviously that wasn't going to happen, but it didn't stop her from trying. She came back from having contact with her mum and decided that she was going to go to the social services office and tell them to send her home. We tried to tell there would be no point as they wouldn't be sending her home anyway so she may as well wait and see her social worker to ask her to move her closer to home, if that was what she would like. But, no, that wasn't going to be good enough, so she rang her solicitor to say that she wanted to go home. Verity said she didn't want to be with us because, at that very moment, we had her tied up and were beating her with a stick. The solicitor wanted to know how she was able to make a call while being tied up, and she said that I was holding the phone for her. The solicitor asked to speak to me. He told me that, if she wanted to be moved that badly, I should get her into a taxi and send her to social services; otherwise, she might make some serious allegations. If Robert and I didn't want to end up in trouble, the best thing to do would be to let her be on her way. So, we phoned for a taxi and sent her off to the social services office, having phoned her social worker to say what had happened and that Verity was on her way. On her way out to the taxi, she grabbed a bedding plant and pulled it out of the ground as a last act of defiance. It was easy enough to put back in. We got a call a little while later and learned that Verity had turned up, but when she was told that she wouldn't be going home, she walked out of the offices, and they had no idea where she went. The next day, we got a call and found out that she had turned up that morning and would be placed with other carers. We were asked if we could take her belongings to their address, which I did. There I actually got to say goodbye properly to her, she might have been a bit of a minx, but she was a lovely girl, and I had gotten quite fond of her. But as long as she was going to be happy, that was fine. At least we were still talking to each other.

It wasn't long before the phone was ringing. Social services were looking for a bed for two little girls. Amelia was three, and Beth was two. They arrived within several hours and were there when Heather came home from school, which cheered her up. She had been going through a bit of a rough time as she had been having a bit more contact with her parents, and she was feeling nervous about getting to know some brothers and sisters that she'd never had much to do with. There were two siblings she didn't even know she had. So when she came home and met the two little girls, she felt cheered and said she was glad to have someone to look after. They settled down nicely and were lovely girls. We took them shopping at the weekend and got them a few new items of clothing.

I was now back on the contact run. I had to take Amelia and Beth to have contact with their parents twice a week at a family centre. I had no problems with their parents and got on really well with them; in fact, after a few weeks, they were able to have contact at their own home as long as I stayed and had a coffee, which worked well.

Through all this, David was still coming to stay every other weekend. He missed Logan, so he was pleased to have the girls there as company. Our weekends were again being taken up going out to parks and playgrounds, which we didn't mind, and the kids all enjoyed it. On some weekends we met up with friends and went to places like Mountfitchet Castle or Woburn Safari Park where they kids all enjoyed the monkeys climbing on the car.

Sadly, Sab's placement came to an end when she turned eighteen. It was decided that, if she wanted to go home, that would be okay. She missed her mum and her sisters, so it was with mixed feelings that we had to say goodbye, although it was what she wanted. So we were pleased for her, but we knew we were going to miss her as we had gotten very close to her. Heather was also going to miss her as she had been good company, and even though Marie wasn't living with us, she had liked Sab and would miss her when she came to visit. Sab said goodbye to Heather before going to school as Heather would be going to a friend's house after school. Sab's social worker came to pick her up shortly after she arrived home from school. We did meet her several times in town afterwards and kept up with how things were going. She had obviously made the right choice as she was always happy when we met her. She was especially happy a few years down the line when she showed off her engagement ring and was able to tell us how well she had done at university, which didn't surprise us. We knew she had the ability to do what she set out to achieve. Again, another positive ending.

Heather had gotten herself a Saturday job, but it didn't last long when she realized that she would have to get up early every Saturday to go there. But at least she gave it a try. She also had a week away to be near her family so she could spend some time getting to know them as they were asking for her possible return to them. But when she came back, she wasn't so sure that she wanted to move in with them just yet; but would like to go there for the odd weekend.

All too soon it was time for the two girls to go home, so we packed their bags and got them ready for their social worker to come and pick them up. They were very excited about going home, so it was nice to wave them off with smiles on their faces.

Suddenly the house was very quiet; there was only Heather left. Now was a chance to do a bit of spring cleaning while we had two rooms empty because we didn't get many chances to do regular decorating. There was nearly always someone in all the rooms, so it was a novelty having space.

Heather was busy taking her exams, and on some weekends, she was away, so we could actually have a bit of a life. We didn't know what to do! We could go wherever we wanted and not worry about getting back by a certain time because of babysitters. It felt weird and as though something was missing. We could have a conversation without interruptions and watch telly without someone walking across in front of the screen, except, of course, on the weekends we had David. Then we realized we were still alive and not dead and gone to heaven.

This hiatus didn't last for long. We soon had a call and were asked to have a three-year-old girl. She was fast asleep when the social worker arrived with her. She carried the child from the car into our living room and put her down on the settee. While we did the paperwork and had a cup of coffee, she didn't move. The social worker must have been gone a good half hour before she finally woke up. I thought, *Now I'm going to have trouble because she's going to wake in a strange place and also with a stranger looking at her!* But she was fine. She got up, looked around gave me a big smile, and asked for a drink, which I got for her. We never looked back. Sherry was wonderful. She had the most gorgeous head of curls. She was of mixed race, but this time I wasn't quite so worried about brushing her hair. Luckily, another carer had a daughter who was of the same mixture, and she was able to help me sort out what type of creams and oils to use both on her skin and hair. She even showed me how to do her hair properly, so this was another learning experience for me. It is important to get that sort of thing right and to acknowledge that there is a difference in how to look after mixed-race children.

We had just got Sherry settled in when we had a ten-year-old boy, John, placed with us. He was a bit nervous when he arrived but, as it was the summer holidays, David was with us, and he volunteered to keep him company and show him around. It was hard to believe that David was getting on for seven years of age.

Our summer was quite busy with keeping up contact for Sherry and John, along with taking David along with his mum and dad to various hospital appointments regarding David's eyesight. He had to wear glasses and eye patches to strengthen one of his eyes.

We also had to attend meetings for all the children. It was more time consuming this year as Sherry's contact and her meetings were being held in Milton Keynes, which involved a lot of travelling. I was having to go there at least twice a week for contact with her mum, and in between I was taking John to have his contact to see his mum two or three times a week.

When I look back, I often wonder when I found time to do housework or shopping. There was never time to do the things that we would have liked because we were constantly running around after everyone else. But that year we were celebrating our twenty-fifth wedding anniversary, and we were determined that we would organize something for ourselves to celebrate with our family and friends. So in between the fostering commitments, we arranged to have a party at the airport as it was nice and central for everyone. We booked the observation restaurant initially for eighty people and sent out the invitations. A few people couldn't make it, so we added others to the list to make the numbers up. Then some of the people who had said they couldn't come got back to us to say they had reorganized their schedules and could now make it. In the end, we had about 130 people turn up, but everyone enjoyed themselves. Because I didn't want to end up with loads of silver ornaments, we told our guests that, instead of buying us presents, we would prefer that, if they wanted to, they could just to put £5 or whatever into a card. We would put the money together and buy a carriage clock that we rather liked. That would remind us of the lovely time we had. About fourteen ex-foster children and their parents came along, and it was lovely to catch up with them. Many were pleased to see each other as some of them been with us at the same time. We still had a house full the next day as some of them stayed overnight. When we went through the cards and counted the money, we discovered something in the region of £900, which amazed us. We were able to get our carriage clock and a new stereo system, which was something that we needed too. The stereo system has since been used and abused, but the clock is still going strong.

Shortly after our party, we had a call from a social worker who told us that Logan was no longer with the carers he had been moved to. In fact, that placement had broken down and ended within months, which is why his social worker hadn't wanted us to have contact with him. She didn't want us to know that the perfect placement had failed. He was now going to a boarding school during the week and to another set of carers at the weekends, but more importantly, his social worker had left and a new one had taken over. There was every chance that we might be able to talk to his new social worker regarding contact as Logan was still asking to see us. We got in touch with our support worker, who got back to us after speaking to various people and said that the new social worker would like to come and see us, to which we agreed straight away.

A few days later,his new social worker arrived with the news that he had heard that we had wanted to foster Logan long term, which we told him was true. He wanted to know if we still felt the same way, and we said we did. He then said that he would have a word with Logan to see how he felt, and he would get back to us. In the meantime, he would set up a contact meeting for us with Logan because he had been asking when he was going to be allowed to see us. All we could do now was wait to hear from our support worker.

It was time for John to move back with his mum, so in the next few weeks, his contact increased until he went home full time. But, as usual, we didn't have a bed empty for long because within a few days we had a fifteen-year-old girl, Veronica, placed with us. She and Heather didn't get on too well because her table manners were atrocious. We felt as if we were sitting down to a meal with an animal. Perhaps she couldn't help it, but it didn't make for very nice mealtimes. Heather, Sherry, and I wanted to go shopping for a change. We asked her if she would like to come along, and she readily agreed. Shopping was okay, but when we went to McDonald's for lunch, Heather nearly got up and walked away. Heather and I were chatting about some of the things we had bought, and when we looked up to include Veronica, we took one look at her and then looked at each other. We couldn't believe what we were seeing. Veronica had put most of her Big Mac into her mouth and carried on eating it without removing it to take a breath. Sauce and all sorts of goo were running down her chin and clothes. We just had to carry on as though it was quite normal. When she had finished, we handed her a tissue and said it was time to go home because we couldn't last out much longer. She didn't stay with us very long as she couldn't cope with living in a village. She said she needed to be in a town. I took her to the train station so that she could go and spend some time with her friends, but that was the last I saw of her. She disappeared for a few days and eventually turned up at the offices asking to be placed in town. They found her a place in one of the children's residential homes where she was happy.

Shortly after our party, our friends Donna and John invited us around for dinner. In between courses, I was told to look at the card that had been put under my plate. It was an invitation for us and a few of our friends to use their villa in Florida for three weeks. Robert and I looked at each other, and we both said "Chris" at the same time. Donna had always been a really good friend, but this was something that was exceptional to us because it now enabled us to keep a promise that we had made to Chris a few years back when he couldn't come with us because of his job.

The first thing we did the next evening was to ring Chris and ask him if he remembered a promise that we had made to him when he couldn't come to America with us, but he couldn't. We reminded him of it and said that we were now making good on that promise. If he could arrange the time, we would love it if he and his partner could come with us. They got back to us a few days later to say that they would love to come, so we had that to look forward to.

In the meantime, we had heard from Logan's social worker who had spoken to Logan. The social worker reported that there had been no hesitation on Logan's part. We would now have to be reassessed as long-term carers, and it would take months to put our application together. While that was in progress, all we could do was work with them and wait. We did ask if Logan could stay with us, but we were told that it might give him the wrong message because, if anything went wrong with the assessment, then he would be really disappointed, especially after being on a holiday like that with us. We went along with that as we did understand, so there were just four of us booked up to go to America, as both Dean and Marie were quite happy to stay at home. By now they were leading their own lives.

The timing had worked well. Veronica had gone and that only left Heather and Sherry. Sherry's contact had increased, and it was felt that it would be more appropriate for her to move back to Milton Keynes so that her mum would find it easier to visit. Introductions to her new carers started at the end of November, and she would be moving about a week before we had booked to go away.

The only other placements we had was a wonderful little special-needs three-year-old for a weekend once a month to give his full-time carer a break. We worked the schedule so our weekends fell just before we left and just after we came back.

Then we had what must have been the shortest placement ever. We received a call one Sunday evening and were asked if we could cope with three siblings. Neighbours had reported that the children had been left on their own in a flat while their parents went out to work, and they were all under the age of ten. The children arrived with a policewoman at about ten o'clock looking very tired and shocked. I gave them something to eat and drink, and then we settled them down for the night. The next morning, someone from social services rang to say they had found the parents and would be over to collect the children before lunch as the parents were prepared to work with social services and make sure that, when they went to work, they would get a proper sitter in to look after them.

This is why it was so difficult when people have asked us how many children we have looked after during the time we have been fostering. Sometimes the figure seems quite high. But some of the children spent such a short time with us that, although we looked after them, the care we provided wasn't the same as the care we gave to a child who stayed with us for months or years. We didn't really have to do much work with the really short-term kids. These latest three were brilliant children, and we would have loved to have kept them longer, but obviously the best place for them was with their parents.

Heather didn't want to move somewhere else for the three weeks we'd be gone, and as she was seventeen, it was felt that, with the right kind of support built in, she would be okay to stay at our house. We made sure that a friend from the village came in every day and made the fire up for the central heating and came again in the evening to build it up for overnight. My sister-in-law made sure that she had enough food. There were so many people in the village keeping an eye on her and she was comfortable with them all. She was quite happy with the arrangements. She did spend the weekends with her friend, so for the first time in twenty years, we went away for a proper holiday without children.

This time there was no problems with passports or visas. Chris had booked the tickets through his airline, so I didn't even have them to worry about. We arrived in Florida as it was getting dark, so we were a bit worried about finding our way to the villa, but we managed.

The accommodations were out of this world! There was so much space and no kids to walk around. We had our own pool, and the best thing of all was that Robert and I had our own bathroom and toilet, which was the highlight of the holiday for me, especially as it was en suite too. As it was so near to Christmas, everyone had decorated their houses with lights and their gardens with holiday figures. It was the first time we had ever seen such outside displays, so we spent one evening just driving around looking at them and taking photographs. Each one seemed better than the last.

The holiday seemed to be over in a flash, and all too soon we were heading home. We couldn't thank Donna and John enough for making it possible for us to enjoy the real Disney World, because this time we were able to stay and enjoy the evening displays instead of rushing back to catch our courtesy coach.

We arrived back home on 19 December, just in time to see Heather before she went off to spend the Christmas holidays with her family. We knew she was okay as we had phoned her several times while we were away.

Both Dean and Marie were pleased to see us, but they had made their own arrangements for Christmas Day, and although we had invitations to go places, we thought we would spend the day at home on our own. Robert had been saying for a long time that he would like to have a quieter Christmas, so now was our chance.

Christmas Day arrived. We got up and opened our presents. We went to the local pub with friends for a drink—something I hadn't been able to do for years. After dinner, we sat and watched television and generally relaxed. I didn't have to worry about making sure that everyone had enough to eat and drink. There was hardly any washing up, and apart from phone calls, there was no one to interrupt conversation. I had a thoroughly good day. Robert, on the other hand, felt that it had been too quiet. He said he had missed the company. So we agreed that, in future, there would be no more complaints from him about noisy Christmas Days.

On Boxing Day, we followed our normal routine of going out for a meal for my birthday. This year we went with Marie and our friends. Then, just as we thought we were going to end the year in peace, we had a phone call and were asked to take a teenage girl for a week.

Heather rang to wish us a happy New Year and said she would be back on 2 January.

Chapter 26

1998 rolled in peacefully. Heather came home. Kathy went back to her carers, and we were asked to have our old friend Verity back for an overnight while she was in the process of changing from one carer to another. She arrived and was pleased to see us. We told her that this time we wouldn't tie her up and flog her, and we would even feed her while she was with us. We took her to her new carers the next day and parted on very good terms.

A few weeks into January we had a fourteen-year-old girl, Trina, placed with us. She was lovely to have around the house when she was with us, but most of the time she was in town with friends. A taxi had been provided to bring her home each night at nine, but nine times out of ten, she would not turn up for the taxi. They would give her another half hour before ringing us to say she hadn't turned up. I would then wait another half an hour before I rang back to see if she had been in contact. I would then ring the emergency duty team (EDT), who handled emergencies for social services that occurred outside of office hours. I would also ring the police to report her missing, which is the procedure. Even though it was a regular occurrence, she still had to be reported missing. She would then go to the taxi office where workers would get a cab to bring her home, normally around midnight. I would then have to call the police to say that she had returned home. I would have to wait until they came out to make sure she was okay. It was usually about two in the morning before I got to bed after listening to the night's events from her and what a good time she'd had. Because she was so lovely, it was very difficult to get angry with her.

We went to the long-term panel and were approved as long-term carers for Logan, so it was celebrations all round. Everyone was really pleased for us. Now all we had to do was start introduction visits to get him home. We started by having him come for tea. Next he came for a day. We gradually built up his visits, and he finally moved home on 20 February.

We organized a coming home party for him in our village hall to which we invited all his old friends whom he hadn't been able to see since he left. David was over the moon and just ran into his arms as soon as he saw him. It was very difficult to hold the tears back just watching them.

Things settled down. Heather was pleased to have him back, although she had enjoyed the peace and quiet when he wasn't here. Trina, the new girl, had been looking forward to meeting him as she had heard so much about him, but for the little time she spent with us, it didn't make a lot of difference to her who was here and who wasn't. Because of the little time she did spend with us, it was felt that it had been a wasted placement and she may as well be moved to somewhere that would provide her with access to her friends without all the taxis, especially when she had started sneaking them in late at night and then trying to sneak them out early next morning. If she had asked, we would have let her friends stay anyway. She had been with us for four months, and we had grown quite fond of her. We knew we would miss her, although it did mean I could start going to bed at a reasonable time. She was finally found a place and moved just before the Easter holiday.

With Trina gone and Heather going to her family for Easter, we decided to take David and Logan to Cornwall to visit Toni and the twins. We dropped Heather off in Reading on our way, and we managed the rest of the journey with only one mishap. Both boys were sick in the back of the car, but we cleaned them up fairly well and arrived at Toni's at about 2.00 p.m. We took them to the beach for a while, but it was very cold, so we didn't stay long. We were soon back at Toni's where it was nice and warm. The twins played with the boys for a while before we finally had some supper and got ready for an early night. The twins took over the normal ritual of reading to both of the boys before they would go to sleep.

It was a busy, fun-packed weekend. We managed to get to Flambards Theme Park. We got in plenty of swimming along with visits to the beach and other play areas. We started the journey home on Wednesday, calling in at Westward Ho! seaside village and Piggy-Land. We arrived home at around 8.00 p.m. The boys were so worn out it was straight to bed for them. We took David home on Thursday as they were both still very tired and we thought they had better get a few early nights on their own. Heather arrived back from Reading on the same day because she had another part-time job working at the Dyspraxia Foundation that she had to get back to.

Logan wasn't too happy about going back to school, but he went without any arguments. His private reading lessons started, which he was quite keen to do, and when his teacher started working with him, he told her exactly what he wanted to be able to do. He told her that would be enough, and she would be able to stop when he had learned what he wanted. She was very good with him and gave him books about things that he was interested in. He used to come home pleased with himself when he noticed that he was reading a lot better, but like he said, when he had learned what he thought was enough, she couldn't get any more work out of him, so in the end she had to stop teaching him. He was fast losing interest and getting more difficult to handle, but he was happy. He could pick up a book and read and was able to keep up with the other children at school, which is all that he wanted to be able to do. He said that maybe he would now get good reports from school as there was a school/home diary, and entries about him were always very negative. School officials would have problems with him at school and ask in the diary that we punish him at home even though they had set a punishment at school. We tried to work with them on this, but we felt that he was spending his home time being punished for the things he was doing at school, and we felt that was unfair as we weren't having that many problems—well, no more than we expected from him. So in the end, we refused to do this. We decided that, if he was being punished at school for something he did or didn't do there, then we would take him to task only over things that happened at home. Also, we would like to see a few positive comments about him in the diary as surely he hadn't been so disruptive for the whole day every that they couldn't find something nice to say about him once in a while. But when we brought this up at a meeting with the school personnel and social workers, the diary had mysteriously disappeared and was never seen again. A new diary took its place, and it did contain a few positive comments, which made a nice change, and we felt we could read it to him and talk about his day at school without everything being negative for him.

It seemed ages before we were asked to have another placement, but it did give us lots of special time with Logan, which helped to settle back with us. On 1 June we were asked to have a mother-and-baby placement, which was okay with us, but when they arrived with the social worker, the mother took one look around the village and decided that there was no way that she was going to stay so far away from her friends. But she wasn't too bothered about her daughter staying so long as she could visit her. So it was agreed with social services that it would be okay as they didn't think she would stay anywhere long, and it was more important to get her daughter looked after, so we ended up with seven-month-old Tracy. She was gorgeous—blonde hair and big blue eyes. Logan was really pleased but asked if we could also have someone his age as well. But I said he would have to wait a little while, and anyway, he had his best friend in the village who was the same age, and also David at the weekends, so he agreed to wait. Heather was pleased to find a baby girl at our house when she came home. She fed her for me while I got supper ready.

Both Logan and Heather were even more surprised when they came home the next day and we had another phone call. We were asked if we could have Jacob, a four-month-old baby boy, overnight. They both helped me get everything ready. Heather was very concerned as this little one had a fractured skull, but when he arrived, she asked if she could feed him for me while I got Tracy ready for bed. He got loads of cuddles that evening between all of us, and the next morning we all went into action. Tracy looked to see where Jacob was and tried handing him a toy. Logan then played with Tracy while I got breakfast, and Heather fed Jacob. We worked well as a team. Soon it was time for Heather and Logan to go to college and school respectively. Logan said goodbye to both babies and gave a special kiss and cuddle to Jacob because he knew the baby would be gone by the time he came home from school. Heather wanted to know why we couldn't keep both babies, but I soon pointed out the impracticalities to her. Also, social services already had a place for Jacob, but the carers just hadn't been able to have him the previous night. Luckily, he was collected just before lunch, so I didn't have to cope for too long on my own.

Logan now had a new routine in the morning. Along with his normal routine of getting up and watching Disney and having tea and biscuits with Robert until he went to work, Logan now had an extra chore. He would play with Tracy when he was ready for school while waiting for the taxi.

Heather was going away for the weekend, so we decided that we would go to Lincolnshire and stay at my brother's house.

Logan loved showing the different things to Tracy and wanted to take her out on the mudflats. Then he wanted us to take them all to the butterfly farm. It was so important to him that he share it all with her.

The following weekend, we were due to have Robert's special needs little boy whom he had fallen in love with, so it was a very hectic weekend. These weekends started getting more and more difficult as the year went on. As Tracy was getting more mobile, she began crawling around the garden, and little Michael kept trying to climb on her back, and he was no lightweight. I had a job to lift him, so Robert had to do the nappy changing. In the end, when Robert had to work on the harvest, we had to say that we couldn't have him for much longer as it was impossible to keep watching him in case he hurt Tracy when she was outside playing. It was sad because Robert had got very attached to him, but we knew his carer, and we were able to keep in touch. And we knew when he was moved to an adoptive family so we were really pleased about that.

During the month of July, we did have a girl for respite while her carers had a break, but she went back quite happily to them. Just before the end of term, Logan came home in a good mood and went off to the cricket field with his friend from up the road. They took a picnic as they were going to watch the cricket team practising. When he came in, he was in a really good mood because everyone had cheered for him after he had climbed a tree to rescue a kitten. The next morning he said to me,

"Yesterday was the best day of his life!" When I asked him why, he said, "Because everyone cheered, me and I didn't get embarrassed!" It was wonderful to see him go off to school with a smile on his face.

We had all settled down to a routine with Tracy. Her mum had been given plenty of time and help to see if she could cope with her, but it was proving very difficult. Tracy's grandfather and his partner wanted to have contact with her, so we were asked if they could come and visit her at our house. We didn't have a problem with that. We were told that they were of the travelling community, but we were prepared to meet them, and we found them very pleasant and enjoyed their company. We looked forward to their visits as they thought the world of Tracy and only wanted what was best for her. We couldn't fault them.

My nephew Joe came around to hang about with Logan at the beginning of the summer holidays. He and Logan asked if he could stay for the night as they had put the tent up in the back garden. We said that was fine. By the end of the holidays, we were saying to Joe that there was only another day or two before they started back at school, and shouldn't he be thinking of going home. It was a good job we all got on well together.

Heather spent her time between Reading, our home, and town. She enjoyed having Tracy around as she was easier than Logan. The only problem we had with Tracy was getting her to sleep through the night. She was still waking up several times. All she wanted was a cuddle, and she would go back down again, but our nights were disturbed.

We did have a visit from a possible mother-and-baby placement. Social services wanted them to move back to this area from up north, but after the visit, the mother decided that she would rather stay up north near the baby's father, so nothing came of our meeting. But it wasn't long before we had another call. We were asked for a bed for an emergency placement, a young girl, Maureen, who'd had an argument with her mum had been sleeping rough because she wouldn't go home. She arrived with the social worker, and it was agreed that she could have a taxi back to see her mum. She could even stay there for the weekends to build up their relationship. The first night she said she really missed her mum, so I said I would organize a taxi for her in the morning. This happened most days, so she asked the social worker if she could go back home to live. Social services believed that it was probably a bit soon. The current arrangement seemed to be working because Maureen had somewhere to go when she felt angry with her mum. So it was set up that she could go to her mum's every day, but she would come back to us to sleep if she wanted, as it was too dangerous for her to keep trying to sleep on park benches. She ended up coming back and staying with us every night until November. In the end, it was decided that their relationship seemed to be working, and she could go home. We heard afterwards that everything had gone well, and she was very happy to be home properly.

As Robert worked all summer helping with the harvest, we couldn't take our holidays until September. Luckily, the schools understood this, and we were able to take the children with us. This year we decided that we would take

Logan, David, and Tracy to Yarmouth as we knew there would be lots for them to do there. Heather wanted stay with her friend, which was okay with everyone. Maureen was able to stay temporarily with another carer as she didn't want to go too far from her mum.

The two boys were delighted when they got there and saw the swimming pool and play area, and it didn't take them long to get down there with Robert while I sorted Tracy and our things. We managed a trip to the beach before supper, and then went to the clubhouse before settling down for the night. The next morning, we couldn't believe that Tracy had slept all night without waking up once. We thought she must have been shattered after the journey, but it lasted the whole time we were there. The two boys had a glorious time. We went out for days or to the beach, then went back to the site for a swim before supper. In the clubhouse every night, the two of them would wander off with a pound each, occasionally coming back for a bit more. David began to look a bit laden down, his pockets being rather full. He asked for another £1 coin as he said he kept winning on one particular machine, but Logan said that David kept putting his £1 coins into the change machine and getting back all the pennies. "He keeps thinking that he's winning!" he told us. We laughed so much our sides hurt. In the end, we had to explain to David what was happening, but he didn't mind. All too soon, it was time to go home.

On our first night home, we put them all to bed. We were totally exhausted ourselves and looking forward to an early night. We thought wrong Tracy woke up twice the first night back. We put it down to her traveller's blood that she slept so well in the caravan and not at home in her own bed. Oh well, you can't win them all.

Heather was having a few problems of her own. When we got back, we were greeted with the news that she was pregnant, so there was a lot of meetings between all of us—her social worker, her boyfriend, his parents and us. It was agreed that the ultimate decision would be Heather's, but if she wanted to keep the baby, that would be okay. But she would have to be moved into a semi-independent unit. She wasn't too pleased about that as she thought she could stay with us as a mother-and-baby placement. We explained that it didn't work like that. The mother-and-baby placements were for young mothers who really couldn't cope with their babies. Going by the way Heather had been with the babies in our house, we knew that she was more than capable of dealing with a baby with a bit of support from us, her social worker, and of course the baby's father. But after a long and very difficult month of working out what she wanted to do, she decided that she wouldn't have it. We asked if she was really okay with that decision, and she said she was. So arrangements were made, and her boyfriend supported her through it. We were very conscious that it wasn't an easy decision, and in the circumstances it was probably the best.

Logan settled down at school a lot better this term as he had a teacher who actually liked him, and they had a good relationship, which was a relief. He still had his problems, but at least we were now getting a more positive feedback from the school. One of the main problems they had with him was, if one of the other pupils was put in the isolation room, Logan would spend his time trying to rescue the miscreant. Or if he himself was put in the isolation room, he would climb up the window to the highest point. Because of this, staff members felt that it wasn't safe to leave him there, and they were constantly trying to find a new way of taking him to task.

With Heather going to her boyfriend's at the weekends and Maureen going to her mum's, we took the opportunity to go to my brother's in Lincolnshire again while they were away in Tenerife, so we took David, Tracy, and Logan up on a Friday evening in October. It was a lovely weekend apart from there being no stair gate to stop Tracy from climbing. We tried barricading her in the living room with several chairs placed on their side, but she tried to climb over them and, when she couldn't manage to do that, we could watch her sitting back and thinking of ways to get through. She really studied the chairs and tried to crawl under them. When that failed, she sat back and had another think. Then she tried to go round them. But eventually she decided to give up when she couldn't get past them. The weekend wasn't long going, and soon it was time to go home

The month of October wasn't very eventful apart from Tracy taking her first steps and having contact with both her mum and her grandparents. We were just waiting for Tracy's court case to go ahead, but that wouldn't be until November.

Logan was still having ups and downs at school, but mostly ups. On the whole, he seemed to be enjoying this year more than last. David was still coming at weekends. Little Michael came for his last respite weekend. Heather was passing the time between our house, her friend's, and her boyfriend's. Maureen went back to her mum's near the end of November. She moved out on a Friday, and Hannah moved in on Saturday. I just about had time to wash the cupboards and drawers in the bedroom, but we were ready for her.

Hannah settled in quite well as she had been to meet us and spent a weekend here so it wasn't so difficult for her. She got on well with Logan, but was not too keen on Tracy as she was becoming harder to look after now that she was running and walking everywhere. We all needed eyes in the back of our heads, although Logan thought she was wonderful. Hannah didn't have a lot to do with Heather as she spent most of her time at her friend's and only came in late in the evenings.

Tracy's case finally went to court in November, and her grandparents were given custody. We were all very happy with the outcome and were prepared to give them whatever support they might need to get her settled in the first few weeks, but there were no problems as she was used to seeing them regularly while she was here.

Logan had to be prepared for her departure as he had become very attached to her. He was quite happy for her as he knew where she was going, and we assured him that we would still see her whenever they came to visit in our area. They did, in fact, move closer to their family locally, so we managed to keep in touch and would often open the front door and find Tracy and her grandmother standing there, which was lovely. We were always pleased to see them.

Logan had a few shaky days at school in November and was excluded for several days. He was given homework to do, which I had no trouble getting him to sit and do.

When I asked him what the problems were at school, as things had been going so well this year, at first he said he didn't know. Then he finally admitted that a new boy had started in school and had been given Logan's seat, and he felt as though he was being pushed out and punished, and he didn't know why. We explained this to the school staff members, and things appeared to change. At least he was coming home in a better mood, and we were having no phone calls from the school.

Heather was coming up to the time when she would have to be leaving care and would be moving into supportive lodgings. She was introduced to the woman who would be looking after her. She went for tea several times and then stayed for a weekend before finally moving on 5 December. We kept in touch with her and helped her through a few rough times until we felt it was better to start backing off a bit, as the more we were helping her the less she was doing for herself. We did keep in contact with her for a number of years, although we haven't heard from her for about the last two years, and we assume that she is doing okay.

Hannah had made friends in the village and joined the youth club, which she enjoyed, especially when they went to Alexandra Palace for overnight skating. She thought it was wonderful to be able to stay out all night and come in at six the next morning. It was decided that, as she had settled down so well, she would be given the chance to change schools and go to our local secondary school in Hitchin where the other children from the village attended. She said she would like that, and arrangements were made for her to visit and have a look around the school and meet the teachers. She was pleased with what she saw and looked forward to starting there after Christmas. This also gave her time to say goodbye to people at her old school.

Logan was given more exclusions, which meant he was sent home. But he never did like December at school when timetables changed to accommodate plays and concerts. He always found it difficult to cope with any changes. It just seemed, at times, that we had no lives of our own as I couldn't make any definite arrangements. During the day I never knew when Logan was going to be excluded. Christmas shopping was very hit and miss as I couldn't guarantee that Logan wouldn't be at home. I tried to keep free from appointments, but as usual we managed to muddle through and got it all done in time.

We were asked to have an emergency placement over the holiday period that turned into a farce because the girl was with us for only about twenty-four hours. She asked if she could go to see a friend on Christmas Day. Social services had already agreed that she could and had arranged a taxi to bring her home. We had agreed to take her there. Everything went okay that day. On Boxing Day, the same arrangements were in place, but she wasn't at the appointed place when the taxi went to collect her. They phoned us to see what they should do, but there wasn't anything they could do. We then phoned EDT and the police. All we could do was wait for the police to arrive. When they did arrive finally, at 10.30 p.m., they got details and searched the house to make sure she wasn't hiding somewhere. They came back 27 December, but there was still no news. A bit later the taxi company rang to say that they had received a call from her. Also, one of their drivers had seen her hanging around the Texaco garage. But we never heard any more that day. The next day the police rang to say that someone had reported seeing her with a known petty criminal, but social services would need a recovery order to get her. They couldn't get that until the next day, so all we could do was wait. The next day one of the family placement workers rang to say that they had managed to get her and would send someone around to collect her belongings as she would now be placed in another county away from her known associates to keep her safe.

We did manage to give the others a good Christmas. We even managed to take David out to lunch for his birthday on 28 December. Sometimes it would be nice to say that we had a boring Christmas and nothing out of the ordinary happened, but then that wouldn't have been us.

Logan and Hannah stayed up to see the New Year in, all with bated breath to see what the next year would bring.

Chapter 27

Soon, 1999 came in very quietly. Hannah was both excited and nervous about starting her new school. Logan was getting bored being stuck at home, so I spent a few days taking him to the pictures or otherwise entertaining him and David. We did our annual visit to the Gordon Craig Theatre to the pantomime. We managed to muddle through until it was time for them to start back at school. Hannah went back a few days before Logan. She came home after her first day really pleased, telling us that everyone had been very friendly and had made her feel welcome. My niece went to the same school, so they both came home together and decided that they would do their homework at my niece's before coming home to our house, which was okay. Logan, on the other hand, was still bored at home especially without Hannah, so instead of having adult time, I was going to children's films and play areas. However, it was soon time for him to start back.

His first day was uneventful, and he even enjoyed it. This attitude continued until towards the end of the month when the phone calls started about his behaviour, and eventually he was excluded for a day. I couldn't fault his behaviour when he was at home during these exclusions; he would sit in our dining room and complete whatever work had been sent home for him to do, and he would stop for a break only when I told him to. Thinking back over his primary schooling, I think he might have coped a lot better with home schooling as I never had problems getting him to do schoolwork; in fact, he seemed to have enjoyed it, and there were no outside distractions that could cause him to be very disruptive as there were in school.

Hannah, on the other hand, was settling in nicely. The biggest problem she had was deciding which of the boys who had asked her out she fancied the most. She eventually settled on one and went with him a few times to the cinema. But like with most teenage romances, it didn't last long, and we were nursing a broken heart most weeks.

February brought a big change to the household; we received a call from a social worker who asked us to be on stand-by as there was a baby due any day. Could we be ready to take it straight away as the mum had made the decision that she wanted it to be adopted straight away. That meant an early move from the hospital.

Logan was over the moon and every day kept asking if the baby had arrived yet. Finally, on 6 February we had a call and learned that the mum had been taken in to be induced; we would be called as soon as they had news. The next day, we had a call early in the morning. A little girl had been born at 6.40 in the evening on the sixth. If we could go to the hospital at about two in the afternoon, the nursing staff would have her all ready and waiting for us. That was all we needed. We had to keep Logan from climbing the walls with excitement. Luckily, it was Sunday, so he didn't have to go to school. He would never have managed a day without some incident!

We finally set off to pick up the baby, who was called Charlee. She was gorgeous, of course just like a little doll. Again I had the job of getting her changed in front of the social worker and nursing staff, but I managed to do it without breaking any limbs. She was twenty hours old as we were walking out of the hospital. As soon as we arrived home, Logan had to sit down and nurse her while I got her food ready. Hannah couldn't get too close as she hadn't been well that morning, and we didn't want any germs being passed on. She had to wait twenty-four hours before she could get a cuddle.

We settled down into a routine for the evening—I worked, and Logan fed the baby. I thought I would get my cuddles during the night-time feeds, but no—not the first night anyway. She woke up at four in the morning. I crept downstairs to feed and change her, but as I got to the bottom of the stairs, I saw a little shadow following me. So Logan got to do the feeding, and I was left with the good job of changing her nappy. Logan was so besotted by Charlee that I thought I would have problems getting him to school, or if he went then I would be getting phone calls to say that he was unsettled. As I expected, he did have a bad day, so they sent work home with him, which he readily got done so that he could feed Charlee. But after that first day, he settled down again, and we had no problems for the rest of the week.

My days were now full with visits from the midwife coming to check up on Charlee, the social worker coming to take photos for her life-story book, and Logan coming home and smothering her in kisses. It wasn't long into the placement when the social worker came to see us and told us that the birth father had decided to go for custody. Therefore, this was not going to be a straight forward six-week adoption placement. Of course we had no problems with this as it meant that we would keep her a few weeks longer.

Charlee was only few weeks old when we took her and Logan to Eastbourne for a long weekend. We had been promising Dean that we would visit him in Hastings as he had just moved into his own flat. As it was too small for overnight company, we stayed in the hotel in Eastbourne and travelled back and forth to see him. We brought him back to the hotel for evening meals with us. Hannah was spending the weekend at my brother's as she got on so well with my niece, so that only left the four of us. It was like going on safari trying to remember what we had to bring with us for Charlee. The staff members at the hotel couldn't do enough for us. Because it was way out of season, there weren't many people there, so they weren't too busy. At mealtimes, we had plenty of offers from some of the regular customers to hold Charlee while we were eating our meals. The staff members even offered to get me a fresh dinner one evening as I had been late starting mine due to feeding Charlee. We took photographs for her album so she could see how young she was when she stayed in a hotel for the first time.

All too soon, we were back home again and into our daily routine. The custody battle over Charlee was going to take longer than first anticipated, so there was a hold put on looking for adoptive parents. The midwife visits stopped and health visits began, but she only came every two weeks. The social worker came once a week to have a cuddle using the pretext that she needed to take photographs. So as far as we were concerned, Charlee was ours for the moment. Logan was as happy as a sandboy. David was nearly as bad and didn't want to go home after his weekends with us in case she would be gone by the next time he came. Hannah was a normal teenager—more interested in her friends in the village than a baby at home, and that suited the boys as they had no competition for cuddles.

The last Sunday in February, Charlee was totally spoiled by some of my family members who came to visit when they found out we had a new baby. I didn't even get a look in.

Between then and Easter, time was taken up with medicals for Logan as he was seen by a child psychologist and had been prescribed Ritalin. Counselling was also recommended after what he had been through. Hannah had parents' evening, which went well. Charlee had to have various medical check-ups, and we had to attend permanency planning meetings in case the custody case went against the father. Social services wanted to be prepared for adoption.

I had a few training sessions to attend, so we didn't have much of a social life. Marie was back and forth. She was now living with a partner, and it looked as though things were going well. She had moved into her own flat in Luton and had been coping brilliantly on her own, budgeting herself really well.

We did manage one outing to the cinema, taking Charlee with us. Logan and David wanted to see *A Bug's Life*. Charlee slept all the way through it; mind you, she was only four weeks old. We decided she could go without the McDonald's menu and would prefer her own bottle.

There was only one incident between Logan and Hannah that had to be dealt with. They had an argument over something, and Logan threatened her with a knife, so we had to be very careful about putting sharp knives away where he couldn't get them. We had to have eyes in the back of our heads. His behaviour did improve once he started on the Ritalin even though he was only on a small amount. Even school personnel noticed that he was a lot calmer.

The Easter holidays were filled with trips to Wimpole Home Farm, Meade Open Farm, Woodside Farm and Wildfowl Park, Woburn Safari Park, and other age-appropriate places. David was with us most of the time as he and Logan were still a bit inseparable. Wherever we went David had to come.

We did have another special event in Charlee's little life. On Robert's niece's eighteenth birthday, she hired a stretch limo to take guests to see the sights of London. We were invited along, which was great. Logan loved it, and everyone else loved Charlee. She was passed from one to the other. It was a wonder she didn't get travel sick with the amount of handing back and forth. We did get some photographs of her both inside and outside of the limo for her life book. This child had been doing so much in her little life; she even came on a visit to the tax inspector with me.

Life didn't seem to be about us anymore; it was all about the kids. We weren't seeing many of our friends as we couldn't go out much. We had to be careful whom we left Logan with as most people had problems getting him to do as they asked. So for the moment, our lives were on hold again. We did get to attend family parties as we could take them all with us. We could relax at these gatherings because my family members took over, and I didn't see much of Charlee, even for nappy changing. And because I was there, Logan normally behaved himself.

We did have another weekend at the hotel in Eastbourne so that we could spend a bit of time with Dean. Logan was pleased as the staff remembered him and played James Bond with him. They even remembered Charlee, and their faces lit up when they saw we still had her.

Life seemed to be going reasonably smoothly, but I knew it wouldn't last. We received a phone call towards the end of May. We were asked to have an emergency placement of a brother and sister. The boy, Antony, was a year older than Logan, and the girl, Ann, a year younger, which worked well, they all got on really well with each other. We were now over the limit of how many children we could have with us full time, so it was decided that one of them would have to be moved. A meeting had to be held to decide which one of the newcomers it would be. Because they had both settled with us, it was decided that the best thing would be to move both of them, which saddened us as they had both started to become part of the family. A placement had been found, and introductions were made, but Ann said that she really didn't want to go. The brother and sister came to me one day and said they had both talked about it and they decided that Antony was prepared to move on his own and let Ann stay with us as she was very happy. He would be moving to his grandmother's as soon as she had moved to a larger flat. He wouldn't be in care as long as Ann would, and she wanted to go back to her mum whenever she had sorted her problems out, which would probably take a lot longer. We called the social worker and told her what the kids had decided. She should have to have a word with them as, obviously, social services were very concerned about the whole move. The initial response was that it wasn't really the children's decision to make, and they would both have to move, but Ann kicked up a fuss with temper tantrums. She refused to get into the car when it was time for more tea visits, and she said that, if she was made to go, then she would just keep running away. Social services finally agreed that it would probably be safer to leave her with us and move Antony to be nearer to his grandmother until he would move in with her full time.

One final occasion for Charlee came shortly before introductions to her adopters began. It was to Mr and Mrs Jim's daughter's wedding to which we had an invitation. Mr Jim had erected a big marquee on their back lawn near the lake. Once again, Baby Charlee was the centre of attraction. It didn't seem like five months ago that we had gone to the hospital to collect this little doll; she had come on so much, and I didn't realize how attached I was becoming to her. People always warn us about becoming attached to the babies. Normally we are able to say that we don't have them long enough as they are usually gone in roughly six weeks. Additionally, the usual routine is full of visits from social workers, health visitors, and finally the adopters, so our time is full and it is as much as we can do to get a look in. But this time, because of the custody battle, the health visitor just managed her routine check-ups, and the social worker popped in about once a week to take photos. The rest of the time she was all ours, so when the social worker appeared one day with a few profiles of adopters to go through to see if we could find a suitable match, it was very difficult to narrow it down to one couple as we felt that all of them desperately wanted a child. The case had gone against the birth father, and papers had been signed to free her for adoption. Logan had to be told as he had gotten very close to her and would miss her terribly. And David would have to be included in any farewells. Having the babies not only affected us; everyone in the house was involved, and their feelings had to be taken into account. I had to attend a planning meeting in which I would be introduced to the lucky couple. The first questions I was asked, as soon as I got home, were what were they like and were they going to look after Charlee? I think I put everyone's mind to rest. Now all we had to do was go through the introductions.

The prospective new parents must have wondered what they were walking into as all the children were sitting around waiting for them and were trying to size them up before they felt they could let Charlee go. The couple obviously passed muster because soon the children were laughing and playing, and I was able to hand Charlee over to them so they could get to know her. Robert and I gave them free range of the house and garden as we took the other children for a walk to give them a bit of space.

Over the next several weeks, we had more visits here, and we took Charlee to their house to meet her new family properly.

Suddenly the day arrived when they came for the final time to take her home with them. It was the first time I felt as though I was losing a part of me. Normally I hand the babies over without any problems, and I feel really happy for the adopters as I knew what they had been going through, having been on that side of it ourselves. This time, it took me several weeks to stop listening for her. I kept picking up toys that hadn't gone with her. The worst thing was the washing and ironing because there were clothes that had remained with us, which had to washed and ironed and put away for later use. But when you are ironing, there is a distinctive scent that comes from clothes that have been worn. Marie can remember me being unusually quiet for a little while, but she was grown-up enough to understand what I was going through. She just remained very quietly in the background.

The summer holidays arrived in time to stop me from having time to feel sorry for myself. Everyone had a very active social life, and I found myself running back and forth to town with one or another of them. If they weren't going out, they were having friends over to stay. The tent was back up in the garden. David had arrived, which definitely kept me on my toes. Hannah had joined the Air Cadets and spent part of the summer away at camp or weekends helping out at car parks for special events. She had also become very friendly with our next-door neighbour and their little girl and had been given permission to go to Cornwall with them. One of our ex-foster children, Vicky, had a daughter who was near enough the same age as Ann, and we were still seeing quite a bit of Chris, Vicky and Nicole. Ann became very good friends with Rosh, Vicky's daughter so the two of them spent a lot of time together either here or at Rosh's house. Logan was Logan and spent time with David or my nephew Joe, who was back down for the summer again sleeping in the tent with Logan and David.

We wanted to find some way of celebrating Logan's return to us, and as it had been going really well, we thought we would save up and take him on that holiday that he had asked us about when he was living with us last time. We had a word with his social worker (he'd had a change of social worker in the last few months), and she was in agreement that he would be allowed to go abroad with us. They would apply for his passport.

We then had a word with David's dad and asked if he could come to Disney World with us. We told him it wouldn't be until the following year as we would have to save up. He was in complete agreement. We helped him fill in David's passport application so that the documents would be back in plenty of time. I especially wanted to do this after the fiasco we'd had with mine. David's passport came through without any problems. Logan's, on the other hand, caused so many problems we thought we weren't going to get it in time. First of all, a letter came back to say that the application form had been received, but there was no birth certificate enclosed. But both the social worker and I knew that it had been included because we had both checked everything before sealing the envelope. It now meant that she had to get hold of another copy of his birth certificate, fill in another form, and send it back. Soon, back came the application again, this time because one of the signatures had gone outside of the box. We eventually got it in the summer of 2000, so it was just as well that we hadn't planned on going any sooner.

One incident towards the end of July upset the children, especially David and Logan. Robert and David had taken our dog, Lucy, for a walk down the lane, and on the way back they met several regular walkers who knew all of them by sight. They stopped opposite our house to make a fuss of Lucy and David, but as they were talking to Robert and David, Lucy decided to cross the road and come home. By now she was getting on, and her eyesight and hearing were getting weak. Unfortunately, as she crossed the road, a car came down the village, breaking the speed limit and ploughing into her. She didn't stand a chance, although she did get up and run into the garden. I heard the screech of brakes, and with my heart in my mouth, I ran out expecting to find David lying in the road. I met Lucy running in, but I didn't take any notice of her. Our next door neighbour had thought the same thing, but when we were told what had happened, we ran back in to find Lucy lying on our kitchen floor. Robert and I wrapped her up so we could get her to the vet. Our neighbours said they would take care of things at home and get information from the driver that we may need.

Finally, by the time we got Lucy on the vet's, table she took only a few last breaths before passing away. At least she wasn't on her own, and we were both with her. By the time we got home, the children had calmed down, but they were very upset about the whole thing. The part of the village we live in has very little traffic because the road doesn't go anywhere, but unfortunately the few drivers that do come are usually lost, and because there are no other cars, they think there is no speed limit. Judging by the looks we get, we, as villagers, shouldn't be out on the road.

Hannah started having a few problems near the end of summer. Her dad had been in touch and was making noises about having her live with him. This sort of thing always unsettles these children. Her personal hygiene had never been very good, but it started to deteriorate even more. She stopped putting her washing in the laundry box. Then the stealing started. One thing that came to light was that she had a lot of money in her possession. When she was asked, she said it was money that people had given to her for a swimming event that she was supposed to do for charity. She had told everyone that she had done it, and of course they all paid up. She had over seventy pounds, which we made her take into school and hand over to the teacher who had organized the event. It did make us more wary the next time children came to us and asked us to sponsor them.

We are not sure if it was the fact that her dad wanted her to go back and live with him or if there was another reason that she started on this downward spiral as she had been doing so well until then. Her social worker came and had a word with her but couldn't find out from her what the problem was. Hannah stopped seeing friends, and we felt that she was beginning to hide in the village, using it as an excuse not to go out and mix. So perhaps a move into town might be the best thing for her as she would be nearer to her friends and would have to go out and mix. So it was arranged for her to move to another carer. We were sad to see her go, but felt it was the right thing at that time. We did hear later that she eventually moved to her dad's, and it worked out well, which pleased us as we did have a soft spot for her

Shortly before Hannah left, we made arrangements to go to Devon for the annual holiday we normally organized after Robert had finished working on the harvest. Hannah had several Cadet camps coming up and asked if she could stay at home rather then come with us. We made arrangements for her to stay with our next-door neighbours as they had already been police checked when she went on holiday with them, and they were happy to have her.

We set off with Logan, Ann, and David. They were all excited to be going, although Ann was a bit nervous at first as she was going to be so far away from her mum and nan, but after they'd had a word with her, she looked forward to the trip. We stayed in a holiday camp in North Devon as we felt there were too many of us to stay with Toni and the twins. But we did manage to see them while we were there. The children all enjoyed themselves, especially in the clubhouse in the evenings. They even won a trophy for their dancing. All too soon, it was time to go back home. Within a few weeks, Hannah would be gone.

We were now down to just Ann and Logan, but not for long. Soon, a fourteen-year-old girl, Natalie, arrived, which pleased Ann as she said she was getting fed up with Logan and David expecting her to play boys' games. Now that everyone was back at school, she wasn't seeing as much of Rosh. Natalie was very nervous during the afternoon on the day she arrived, but soon relaxed when Logan and Ann came home. They all hit it off straight away. Natalie was never going to be an easy placement as she had a twin sister from whom everyone felt she should be separated. The twins encouraged each other in very negative ways, doing things like breaking and entering into their mum's home when she wasn't there. They had caused no end of problems at school, living on the brink of exclusion every day. But having Natalie wasn't too bad to begin with. She did settle down, especially as she was allowed to bring her friend home for overnight visits at weekends.

In November, we had a lovely visit from Charlee and her new parents. Logan and David were amazed at how much she had grown. I had lots of cuddles, but it actually helped me to realize that she didn't smell like "my" baby anymore, and I very happily handed her back to her mum when it was time for them to go. Everyone was pleased with how the reunion had gone. The boys saw how happy she was, and that was enough for them. Robert was also pleased to see her, although he hadn't got as attached as much as I had because he didn't have as much to do with her day-to-day routine.

We seemed to swop one problem from another. At first Ann and Natalie got on really well, but as Christmas approached, Ann started to play up, especially a few days before she was to go to her nan's for Christmas. I had to have a few words with her before leaving her there. I phoned later to see if she was okay, and her nan told me that Ann had told her that she was frightened of Natalie as she was making her do things that she wasn't comfortable with like stealing and telling lies. It had got to the point where Natalie was making her get up during the night to go out to the back garden to have a smoke. I said I would have a word with her when she got home, but in the meantime, she was to have a nice Christmas. Natalie's mum came to collect her on Christmas Eve, so that left us with only Logan.

We had a very quiet Christmas. Logan was determined to wait up and set a trap for Father Christmas. Luckily, he fell asleep at around eleven, so we managed to get all his presents out and under the tree before going to bed. He was really pleased with everything he got, but he read every label very carefully before opening things, and at the end he said that they weren't from Santa because he recognized my handwriting. But he was pleased with them. That was that. Next year we wouldn't even try; we'd just let him grow up. He did promise that he wouldn't tell David; it would be our secret.

There were a lot of things going on for David. His mum and her new partner had returned from Blackpool and wanted custody of David. His dad had been having problems trying to cope and had already asked social services if we could foster David on a full-time basis. That left him in a vulnerable position. Before a move could take place, there would have to be an assessment. A court welfare officer was appointed for David. We took him to see her during the Christmas holidays. She had a long chat with him. Without telling him that his dad had asked if he could to come to us, she asked him where he would like to live. He thought about it for a while before answering.

Then, in a very adult way, he told her that his heart was telling him that he wanted to stay with his dad, but he knew his dad was finding it very difficult. His head was telling him that his mum would be able to look after him better. Later, when he came asked us if he'd said the right thing, we told him that, if he'd said what he felt, then, yes, it was the right thing. But he said that what he really wanted was to come and live with us so that we could look after his dad as well. So we told him that whatever decision was made, we would always keep an eye on his dad for him. He was happy with that.

This year was the beginning of the new millennium, and all sorts of things were expected to be happening. We were asked if we would go on the emergency placement list over the holiday period. We agreed as we would normally have been on call anyway, so it didn't make much difference to us. We weren't going anywhere.

Before we picked Ann up from her nan's, we had a chat with the children's social worker and our support worker. It was decided that the right thing to do would be to have a word with Ann and explain that Natalie would be moving to the downstairs bedroom, and they would not be allowed to sleep in each other's rooms. We would also be keeping a very watchful eye on the situation. When Ann heard that, she was very relieved and said that she would tell me in future if anything else happened. I told her that I was there to look out for her, but I couldn't do that if she didn't confide in me. When Natalie came back from her mum's, she was told that she must now move downstairs and she could have her friends stay over as she would now have bunk beds in her room, which pleased her.

David was staying with us over the New Year as there was a big celebration organized in the village hall, but before that happened, we had a telephone call on 30 December. We were asked to take an emergency placement of Trevor, a seven-year-old boy. He arrived with his nan and his social worker looking very nervous as he was the middle child of five and was worried about not being with them. But as soon as Trevor arrived, there was a welcoming committee waiting to take him under their wings. They took him off and showed him to the room he would be sharing with Logan and, for the moment, with David. Ann and Natalie got him a drink and some biscuits. By the time his social worker and nan had left, he was feeling relaxed and was happy to wave them off. I didn't see any of them again that night as they went off to entertain him and get him ready for bed.

The next day was New Year's Eve, and all the children were excited about staying up and seeing in the New Year *and* the New Millennium. They all took Trevor around the village and introduced him to people and offered to help get the village hall ready, but they were politely refused. The time soon came around for us to head off to the hall where everyone else in the village turned up. We had a marvellous time between the hall and the pub. I don't think there was one face that we didn't know. Photos were taken, and at the stroke of midnight, everyone held hands and sang. Some were more tuneful than others, but no one was bothered. The fireworks display was amazing and rounded the celebration off nicely. It all came to an end too soon, and we eventually got everyone together and headed off home to tuck them up shattered but happy at 2.00 a.m.

Chapter 28

T he Year 2000 was going to be very special as Marie was pregnant, and we were going to have our first grandchild. The boys were looking forward to having a niece or nephew, as they thought of Marie as their sister. But we had a while to wait. She wasn't due until June. In the meantime, we still had our lot to keep us busy.

Trevor settled in nicely. The only problem we had was that, because he had been an emergency placement, we weren't sure how long he would be allowed to stay with us. Everyone enjoyed having him around. When David came at weekends, he, Logan, and Trevor were like the three musketeers. They would wander off up the village like three little steps: Logan was eleven; David, ten; and Trevor, nine. They would go to the cricket field to play football or make a camp just inside the woods. Ann would join them when she was with us, but she was spending more time at her mum's, and it looked as though she would be going home fairly soon.

Trevor had settled with us so well, it was decided that he would be allowed to stay. There was one incident in which his mum turned up to take him home, but after a few days, she agreed that it was in his best interest to leave him in care until she had sorted her problems out. She was very happy with him being with us, and she was allowed regular contact with him. Also, his grandparents would take it in turns to come and visit him.

Around Easter, the whole household was devastated when we got a phone call from David's stepdad to say that David's dad had died in a house fire. Our first question was where was David? Although it had been decided that his mum would have custody, he had been allowed to stay with his dad sometimes. Luckily he had been with his mum that particular weekend, so he was safe. The next morning, I had to tell the others, and they were all concerned both for David's safety and how he would take the news. He loved his dad very much. The following weekend, he came to stay with us, and they all talked about it with him, giving him an opportunity to talk about how he felt. They were like little counsellors for him. He was obviously devastated, but the support he got from the children was wonderful. They let him know that, any time he wanted to talk or cry, not only were Robert and I there for him, but the children were too.

As there were such bad feelings between David's dad and his mum and stepdad, his mum asked us if we would take him to the funeral because they didn't want to attend. We made sure that there were flowers sent in his name and that he was suitably dressed in a suit and tie. His dad would have been proud of him. We waited at the graveside with him until everyone else had gone and let him cry and say a final goodbye. He placed a beanie baby on the coffin so that his dad would not be alone. Life then had to go on as near normal as possible. We seemed to be having him nearly every weekend, and as often as we could, we would take him to the grave to put fresh flowers there. He took the others up to show them where the grave was, and sometimes he would ask them to keep him company there for a few minutes, which they did willingly.

Soon it was time for Ann to go home to her mum's. On the first of May, we loaded her things into the car and dropped her off at her mum's. The boys helped her carry her things in, and each of them gave her a cuddle and wished her luck. They told her we were all going to miss her very much.

Logan wanted to know why David couldn't come and live with us now that we had a spare bed, but we explained that it didn't work like that. And actually we didn't have a spare placement as we already had three, and we had four only because Trevor had come to us in an emergency. He'd been allowed to stay only because we all thought that he had settled so well with us, and either Natalie or Ann would be going back to her mum's fairly soon.

Natalie didn't seem to miss Ann as much as I first thought she might, although she did sleep in Ann's room on the last night to have a girlie night. Natalie was very busy doing her own thing, which was going between her dad's in Cambridge, her mum's, her sister's in town, or taking it in turns to either stay with her friend or have her friend staying here.

Natalie went on a holiday with the school to Germany at the beginning of June. We had only one phone call from one of the teachers to ask if she was up to date on her tetanus injections as she had broken her toe, and the local hospital needed to know. Apart from that, she came back safely with everyone else and at the same time, which was an accomplishment. She said she had enjoyed herself and didn't even mind the broken toe.

I spent most of that summer with Marie and even went to antenatal classes with her, which I found very interesting as it was something I had never experienced before. It wasn't what I was expecting. I thought it was going to be about breathing exercises and such, but in fact it was very much about how to handle and feed babies without feeling nervous. They operated under a very practical theme, which I thought was a really good idea. I thoroughly enjoyed going, especially when they organized a trip around the hospital to familiarize the moms to be, with where to go when the time came.

It was getting near to the time when Marie's baby was due. Everyone was getting excited. After about 20 June, the first thing everyone asked when they came home from school was if Marie had had the baby yet. But of course the answer was no, which led to very disappointed faces.

On Saturday, 24 June, Natalie was staying at a friend's house. She planned to stay until Monday morning when they would go to school together. Trevor had contact with his mum. She took him to his school's summer fête. Logan came with us to Marie's, but we had to leave at 5.00 p.m. to get home for Trevor. Both boys had supper and got ready for bed. At 10.00 p.m., Marie's partner rang to say he was taking her to hospital as contractions had started. She was asking for me to be there. The boys had heard the phone ringing; they were all excited and wanted to know if they could go with me, but we told them that wouldn't be possible. They made me promise that I would ring home as soon as the baby was born.

I arrived at the maternity unit and was allowed in. I found Marie and her partner and the midwife. We spent most of the time holding Marie's hand and listening to her saying that she had changed her mind—she didn't want to go through with it anymore! She just wanted to go home. We all told her it was too late now, and she would have to carry on. I had seen my next-door neighbours little boy's birth and thought then that, as wonderful as it was, I was pleased that I had my two arrive with their little carrier bags. It was less painful that way. But as soon as our granddaughter put in an appearance, I could understand why people go on to have more children after the first. The absolute joy you feel is very hard to describe. It was made all the more special when they asked me to cut the cord. As soon as baby was wiped over and wrapped up, we left her in the capable hands of her dad while I went to help Marie have a shower and freshen up. As soon as they were all settled, I went outside and called home to let them know that we now had a little girl to add to our family. After giving both mother and daughter a big cuddle, I set off home, leaving the new family on their own to settle for the night.

When I got home, the house was very quiet, so I managed to get to bed without waking them up. The next morning was bedlam. The children insisted I call David to let him know. Then we had to make phone calls to Dean and the rest of the family. Finally, we had to go and collect David as we couldn't go to the hospital without him or we'd never hear the end of it. Logan said he was so happy he could cry. We had a lovely visit at the hospital, but we didn't stay too long as they were being discharged, so we went to see them settle at home.

Logan came downstairs the next morning with a big smile on his face, and when I asked him what he was so happy about, he said he was feeling very grown up now that he was an uncle. When he came home that evening, he and Trevor went out and about the village telling everyone that he was now an uncle to Baby-Marie. The following evening, Marie and family came over for dinner. Baby-Marie had her first visit to Nanny and Grandads'.

The next evening, Logan went to the cricket field on his own for a while and came back looking for a carrier bag. Then he went off again on his bike. A little while later, he came back with a carrier bag swinging from the handle bars. He got off his bike and called us out into the garden to show us what he had. He put his hand into the bag and pulled out a hedgehog. He said, now that Marie had her baby, he wanted to have a pet of his own. We explained that it was a wild hedgehog and wouldn't like being kept captive. But we told him that he could leave it in the garden and could put food out for it. When he came home the next day, he went out looking for it but couldn't find it. Then we were all out in the garden looking, but it was nowhere to be found. He kept looking for a few days but then gave up and was happy to just be an uncle.

A lot of my time was spent on the telephone talking to birth families, especially when they were having problems. As much as their problems should not be ours, we sometime felt that we could not always help the children until their families had sorted their problems out.

This can be quite time consuming. One night, Natalie's mum rang me to let off steam about the problems she was having with Natalie during contact. I ended up on the phone to her for just over an hour, and I had no sooner put the phone down than Natalie's dad's partner rang to say virtually the same thing about what they were having to deal with when they had contact with both Natalie and her sister. So there was no relaxing for me that evening. By the time I got off the phone, it was bedtime, but to us, it was all part of the job. There were times when Robert would have happily disconnected the phone as he said that every time he came in, I had it attached to my ear, and he often felt like calling me on the phone just to talk to me.

As if we didn't have enough children in the house, some of the younger ones often brought imaginary friends in that we had to accept as part of the family. Trevor introduced us to his friend, who was named Claudian. Trevor explained to me that his friend couldn't sit down to meals with us because, every time he tried eating the food, it would fall out between his bones. It seemed he was a skeleton, which made a change from the normal, and we decided that he would be good company when Halloween came around.

Before Halloween, we had our overseas holiday to organize. We made arrangements with social services for Natalie and Trevor to go on respite as we had already made the arrangements for our trip the previous year before either of them had come to live with us.

The school summer holidays seemed to follow a pattern of contact with families and friends, and this year was no exception. Logan said that he was feeling as though he had been abandoned by his family as he was the only one not seeing a family member. He wanted to see his brother. We had a word with his social worker who managed to contact him, and it was agreed that arrangements would be made for them to meet up. If that visit went well, they could see each other on a regular basis. Logan's brother was in a permanent relationship and was living with his partner and their daughter. After several visits, it was agreed that Logan could have overnight stays. This worked for quite a while, but like all things for Logan, things eventually went wrong as his brother's relationship came to an end and he had to move out. That left him with nowhere to have Logan on a regular basis. All we could do was be there for him. To take his mind off things, we started to concentrate on our holiday.

Donna and Joe came up trumps again and let us have their villa for next to nothing. Not only that, but we could also have the use of their people carrier, which was parked in their garage for their own private use. So we had to worry only about our fares and entrance fees to the theme parks. Both David and Logan had been saving for a year and had managed to save £50 each. This we doubled for them; we had told them we would contribute an amount equal to whatever they had saved. We felt also that this holiday came at the right time for David as he was still hurting from his dad's death.

This time we would travel without any stress as we had left a good hour and a half between connecting flights. Another friend, who was living near to Donna's villa, would pick us up at the airport and take us back at the end of our holiday.

We set off full of confidence, and the two boys were excited. We got to Gatwick without any problems—a good start. We checked in and waited for our call. Unfortunately, there was a one-hour delay, which cut our changeover time to half an hour, but we figured we'd be okay. Because of rescheduling, the flight path was going to be altered slightly, which would add another ten minutes onto flight time. We could surely make our connection in twenty minutes! The boys were really good on the flight; we had no problems with them. When we started the landing procedure, David started crying as his ears were hurting. We had to keep giving him sweets to get him to swallow. We eventually landed safely. Now for the sprint! We found our luggage, got through customs, and were told which conveyor to put it on for our next flight. "You may have already missed it," said the attendant, "but it's worth a go!" We ran the whole length of Atlanta Airport (it's long!), and we finally arrived, red faced and out of breath. The stewardess greeted us: "Ah, we have been waiting for you and have upgraded you to first class to make the flight easier for you." The boys were ecstatic when we were shown to our seats, which were like armchairs, and each one had a private computer screen. We were waited on hand and foot; the boys had whatever they wanted. Sadly, this leg of the journey lasted for only an hour.

We were met by our friend, and he took us to the villa. By the time we got there, it was quite late, so we just concentrated on getting something to eat and getting ready for bed. The first day we stayed near the villa and ventured out only to get some basic shopping. We divided the following days between the parks, shopping, and "break days" at "home", only going out for a meal in the evening. The first several days weren't too bad, but once we went to Disney World, Logan started playing up. He would try to lose us, so we had to watch him like hawks. He was very sulky and would try and cause arguments by refusing to say what he wanted to eat. Or he wouldn't eat what we ordered. David, on the other hand, was so good. His face was a picture when he met the characters and they interacted with him. He loved nearly every minute of it. The only time we had a problem was when we were queuing up to go on the Men in Black ride. He was okay until we got to the front of the queue. He then said that he had changed his mind and didn't want to go on it as it looked scary. We promised him that it would be okay. In the end, we picked him up between us and carried him on. By the time the ride finished, he wanted to go on it again. After that, he trusted us when we said the rides wouldn't hurt him. His favourite one was It's a Small World, which we went on a few times.

On one day, we did manage to lose each other. Robert was in the lead, David was next, then Logan, and then me. Logan bent down looking for small lizards. By the time I got him back up, there was no sign of Robert or David, so all we could do was to stand where we were until they eventually came back looking for us.

The three weeks went too quickly for David, but Logan was pleased when it was time for us to go. I had rung Trevor and Natalie halfway through the holiday to let them know that we hadn't forgotten them. Now all we had to do was survive the journey home.

The first flight was on time. So far so good. We got off the plane in Atlanta and went to collect our luggage. We waited and waited for it to come. All the other people who had been on our flight had collected theirs and gone. In the end, we went to ask at an enquiry desk and were told that our luggage would have automatically been transferred. All we had to do was claim it when we got to Gatwick. We then had another mad dash to get to our departure gate, which we managed with about ten minutes to spare. One day we'll get it right.

When we got home, we swore we would never take Logan on another holiday. It had been far too stressful, although we did think that particular holiday may have been too much for him. But we felt shattered by the time we got home. The only silver lining had been watching David.

When we were talking to Logan several years ago, he said that he had been pleased with the holiday. It was just that all his allusions had been shaken. He had thought the characters from the Disney films were real, and when he met the characters, he was very disappointed when he realized that they were only people dressed up. Obviously we have forgiven him and hope that he has forgiven us for putting him through it.

Shortly before we went away, Dean moved back from Hastings. It had all gone wrong for him down there, and he wanted to come home. We knew it would be no good for him to come back to the village as he had no way of getting a job there, so Nicole very kindly offered to put him up until he found himself a job and somewhere to live. It was lovely to have him back, but our being away for three weeks seemed to make it hard on him as he had expected us to be there. He coped as well as he could, but we weren't back long when we got a phone call from his doctor to say that he had taken an overdose and had been admitted to the hospital. We went up to see him straight away. He was fine, but there would be the ongoing worry about how he was going to cope as he was suffering from schizophrenia. The doctors admitted him to the psychiatric ward where he would get the help that he needed. He was there until after Christmas, and staff there were able to help him get sorted out with the right medication. Finally, he was back on an even keel.

Natalie and Trevor were pleased to have us back and were even more pleased with their presents. We were soon back to normal. One of the highlights was seeing Baby-Marie after being away from her for so long. It had been only three weeks, but it seemed so much longer, and she seemed to have grown so much in our absence.

The return to school was not without its difficulties. Logan was still a bit angry over the holiday and was taking it out on everyone at school. Trevor was having problems with his contact; he wasn't sure if he wanted to keep seeing his family. He felt that they kept letting him down. Like Logan, he was taking it out on the teachers.

Meetings were set up to discuss Logan's schooling next year as he would be leaving primary education and going on to secondary. The school personnel were pushing for him to go to another special-needs school, but the only one in the area had a really bad reputation, and we didn't feel too happy about him going there. We asked if there was any chance he could go to our local secondary school with additional built-in support. It was agreed that it would be looked into. The secondary school was agreeable provided that permission for the support could be granted. The primary school administration was still against it and felt that it would be setting him up to fail. Indeed, they even felt he would probably still fail at the special needs school. We asked if he would be able to go to the special needs school if he failed at the mainstream school. It was agreed that he would. We then asked what would happen if he went to the special needs school first. If he failed there, where would he go? Nobody knew what options would be left to him, so we reasoned would it not be better to at least give him a chance at mainstream with at least an alternative option if he did fail? So after endless discussions, it was agreed by everyone that he would be given the chance of attending the mainstream school with his classroom assistant moving along with him. We felt quite happy with this decision.

Natalie was being herself and playing up at school anyway. We were only a few weeks into the second half of the term when Trevor was excluded for two days. Natalie brought home a letter to say that she was being excluded for three days. On Friday, Logan came home with a letter saying that he was being excluded for two days the following week. Then Trevor brought his letter home on Logan's last day of exclusion to say he was being excluded for three days! And so it went on for the rest of the term. There was at least one of them at home every day until the final week when I actually had the last two days of term without any of them. I hadn't had a chance to go Christmas shopping so it was a mad dash in those last few days. I was hoping that none of them would be off on the last day so I could finish the final things I needed to do.

Christmas was with us once again. This year we paid a visit to Marie's before heading home to get our Christmas dinner. The rest of the holiday went okay apart from an emergency placement New Year's Eve of a brother and sister, four and two years old respectively. Logan was not impressed with them, but Trevor took them under his wing and showed them around the house telling them about how he had felt when he arrived the previous year and how it helped him when everyone showed him around and helped him to settle in. He told them that it was his turn now to do it for someone else. This placement didn't last long as the next day their grandparents arrived to take them home with them.

It is amazing how quickly the years seem to go by. That year was my fiftieth birthday, but because it falls on Boxing Day every year, we arranged to have a little party a few days later on 28 December, but the day didn't start very well. It was snowing, and the motorway was closed, so that meant that my family members couldn't get to our house. But we still had a good turnout with our local friends. Near the end of the day, we were just thinking that, apart from my family not getting here, we'd had a lovely day. Just then the phone rang. It was my brother Dermot in Ireland to let us know that our sister Pat had just died from pneumonia, and the funeral would be in three days. There was no way either Robert or I could get there, so all I could do was to think of her and send my love to the rest of the family.

Chapter 29

The year 2001 came in very quickly and very quietly. Baby-Marie was growing more beautiful every day. We were able to concentrate on her quite a lot as there were no new placements in the early part of the year. Logan, David, and Trevor were still getting on well together and were often out and about together or playing upstairs. Natalie spent most of the time at her mum's, which we thought was great as it must have meant they were getting on a lot better.

Logan joined the village youth club, which he thoroughly enjoyed. He enjoyed it so much that one evening when he wasn't very well and I said he would be better not going, he went upstairs in a temper and trashed his room. Luckily, he didn't break anything, but his clothes and belongings were thrown all over the room.

Trevor still wasn't allowed back to school full time. He would go in for the morning and then go to another carer for the afternoon. He wasn't too bothered about this as he wasn't very happy at school anyway.

In Ireland, a month after a person passes, a celebration mass is held for him or her. As I hadn't been able to go to

Pat's funeral, Elizabeth and I and two of our nieces went over for the weekend to attend and meet up with more of the family members. Again, Robert was left to cope with the children with help from Marie. I was back in time for Marie's twenty-first birthday, for which we all went out for a meal.

As if we didn't have enough to contend with, our car was stolen from outside Sainsburys. We had gone shopping, taking Logan and Trevor along, and when we came out with our trolley full, we couldn't find our car. We had a good look around the car park thinking we had just forgotten where we had parked it, but it was nowhere to be seen. It was a freezing cold night, so we were not amused. We first reported the theft inside the store, and then we rang the police. Then we rang Marie. Her partner came out to pick us up and take us home. We heard from the police several days later that they had got it back, but it was not in very good shape. It had been used for a spate of petty crimes. The insurance company paid out in a reasonable time, but in the meantime, we were back to relying on the good will of everyone in the village to take us shopping. Social services did let us use taxis for important appointments for the children, which was a help. We were back on the road by the end of March. We bought a Vauxhall Albany, a seven-seater. The kids loved it as the seats were like armchairs. It even had curtains on the windows.

In the meantime, Natalie had her review, and it was agreed by everyone that, if she was still in care by the same time the following year, a move to town would be arranged as that was where her school and her friends were, so being there would be easier for her. There was one serious concern over her, and that was that she had started corresponding with an eighteen-year-old prison inmate. But, as it is with everything else, we could only ask them to be careful and not get involved. We could not live their lives for them or monitor them twenty-four hours a day. Although we had no letters arrive at our address for her, that didn't mean that she wasn't receiving them at a friends' addresses.

Logan was having more problems at school. He was coming home and taking it out on Trevor. He told staff members at school that he was worried about me as one of my brothers was ill, and it was upsetting me. This was true in a way; one of my brothers had an aneurysm and had gone into a coma during an operation. He was still in the same state after several months. Since he went into the coma, our sister Pat had died, and now my oldest brother, Patrick, wasn't very well and was in hospital in Harrow. I didn't realize at the time how much of this information had filtered down to the children, but Logan had always been very intuitive and had obviously picked up on this more than the others. In fact, Patrick did die in April. This time we were able to attend his funeral as it was in England. There were still problems surrounding our arrangements. We had organized somewhere for Logan and Trevor to go after school on the day of the funeral and had asked Natalie to make arrangements with her friend or her mum, whichever she wanted. But she never bothered, so she got annoyed because we made arrangements with our next-door neighbour for her to go there. It would have been nice, just once, to be able to go to something important without all the drama.

I was contacted by Logan's school on more than one occasion. He was often put into isolation, and we were told afterwards that administrators felt that he was a danger to himself and couldn't be left unsupervised. When he was in isolation and a teacher went in to check on him, they often found him up on the highest window ledge just sitting there waiting. Other times when his friends were in isolation, Logan would try all sorts of tricks to try and rescue them. During one phone I learned that he was acting inappropriately in the hallway. When I asked what he was doing, I was told that he was jumping out in front of staff members pretending to be James Bond. I couldn't understand why it was considered unacceptable for a ten-year-old boy to imagine he was James Bond.

I don't know if it was to do with his problems at school or if there was another reason, but Logan started bullying Trevor. Respite was organized for Logan. He would go to another carer about once a month to give everyone a break. He quite enjoyed this and got on well with his respite carers. Trevor went for an interview at the same school Logan was going to; it was agreed that he would be able to start there.

David was still coming most weekends, but I did see a lot more of him as he wanted me to work at his school. So I volunteered to help out and started as a classroom assistant, which I thoroughly enjoyed as it was nice to get home and not have to think about any problems there until the next time I went there. Initially I could go in when I wanted, but it wasn't long before they were ringing me most days asking if I could go in.

As we had been going back and forth to Harrow to see my brother in hospital, we decided after the funeral that we would take the boys away for a short break. My brother Sean and his partner went to Tenerife leaving us their house keys, so we packed the three boys into the car and went off to Lincolnshire for the weekend. Natalie didn't want to come with us, so we made arrangements for her to go to another carer for the weekend so that she could stay near her friends and her mum.

We arrived in Wisbech on Friday night and took the boys for something to eat. The next day, we took them out on the mud flats where they ran off any excess energy. On Sunday, we went to the butterfly farm. Logan was always fascinated with the terrapins, and we had to make sure he didn't take them out of the pond. We started the journey home on Monday, stopping for a bit at the fun farm and play area. By the time we got home, they were actually ready for bed.

Things with Natalie had started to deteriorate. She kept trying to make last-minute arrangements to stay overnight with friends. We did understand, but we needed her to make proper arrangements. Instead, she kept coming up with people we didn't know. Obviously we couldn't give permission for her to stay overnight with anyone that neither her mum nor we knew. Eventually, towards the end of May, she was supposed to be staying at her mum's, but one of her friends' mum rang me to say that she had turned up there in a drunken and distressed state. Natalie had admitted that she'd had unprotected sex and was worried about going to her mum's. I rang her mum and explained the situation. We agreed the best thing would be for her mum to collect her and make sure that she was taken to the doctor the next day for the morning-after pill. I then rang her friend and explained what was going to happen. It was a very rocky week as she was determined to stay in town.

At the beginning of June, I was awakened by police officers knocking on the door. They wanted to know if Natalie had returned home. I told them she hadn't, but I hadn't been expecting her as she was supposed to be staying with friends. They said they'd had a call from one of her friends' mums to say that Natalie had been drunk and was last seen with two boys who said they were going to put her in a taxi and send her home. But she obviously hadn't arrived at our house. The officers had to search the house to make sure she wasn't hiding somewhere. I then gave them several addresses of places where I thought she might be and the name of the two taxi companies that she might use. But no one had seen or heard from her. There was no sight of her that night. The next afternoon she rang her mum asking her to pick her up in town. Her mum rang to let me know. The police then rang to let me know that she was back at her mum's. EDT was also informed.

The following day, Natalie's mum rang to say that she'd had enough and was going to put her daughter in a taxi. If she didn't come back when she was supposed to, then she would just lock her out of the house. Natalie did return to us, but in a very subdued state; she wasn't saying very much. She began to be a bit more sociable after a few days. Then she made arrangements to go to her dad's for the weekend. I was finding it more difficult to get her up in the mornings; she would keep the taxi waiting, which annoyed the drivers as they often had other jobs to go after the school run. Someone from her school would ring to say that, although she was registered as being in, she was often missing from her lessons. Some days after school, she would go straight around to friends' houses without telling anyone. She just wouldn't be there for the taxi to bring her home. It was getting to be a habit to have to ring EDT and the police to report her as missing.

Her social worker came to see her, and he promised her that he would start looking for a placement in town, but in the meantime, he asked her to work with us. We had no problem with her going to friends' houses after school, but we wanted her to tell us so we could organize the taxi to pick her up at her friend's house instead of straight after school. She was fine for a few days, and everything worked well, but it didn't last for long. Eventually, toward the end of June, she went missing again. This time she had been seen getting into a taxi with someone that her sister knew. But she also knew that this person didn't have a very good reputation. We, again, had to call the police and EDT. This time, she was missing for a couple of days. Her sister came up with an address, and when she went to pick Natalie up and take her to her mum's, she didn't want to leave.

I had a word with her social worker and our support worker, and we all agreed that, as she had been staying with a known criminal who had been in prison on drug charges and also had been involved in an armed robbery, it was probably for the best that she wasn't brought back to us. After all, we had the younger children to think of.

We could only assume that this was the person that she had been writing to while he was in prison, and she had met up with him when he was released.

Marie and I packed her belongings up and dropped them off at her mum's. We couldn't believe the state of her room. There were half-empty lager cans in her chest of drawers in between her clothes, and we also found a carrier bag that contained a load of vomit. Needless to say, I had to set to and give the room a good cleanout with plenty of disinfectant. Over the years, I learned to never be shocked at what I find in the bedrooms at the end of placements. I am just amazed that kids can let themselves get into that state, which is why I always like to give the bedrooms a good clean and wash everything down between placements.

While all this was going on, we had Baby-Marie's christening, which turned out to be a wonderful day. Both David and Logan behaved themselves, and they both looked really smart in their best clothes. We felt quite proud of them as they took their places as Baby-Marie's godfathers. My friend, Donna, did us the honour of being her godmother.

We also had a new placement of a six-month-old girl named Megan. Marie, Baby-Marie, and our support worker came with me to collect her from the hospital. She had a fractured skull, and there were some concerns over how this had happened. She was absolutely gorgeous, but then I always think the babies are wonderful. We were supposed to go out for a meal with Toni and the twins that evening, but we had to cancel, and they understood. Everyone had to come back to the house to do the paperwork. As soon as we met Megan's mum, we took an instant liking to her, and we knew we were going to be able to work with her. By the time all the paperwork was done, it was seven in the evening. We then had to go shopping to get nappies, food, and a few clothes to keep us going. By the time we managed to settle her down it was 9.30. The boys were delighted with her; each of them tried to outdo the other in being helpful. Logan had been to youth club and felt that, because he had missed a few hours, he should be given more time with her.

Mum had contact with Megan the next day, which was a Saturday. I had to fit that in around taking David to a party, but we managed. Then we had a BBQ in the evening. Marie, Baby-Marie, and her dad came too. Baby-Marie was fascinated with Megan and kept wanting to play with her. On Sunday, we went to Woodside Farm and Wildfowl Park for a picnic. As this was half-term week, we had a lot of outings arranged but we now had to organize them around Megan's contact with her mum, who was allowed to see her every day. And we also had to be kitted out with a cot and pushchair as it had been several years since we had needed of one.

It was decided that Trevor would benefit with counselling, so we had to have an interview with Child and Adolescent Mental Health Services (CAHMS) to work out what would be the best way to go about. It was agreed that he would respond better if I went along to his sessions with him, and as it worked out, this was a good idea as he found it difficult to open up to people. When he was asked a question, he would look at me then tell me the answer. Everyone was happy to let it carry on like this while it worked. He was having regular contact with his mum and grandparents, so apart from his relationship with Logan, he was quite happy. We had to keep a close eye on the two of them. But having said that, I must say that there were still problems.

Both boys were both looking forward to Trevor starting at Logan's school. He started near the end of June as everyone thought going for a few weeks to the end of term would make it easier for him when he went in September. Trevor was hoping to start off going in the taxi with Logan, but I explained to him that, as it was his first day, I would take him in and get him settled, which he understood. He looked forward to going every day after that in the taxi with Logan. He made a bit of a shaky start, but towards the end of term, he finally started to settle down.

Logan had his introduction day at the secondary school and couldn't wait to start there in September. Things settled down a bit once Natalie had gone, as we now stopped having telephone calls in the middle of the night or having to stay up until the police called around.

David didn't want to go home after the half-term holiday in case Megan would be gone by the next time he came over. Also I had to give up working at his school because Megan was taking up a lot of time. It was especially difficult trying to keep up with contact about three times a week. At least all contacts went ahead as her mum was very reliable at being there, unlike a lot of parents who quite often wouldn't turn up.

We celebrated Baby-Marie's first birthday with a trip to Whipsnade Zoo. It was a lovely day, and a good time was had by all. At around this time, Trevor had to be told that his two younger brothers were going to be adopted. Arrangements were made for him to have a goodbye meeting with them, which was very sad and emotional. I don't know how much of it really sunk in with them. I also took him to the hospital to visit his mum and his new baby sister. At first he was really pleased and excited to see them, but then it all got a bit much for him, and he began to say that she wasn't his sister; that she was a stranger. He carried this on for a while. We assumed it was his way of dealing with the loss of his two brothers, and also he realized that there would be a point when he would also lose this little sister too, and it would be easier for him not to get attached, because this is what did happen he was allowed to see her several times more before he had his final visit with her.

The summer holidays started in the normal way. My nephew came down on the first day, and the boys asked if he could stay the night as they were putting the tent up. I said that would be fine, and his mum had no problems with it. Towards the end of the holidays it was the same as last year— a case of "Joe, you start back at school in a few days' time. Hadn't you better go home and get your stuff ready?" Mind you, he did go home a few times to get clean clothes and say hello to his mum.

During the summer holidays, Megan's contact carried on about three times a week, so we had to organize anything else around those visits. The boys didn't mind; they were just so pleased to have her in the house. It was handy having the seven-seater car as we could have a good day out which included Marie and Baby-Marie. We also had to equip Logan out in his new school uniform. Unfortunately I picked one of his off days to do this. We parked the car and paid for three hours as we had other things to do around the town. We left his uniform until last, giving ourselves an hour, which we thought would be plenty of time to get a pair of shoes, some shirts, and some trousers. We managed the shoes and shirts in not too long a time, but to try to get him to try on a pair of trousers was a nightmare. First off, he refused. Then he went into the dressing room and took ten minutes putting them on over his jeans. He took another ten minutes to take them off again, only to come out in his jeans with the trousers in his hands. I sent him back in again to take his jeans off and put the trousers on. We eventually managed to get him a couple of pairs, but when we got back to the car, we had over-run our parking time by minutes and ended up getting a £30 fine. Those trousers turned out to be very expensive.

It was suggested that it would do Logan a lot of good to go to a small summer school for a few days and get to know some of the other children who would be starting in September. He readily agreed and really enjoyed this.

Megan had to attend an appointment at Guys Hospital for a check-up as she had a hole in her heart. Her mum and I both took her. They medical professionals were very pleased with her. The hole wasn't big enough to worry about at the moment. They would be looking at her possibly having an operation when she was about three or four. In the meantime, she would be fine. She did have an operation later on when she was back safely in her mum's care. While she was with us, she had to be on special milk, which we had to order through our surgery. Every time I went to pick it up, the ladies in the dispensary would ask to see the "special milk baby". For ages after she had gone back home, they would always ask me how the special milk baby was getting on.

A good friend of ours had moved to France and had been asking us to go over there and see him. We'd always put him off because we didn't like to go anywhere without the children as we felt they needed holidays too. But this year Robert and I decided that we would try to have a week away from them together. No one wanted to move the boys anywhere else for a week, so it was decided that Megan was young enough to go to another carer. But it was one we had socialized with, so Megan was very comfortable with them, and they also knew her mum as we had introduced her to them during the summer. Everyone was happy with that arrangement. Placing the two boys temporarily was going to be more difficult as Trevor was settled with us, and it was very difficult to get anyone to have Logan. So Marie came to our rescue and offered to move back home and look after them. They would be at school all week, and the plan was approved by social services and our support worker, who said she would keep an eye on them. Marie was to have her number and should call if she was worried about anything. Plus, Marie had split up with Baby's father earlier in the year, and after a few months on her own, she had met someone else who would be on hand to help her out.

Well, I ended up wishing we had never gone away. We left on a Friday night after the boys went to bed. We had explained to them where we were going, and we told them we would be back before too long. They seemed okay as they gave us a goodbye hug before going off to bed.

On Saturday, when both boys got up, Trevor wanted to know where I was. When Marie told him, he said, "What, today?" They both played up, Logan being the ringleader. As it was raining, he had them both running in and out in their socks refusing to put any shoes on. They wouldn't do anything they were told, and the refused to go to bed at the end of the day. Marie finally managed to get them upstairs at 11.40 p.m. Trevor said he missed Megan. Logan said I shouldn't have left him, and he wasn't going to school.

The boys woke up on Sunday in the same mood. They had removed the sheets from the spare bed in the middle of the night. Logan chucked his Rice Krispies on the floor because there was no stardust cereal for him to have. He told Marie that he could remove the sheets if he wanted as he was master of the house now, and Trevor would have to do everything that Logan told him to as Trevor was now his slave. As a last resort, Marie rang me in France so that I could have a word with them. It seemed to work. They both quietened down until bedtime when she had a job to get them to stay in their rooms.

On Monday, they both got up okay, but Logan's behaviour soon went downhill. He refused to get dressed for school, and he started wrestling Trevor to the floor even though Trevor asked him not to. When Marie had to pull him off, and he told her to f***k off! He had pepperoni for breakfast. He wouldn't go out for the school bus, refusing to leave the kitchen. She eventually managed to get him outside, but he pushed Trevor over as he left. Once he was outside, he started banging on the windows. The girl from next door came out and got him to walk up the road with her to catch the bus. Marie didn't see him anymore, so she assumed he had gone to school. Trevor was a lot quieter and got himself ready for school and helped Marie with Baby. As he was leaving to catch his taxi, Marie thanked him for being better behaved and for helping her with Baby. As he left, he told her that Logan was never that bad for Marie(.meaning me)

My nephew Joe came around in the evening, and they played on the computer, which kept them quiet, apart from one incident of Logan kicking Trevor. That evening was a lot better than the previous two. The only incident on the Tuesday was Trevor coming in complaining of a wasp sting, so Marie had to tell both of them off for playing with a wasp nest. On Wednesday, Trevor's behaviour was excellent. Logan mucked about in the morning but managed to catch the school bus. At lunchtime, the school rang. Logan and another boy had gone missing, and the teachers were trying to find them. Marie phoned our support worker to let her know what had been going on over the last few days. She was told to ring back and let her know what happened. Someone from the school phoned at two in the afternoon. They weren't having any luck and were now going to ring the police. They rang back at 2.30 in the afternoon to say that the other boy's granddad had found them and brought them back to school. In the meantime, our support worker had phoned Logan's social worker who said that she would come and see him on Thursday evening.

When Logan came home from school, he was in a foul mood. Marie asked him to go to his room. He carried on swearing, went to the spare bedroom, and stated throwing things about. When she tried to stop him, he took a swing at her. She managed to get him into his own room, but he came downstairs ten minutes later and walked out of the house. A neighbour from down the road knocked at the door to let Marie know that she had seen him in the next village and didn't think he should be there. Marie took Trevor and Baby next door so our neighbour could watch them while she went with the other neighbour to find Logan. When they caught up with him, he got into the car without making a fuss. At home, he had dinner and went to bed without a fight.

On Thursday, Trevor was well behaved again and caused no problems at home or school. Logan was okay when he got up, and he went off to school, but in the evening the school bus company rang to say that Logan never turned up at 3.30. Then he arrived home saying the bus went without him, and he had got a lift home in my nephew's taxi. The school rang to say that the bus had waited ten minutes and had to leave without him. So no one was sure what actually happened, but at least he arrived home safely. He was in another foul mood. He started chucking Trevor's school things around and swearing. He went out but came back at 6.30 p.m. in a better mood. He had dinner and went to bed without a problem.

Marie had a job to get Logan out of bed the next morning, but he managed to get the school bus on time. Then he told Marie that he didn't want to go to respite as he wanted to be home to get the presents from Mum and Dad when they got home. After Marie and Trevor managed to get him into the taxi at 5 p.m., they both heaved sighs of relief. Marie's final account in our diary reads, "May the Lord have mercy on his soul." I quite understood what she meant when I read it.

But Marie wasn't quite finished yet. She still had until we got home. On Friday, after Logan left, she received a telephone call at 6.30 p.m. from one of the social workers. Marie learned that it was rumoured that Trevor's mum was going to abduct her kids because she had found out where the baby was being fostered from some medical records that had been left behind by accident. Marie was given an incident phone number to ring. At 6.50 p.m., Logan's mum phoned and asked to speak to him. When Marie told her he was in the bath, she said she would phone back at about 7.10. Marie then phoned the police on the incident number, and a child protection officer came at around at 7.30. But his mum had not phoned back. The officer told Marie that Trevor's mum had a sister. An article in the paper reported that she'd left her husband for a twenty-million-pound lottery winner. The mum of one of the older children told that child that she had come into some money, and a man would be arriving in a blue van to get them. Trevor was the only one that she had tried to contact. There were no further incidents for the next twenty-four hours.

I don't know what I was expecting when we got home as Marie had been ringing me to keep me up to date, but all I can say is how proud we are of her for the job she did. We know there were a lot of carers who couldn't have coped as well as she did.

Trevor was in bed asleep when we got home, but he was really pleased to see us when he got up the next day. The first thing he wanted to know was when Megan was coming home. We took Marie and Baby home so Marie could have her mental breakdown in peace. We then took Trevor swimming and for a meal to thank him for being good for Marie. He was a bit worried about Logan coming home. We all had to face that.

Logan arrived home about 7.30 p.m. The first thing he said to Robert was, "You're home from your holiday then." Robert said we were, but we weren't very pleased with his behaviour while we were away. Logan told Robert that he didn't care. Robert told him not to push it. Logan said that, if Robert pushed him, he would report him for child abuse. I told him to get something to eat and just go to bed.

I had no problem getting him up the next morning. They both went off to school. But that evening was Logan's parents' evening at school. The school administrators weren't very pleased with him either, as he was constantly being rude to the teachers. They had tried detention and a few other punishments, but nothing seemed to be working. They asked me if I had any suggestions. I knew how much he liked going to that school, and he was sitting right next to me, so I said that, if he couldn't handle the school rules, then they should chuck him out and send him to the special-needs school. I said that it didn't matter what punishment anyone came up with, if Logan didn't want it to work, then it wouldn't. And only he could make it work. Finally it was agreed that they would give him another month to see how it went. He came home in a very subdued mood. He was a bit quieter for the next few days, but as normal, it didn't last long. On Thursday, I had a call from the school. There had been a serious incident. Logan had been seen leaning over the banisters. I was asked to keep him home the following day as they were going on a field trip and couldn't take responsibility for his safety. All of this was because of his behaviour and attitude. He was very disappointed when he got home, and he went straight to bed.

In the meantime, I had a phone call from Trevor's mum. She wanted to talk to him. I had a chat with her after she spoke to him, and she told me that it was not her sister who had gone off with a millionaire. Rather, it was the older sister of another girl who was in care. The weekend went off without any major incidents. Trevor played with Megan and Baby-Marie, and Logan had John down to keep him company.

I took Logan back to school on Monday. We started the day with an appointment with the head teacher. But because of his behaviour over the last few weeks, the teacher asked that we keep Logan out of school for the following week to give him time to realize how serious the situation was. Hopefully he would come back with a better attitude. Logan was fine for the weekend and all the way through until it was time for us to go to Trevor's parents' evening. Marie came over to look after the boys. Trevor didn't need to attend the meeting, so she had both of them. Logan started as soon as we left the house. The first thing he did was put his fingers into Trevor's dinner. Then he pulled Trevor out of the drinks cupboard (while he was getting a drink to go with his dinner) by the back of his collar, ran off outside when he got told off, got up on top of the shed, and started throwing stones. Marie finally managed to get him in. He went straight to his room. The following day he was as good as gold and actually did the work that his teacher had sent home for him.

Trevor's parents' evening wasn't so good. He had been playing up the last few days. We wondered if it was because Logan was off school. Did he think that, if he played up, then he would be sent home? The next day I told him that, whatever he did that day, he wouldn't be sent home. He came home that night with a very positive note in his diary; his behaviour that day had been completely different.

On Friday, I had to leave Logan at my sister-in-law's as I had to go to Guy's Hospital with Megan and her mum. Because of the hole in her heart, she had to have regular check-ups. They, again, were very pleased with her and were going to transfer her to the Lister Hospital as there was no need to keep taking her to London for regular check-ups; they would need to see her only twice a year.

David arrived on Friday. The children were all pleased to see him, but the peace lasted only until Saturday when David and Trevor came home on their own. Logan was being too bossy, and they both kept their distance from him for the rest of the day. On Sunday, Logan went to see his grandparents for the day, so Robert took David and Trevor swimming while I looked after Megan.

The entire half-term week was peppered with a series of fights and arguments between Logan and the other two boys. I was constantly having to watch them to make sure that Logan didn't hit Trevor when he wouldn't do as

Logan told him. It was easier when David was around as he would come and tell me what was going on so I could deal with it. Apart from an upset tummy, Megan sailed through the week, which was just as well.

We had finalized Logan's independent education plan (IEP), which is now known as personal education plan (PEP). It was agreed that, if Logan wanted to, he had the potential to make it work at this school. They gave him three targets to reach before they met up again and explained to him how important homework was. But when we got home, he said he wasn't going to do any homework because he didn't feel like it. I had to argue with him to get him to do it.

Things were not getting any better between the two boys. Logan kept trying to keep Trevor from watching television in the dining room. He'd sneak into Trevor's bedroom and scatter his toys or throw them downstairs. I was finding it more and more difficult to keep them separated. I had a word with our support worker and both boys' social workers. The only idea they could come up with was to try to get more respite from Logan.

We took Logan shopping to get him a bike for his birthday, but he wouldn't even look at them let alone try one for size. When we asked if he would rather have something else, he said no, he wanted a bike. So in the end, we had to pick one for him. He started a spate of running off. One evening after he'd had a particularly bad day at school because he refused to take part in his lessons, he said he'd had enough and was going to run away. He banged Trevor's head against the wall and ran out. This happened at about 6.00. I waited until 7.00 before I rang EDT and the police.

There was still no sign of him. The police turned up at 7.30, and Logan returned at 7.45. The officer tried to talk to him, but Logan just told him to go away as it was nothing to do with him. The officer tried telling him that he was wasting police time by not talking, so Logan told him to go away and do something else then. The officer did give him a warning about hitting Trevor and said that, if he injured him, he could be charged with actual bodily harm (ABH) as he was now over twelve years of age. Logan promised to Trevor alone, which he did for a few days.

It seemed as though Logan was really making us pay for having gone away for that week. It felt as though the whole household was centred around Logan. Megan was no trouble. We were getting on well with her contact. Apart from trying to keep Logan from tormenting him, we had no major problems with Trevor, but things couldn't continue the way they were. We had committed to Logan for the long haul, but we were finding it very difficult to know what to do with him. Every time we tried to talk to him about the problems, we got nowhere. We could only ask for advice and help from social services, but I think they were at a loss too. More respite wasn't the ideal answer as it was sending him away all the time, but we were all at our wits' end.

Finally, I think Trevor had enough. He went to visit his older brother for tea, but when the social worker went to pick him up, he refused to come back while Logan was with us. We completely understood as it was getting harder for me to keep them separated. Trevor wouldn't always come and tell me when things were bad. I kept telling him to shout out loud whenever Logan went near him, and I would be there, but he said he didn't like to.

He ended up staying at another carer's for a few days. We were told that we either had to carry on and try to cope or Logan would have to be moved. We weren't very happy, but we weren't left a lot of choice. We really couldn't cope for much longer with things the way they were. We didn't want to lose Logan after the trouble we had getting him back. Yes, we had wanted him for the long-term, but there wasn't much else we could do. As it turned out, they couldn't find any other carers who would take him as his reputation was well known within the fostering community, so we had to try to cope as best we could.

Trevor wanted to come back as he was missing us and Megan. It was only a few days before Christmas. Logan's brother had settled somewhere and offered to have him over the holidays, which was a big help. We managed to get Trevor back in time for Christmas. We ended tha year feeling very tired and concerned about Logan as we had no idea what to do to help him. We could only hope that the New Year would bring us some luck in helping all of us. We were in this together, and we really wanted it to work. We were asked if we would be on emergency duty over the Christmas period again this year, which was okay as we weren't going anywhere so far that we couldn't get back. We thought we were going to escape having any placements, but on 30 December we received a phone call and were asked if we could take Mary, a fourteen-year-old girl from the travelling community. They weren't sure how long it would be for as it looked like a case that would have to go to court, but that would be sorted out when everyone went back to work. In the meantime, we helped her to settle in, and she saw the New Year in with us.

Chapter 30

January 2002 wasn't too bad. Mary settled in well. There was only one incident between Logan and Trevor when Logan complained that Trevor wouldn't sign a contract to say that he would be Logan's slave for the rest of his life. Logan did get a bit upset when he realized we were keeping a very close eye on both of them. Apart from a cold, Megan had no problems. Her contact was constant and reliable, and we were all just waiting for a vacancy at the assessment centre. Mary joined the youth club and went along with Logan every week.

There weren't many phone calls from Logan's school except one. He had spilled some Tipp-Ex correction fluid on a girl's jumper, and if it didn't wash out, he might have to pay for it. He swore it was an accident, but everyone else said he had done it on purpose. Towards the end of the month, there were a few arguments between Logan and Mary. They were both trying to be the big boss in the house. It came to a head one night when we were at our support group. We had a phone call from Mary who told us that Logan was refusing to go to bed for the sitter. I had a word with him after I had a word with the sitter.

When I asked him why he was playing up, he said that Mary was bossing him around, and she was a bitch. I said I would have a word with her, which I did, telling her to leave him alone as it wasn't her place to tell him what to do. They both agreed to do as they were told. I received another call about twenty minutes later. Logan had put his fist through his bedroom window, but he was not hurt. I had a word with him and told him that we would be home soon. He said he didn't want us to do that. In fact, he didn't want to see me either that night or the next morning. The social worker would have a word with him. By the time we got home, he was in bed fast asleep. He came out of this room very quietly the next morning and went off to school without a word to anyone. He was very quiet when he came home in the evening. He went straight to his room and came out only for something to eat.

Mary's social worker was waiting to go to court to get an order to keep her in foster care. Because we were over our allotted number of placements, we had a meeting in which it was decided that an exemption would be given for her to stay with us. Because Megan was in our room, Mary would have her own bedroom so there would be no problem. As it turned out, her time with us didn't last long. One day in the middle of February, the kids asked if they could play outside, and I said that would be okay. Trevor came in after about ten minutes and told me he thought Mary and Logan were going to Joe's. He had seen them cycling up the village. I rang my sister-in-law at about 7.00 that evening when they hadn't returned for dinner, but she said she hadn't seen them. She had, however, seen two cyclists going the towards the next village when she was coming back from shopping. She thought that one looked like Logan, but she had never met Mary so didn't recognize her. But then she'd thought it couldn't have been Logan as he had never biked down that way before. Robert drove around but could see no sign of them. We then had to call the police and EDT to report them missing. Two police officers came around at about 9.00 and took down all their details. Then the searched the house and garden to make sure they weren't hiding. The only place we could think that they might have gone to was Mary's family near Slip End, but we didn't have a proper address as it was a campsite.

The police brought Logan home at about two in the morning. He said he had followed Mary to see where she was going and ended up in the middle of the big town. They had then dumped the bikes near the Galaxy Leisure Centre and had walked to Slip End. Mary then left him there, saying she would be back for him, but she never returned so he knocked on someone's door and asked if they could call the police. He couldn't remember which house it was so we could not go and thank them. They could just as easily have shut the door in his face.

Robert and Logan went back the next day to collect the bikes. Luckily, they were still there. The police came back that afternoon to ask him some more questions and take a formal statement. From that day to this, we have never seen or heard from Mary.

One thing that was puzzling us for a few weeks around this time was a small puddle of water that used to appear outside our kitchen window. Although we asked if anyone knew what it was, no one seemed to know anything about it. Well, we soon found out when I went to clean Mary's bedroom, which was the one directly over the kitchen. As I was emptying the wardrobe to pack her belongings, I found a pint glass full of urine. We assumed that Mary used it during the night and emptied it out the window in the morning. We never ceased to be amazed by the things we found after a placement has left us.

Not long after this incident, my brother Mick, who had been in a coma, died. We attended his funeral. Thankfully the timing worked well. Had Mary waited another week to run away, we would have probably ended up missing it.

Things were still a bit strained between Logan and everyone else in the house, even including David, when he was with us. This really surprised us as they had usually been so close.

We had reviews and professional meetings to see if anyone could come up with an answer that would help Logan and us. The only suggestion that seemed anyway feasible was that, as it looked as though he would have change schools anyway, a residential school might be found for him. We agreed that it could work. We would have him back at weekends and holidays. So the search was on. I went to visit one particular establishment with his social worker. It appeared to have a lot going for it. It also had a good reputation and had been used before by social services, so it was agreed that an application would be sent.

Trevor's social worker was waiting to go to court to get the freeing order they needed to make long-term plans for him. His two younger brothers were now placed with their adoptive parents, but a meeting had to be set up for Trevor to have a final goodbye as he was finding it hard to accept that they were no longer around for contact. As they had been moved further up north, it was agreed that we would take him and have an overnight stay in a motel so we could meet up with his brothers the next day. Respite was organized for Logan, but Megan came with us. It was such a moving time watching them play together. They all knew that it would be many years before they would possibly meet up again. It was sad, especially as they had been such a close family. Sometimes we wondered if the right decisions were always made.

Megan was getting bigger every day. She was running around now. She and Baby-Marie were becoming very close as Marie and Baby were at our house most days, and Baby would stay overnight sometimes. They played really well together. One day they both hid under the dining room table when they heard me coming from the kitchen. I knew they were there, but they were both so quiet, I had to pretend that I didn't know where they were. It wasn't long before the giggles started. It was lovely to see them together, but I knew that Baby-Marie would really miss Megan when she finally went home.

We were still attending child protection meetings as Megan was still on the "at risk" register. These meetings were held regularly to see how things were going. Some of her contact had to be supervised by a social worker who had been assigned to do a risk assessment and write reports on how contact was going. But Megan was still allowed to have some contact with her mother with me supervising, which resulted in a more relaxed time for everyone.

Trevor was settling down much better at school and had even made a good friend. Quite often they would socialize outside of school. As his friend had Asperger's syndrome and found it more difficult to go to strange places, it was easier if Trevor went to their house. This was fine, and the boy's parents were even cleared by social services so that Trevor could stay overnight sometimes. It was lovely to see him have a good and happy social life.

Life in our house was very up and down. Sometimes Logan would play nicely with Trevor and David, and we could go out and have a really good day, but then there were times when we were ready to strangle Logan because he could be so awkward and disruptive all at the drop of a hat. At those times, we could see no reason for the sudden flare up. I suppose the biggest problem was that he had such a wonderful character that people couldn't help but like him. For that reason, we did put up with a lot more from him than we could have done from another child. And we really didn't want him moved somewhere else. But at the end of the day, there were a lot of other things to be taken into consideration, and it made it all the more difficult because he wouldn't work with his counsellor or any of the professionals who were introduced to try to help him and us.

Megan was still waiting for that vacancy in the assessment centre, so her placement was lasting a lot longer than we initially thought it would. In the meantime, everyone was getting more and more attached to her, especially Logan, Trevor, and David. Even my family members were very fond of her. We took her to quite a few family gatherings, and I wouldn't see Megan from the time we arrived until it was time to leave. She would go to a group of people, look up at them and say, "Hello!" in a loud voice. That was all it took. She would be swallowed up by the group, and they would spend time chatting to her. Then, when she'd had enough of them, she would wander off to another group and the same thing would happen again. Even nappy changing was often taken over by someone else. They all wanted to know if we could keep her, but obviously we had to say we couldn't.

I started a six-week training course in therapeutic crisis intervention (TCI), which was very demanding. But it was a crucial training course. My brother Willie and his wife stepped in and looked after Megan for me one day a week so that I could attend. It was a very interesting course, and it also enabled me to get to know other carers. It was very much a team effort as we brought out what we already knew and learned new ways of dealing with the problems of the children. We often had to put ourselves in other carers' positions so we could see things from their side. We did receive certificates at the end of the course; in fact, we now received certificates for every course we attended so that we could keep a record of what training we had done and which others we possibly needed. We also had a record of the dates on which we took a particular training course so that we were also aware that sometimes we could do with a refresher.

We were just coming to terms with Mick's death when his daughter, Stefany, had an aneurysm and died. This put us all into shock as no one was expecting that. She was buried next to her dad. It also brought home to us that it could just as easily have been any one of us as we had always made jokes about who was going to be next. But those jokes were always centred on my generation and not the younger one.

Life went on, and arrangements were made for Logan to go to his new school in Gloucester. I think the only person who was really happy about it was Trevor, but we could understand how he felt.

While we were trying to sort all the problems in our house, Dean was going through some tough times. He had been admitted into the psychiatric ward at the hospital to get some help. He coped exceptionally well and was soon discharged to a hostel. While he was in the hospital, he met Cal. She came with a friend of theirs to visit him, and he and she just seemed to hit it off. When he was discharged, they kept in touch, and he carried on seeing her. He was then given a studio apartment, which we helped him furnish to make it comfortable. It wasn't long before Cal moved in with him. It was great to see him settling down with someone, and we could see that they were good together.

Logan's arrangements were moving along nicely. He had to stay at the school for a week in July, which gave his school a break as he was still getting the odd exclusion for his disruptive behaviour. One day, one of his friends brought a replica gun into school, which was confiscated. It was put away in the study of the head of year, but it wasn't there long before Logan had quietly sneaked in and, as he saw it, "rescued" it. Sometimes some of the things he got up to would have been very funny if they weren't so dangerous. He nearly got banned from the youth club for dangerous behaviour. They had moved from our village hall to the church, which was now our community centre. It was next door to the village school. Although the children had all been told that they were not allowed on the school premises, the school staff members would frequently have to go and get Logan back as he would have climbed up on the roof of the school. In fact, a few people still talk about the things he got up to, and it is always with a soft spot for him as he was well liked within the village.

I attended a few more training sessions. One of them was on preparation for court, which was held in county court. Many of these training sessions could be very interesting, and they also got me away from the kids so I had a breather.

Before school broke up for the summer holidays, Robert and I thought it would be nice to have a day out with just Baby-Marie and Megan, so we took the pair of them to a park where we had a lovely picnic. They both enjoyed the day; it was lovely for us to be able to give them our time without having to watch what the older ones were up to.

Just as the schools broke up for the summer holidays, we were asked to have Sheila, a girl of thirteen, who needed an emergency placement. Her three siblings were also taken into care, but they couldn't be kept together because no one had enough beds for four. Unfortunately, they had to be separated. Sheila's little sister, Diane, was placed with a carer in town whom we knew really well. As Sheila had cried most of the first night and was refusing to eat anything as she missed her family, I got in touch with her sister's carer. We made arrangements to take Sheila there so that she could see that her sister was safe and happy. When we got there, they played together for a little while. Then Sheila started talking to the carer's own daughter emma. When they discovered that they liked each other, they wanted to spend a bit more time together. We ended up bringing Emma home with us, but Sheila was still upset the next morning and would burst into tears for no reason except that she was unhappy. We took them both to the pictures and for a McDonald's, but she hardly touched hers. Emma came back home with us and spent another night here to keep her company. She was still crying when her social worker came to see her the next day. The social worker gave her permission for Sheila to have sleepovers at Emma's house as her mum was a carer. Additionally, that would ease the load at our house. We took it in turns to have them, but there came a time when it wasn't convenient for Sheila to go to Emma's or for Emma to come to us, and so the tears started again along with the refusal to eat. Sheila said she was used to having company all the time and couldn't cope on her own, and she definitely didn't want to spend time with the boys.

We also used to have days out with other carers, and I told Sheila that she would meet some of their girls when we went out with them. We had a few days out with two other families, and she got on really well with one of the girls, whom was placed with Jane. So she asked if she could go there as it was only around the corner from her where her sister was staying. We said we would have a word with the social workers, and it was agreed that it would be a good idea as it solved the problem of contact as well as Sheila having the company of another girl. We all met up at one carer's house for an afternoon, and when it was time to come home Sheila went off to live with Jane as her placement, and I dropped her belongings off as we passed her house. Everyone was happy.

The weather during that August was exceptionally hot. It had been arranged for Trevor and Logan to have a few days out at the Mariners' base. They were really looking forward to it. I watched them go off with my heart in my mouth and could only hope they stayed out of trouble, which they did. But on the first day after they were back, Logan was soaking. He had deliberately left without a change of clothing, which they were asked to bring, so he had to have a bath as soon as he got home. The next day, I made sure he took his change of clothing, and both boys were nice and dry when they got home. But Logan then proceeded to go for a walk up to the village where he wrote his name in some wet plaster that a villager had spent some hours smoothing out. Needless to say, the man was not amused. The third day, they went off again with everything they needed, but this time, when they returned, I could smell them before they even got to the back gate. They were carrying a plastic carrier bag. When I asked them what on earth had they got in it, they opened it up and showed me the biggest, smelliest dead fish that I had ever seen! I asked them how on earth they had managed to get the taxi driver to let them into the car with it, and they said they had asked him, and he'd said it was okay. After all, he had been young once himself. I still don't know how they managed the journey with the smell. And it must have lingered in the taxi for days afterwards; it was bad enough when I smelled it when was out in the open. Needless to say, they had to get rid of it as far away from the house as possible. We were really going to miss Logan when he had to go.

We had some new bedroom furniture delivered. It came in big cardboard boxes. The boys immediately took possession of the boxes and made a fantastic spaceship in the back garden. They spent a lot of time playing with it between arguments. We ended up leaving it there until after they had all gone back to school.

The time went by quickly, and soon it was time for Logan to go to his new school. The day before he was due to go, I took him, Trevor, David, Megan, Marie, and Baby-Marie for a meal at Pizza Hut. They were all very well behaved, and at one point, they got a bit emotional as Logan thanked them for coming and for being his friends. He gave them all little presents. He then thanked me for looking after him and for being there for him and for taking them out to lunch. It's no wonder that we felt so much for this child. This was the Logan that we knew, even if social services and other carers never saw that side of him. It was what made him so special to us. We finished our excursion off with a trip to Toys "R" Us and they returned home for a very peaceful evening without any arguments.

The taxi arrived, and we were loaded up and ready to go by 9.45 a.m. We arrived at Logan's new school at about one in the afternoon and were once again shown around the school. We found Logan's room, and the worker told us that they were off to Cornwall the next morning for ten days, which pleased him. He gave us lots of hugs and kisses. We promised him that we would visit him in about a month when he'd had a chance to settle in. This also pleased him. It was a very quiet journey home as it was just sinking in as to how much we were going to miss him. Life in the village would never be the same again.

Trevor was a bit lost for a while, but he cheered up when David came to stay. But then David missed Logan! It took a while for everyone to get used to Logan not being here. I must have been more keyed up over the last year than I'd thought because, for a few days after Logan left, I had a job to lift my head off the pillow. I think I slept for three days! Robert and Marie managed to look after everyone, and I was soon back to normal.

David went home, and Trevor started back at school. The carers with whom I'd done the TCI course organized a reunion lunch, which was lovely. It made a nice break to have adult company. Our yearly village fête was held on the first Saturday in September, and it seemed really odd to go there without Logan. My brother went on his annual holiday to Tenerife, leaving us the keys to his house, and we thought it would be nice to take Trevor and David there for a weekend. They were eager to go, but once we were there, I think we all missed Logan. It just wasn't the same without him, but we were soon back home.

Within a week, we were doing introduction meetings with Andrew, a nine-year-old boy who had been living with his grandparents and his older brother. There was a lot of trouble with the older brother, and the living situation was breaking down because the grandparents couldn't manage him. But social services were not prepared to take only one of the boys into care as it wouldn't be fair. So both boys had to be brought in. We had only the younger one, and the older boy was placed with other carers. We attended introduction meetings with both boys and their grandparents, which involved them coming to meet us and the other carers. Again, we were lucky that we knew the other carers very well so we would be able to let the boys have good contact with each other and also have plenty of contact with the grandparents. It was rather sad as Andrew was very close to his grandparents and didn't want to leave them, and they had a really good relationship with him. It must have hurt them so much to be separated from him, but we would do our best to make sure that they kept up contact. We would work closely with all concerned.

Andrew came for tea a few times and then had a weekend sleepover. When everything seemed to be going well, he finally moved in on 22 October. By that time, I think he finally had come to terms with the fact that he was going to be leaving his grandparents and coming to live with us because, for the first few nights, we got very little sleep. I would awaken when I heard him crying and screaming at the top of our stairs. I would have to get up and put him back to bed after giving him a cuddle and then staying with him until he finally dropped off to sleep. We had permission to let him share a room with Trevor for a few nights until he did settle down.

Andrew moved in over the half term, so we didn't get to take them out that holiday, but we did have David over, and all three got on well together, although David was still missing Logan. I rang the school and asked when we could go and see Logan. We were asked to wait a few more weeks as he wasn't quite settled yet. After Andrew moved in, I started the round of medical, optician, and dentist appointments along with reviews, so that kept us busy for a few weeks. It also gave us time to let Andrew settle in.

We were finally given a date for Megan to go to the family assessment centre with her mum and brother. We knew she would pass with flying colours, so we had to be prepared for her to move back home. I took her to the centre on 18 November and saw her settled in. Her mum was already there. I wished them luck and was told I could visit them the following week, which was lovely. It was good timing, too, as when I got home, I had a phone call from Logan's school. We could go and see him that weekend.

We arranged for Trevor to stay with his older brother, and Andrew was allowed a weekend with his grandparents, so it was just us and David because we daren't go without him as we would never have had heard the end of it from either him or Logan.

We set off on Saturday morning and arrived in time for lunch. We had made arrangements to stay overnight in a motel. But we couldn't wait to see Logan, so we went straight to the school. Both Logan and David were so pleased to see each other. There were hugs and kisses all round. We asked if we could take Logan out to lunch and were told that it would be okay; in fact, they were quite happy for Logan to stay out with us until the following day. It was wonderful to have him for so long. We went into town and took them to the pictures as that was what he wanted to do. Then we went to the motel and booked in. After that, we went to have a lovely meal before going back to the motel to play board games, which luckily, we had brought with us. Soon they both fell asleep after talking themselves to death.

The next day, we went for a drive around the countryside, and Logan showed us around the area nearest to the school where he was allowed to go out. We even had to have an ice cream with him, as that is what he had been looking forward to most of all. We had to sit outside in the freezing cold, but it was worth it just to see his face. All too soon, it was time for us to go. He asked when he would see us again, and I said that I would ring and ask when we would be allowed. He wanted to know if he could come home to us for Christmas, and I said I would ask as it would be lovely to see him then. And it was only about four weeks away. We asked one of the staff members about a Christmas visit, and he said he didn't think it would be a problem, so we left it that we would find out as soon as possible and let Logan know. He was happy with that.

We all came away with the same choking feeling as we tried to keep the tears out of our eyes as we said cheerio to him. It was so sad to look back and see him standing there waving. It is a picture we will never forget. David was in tears, but he cheered up by the time we stopped to get something to eat.

The following week was quite busy. I had Andrew's personal education plan (PEP) meeting with the school. Trevor was suspended for a day. I also had to take Trevor for a medical assessment. Marie's new partner laid a new floor in our kitchen, which I greatly appreciated. I did manage to phone Logan's school and his social worker to find out what was going to happen over Christmas, and they both said they would get back to me. The following week was Megan's second birthday, so I took Baby-Marie to see them. We had a lunch out and gave her the birthday presents that everyone had bought for her.

Megan's assessment finished on 11 December, and it was agreed by all that, as they had done so well, there was no reason she could not move back home. There were no more concerns. We were all very pleased even though we hadn't expected anything else.

I eventually heard from Logan's social worker that he couldn't come to us for Christmas as none of the other children there went home, and arrangements had been made for them all over the Christmas period. I then had to ring Logan to tell him. He was very upset as I thought he would be, but I said we would organize another weekend to come and see him as we were not allowed to have him back at weekends, which he was okay with.

Christmas was fast approaching. Megan and her mum managed to get in a visit to us just before the holiday, and everyone was pleased to see them. Andrew was allowed to stay at his grandparents for the holidays. His mum and dad had been having some contact with him and were allowed to collect him from his grandparents' and have him overnight. They brought him back to us on 29 December. He was obviously upset at leaving his family, and it took him another night to settle again.

Trevor was here with us for the day. He woke very early but didn't come downstairs until 7.30. He was very pleased with all his presents. His grandmother came to see him for a while, and his granddad and his brother both rang him to wish him a happy Christmas. We phoned Logan to wish him a happy Christmas. Trevor spoke to him for about half an hour. When we spoke to him, we asked him what he had been doing all day. He said he had been watching telly as only he and one other boy were there. Everyone else had gone home to their families. I couldn't believe it! He was very angry that he hadn't been allowed to come to us. As far as we all were concerned, we were his family. I managed to calm him down. I told him that I would have a word with his social worker and see if he could come home for a weekend or if we could go and see him again. Dean and Cal had come for dinner and overnight, so they had a word with him too, which pleased him.

The following day we went for lunch at the Raven with Dean, Cal, Marie, Baby-Marie, and David as it was my birthday. Over the years it had become a tradition that we would go out to give me a break.

The following day, Trevor went to stay at his friend's house for a few days. When his friend's mum brought him home, she told me that they had been very disappointed in his behaviour as he hadn't been his usual self. But we couldn't come up with a good reason for this. It didn't help matters that Andrew's behaviour wasn't much better, but when we spoke to Trevor about his behaviour, he said that he had been told that he would be moving to live with his older brother. I said I didn't know anything about that, but I would have a word with his social worker as soon as they were all back to work. Andrew's social worker was coming to see him the following week, so we would have to wait and see what was going on.

We managed to see the New Year in. Marie, Baby-Marie, and David were all with us, so it was a lovely evening as they all decided to be on their best behaviour.

Chapter 31

T he year 2003 crept in nice and peacefully. It was too wet to go anywhere on New Year's Day, so we ended up spending the day playing board games with the children, and there weren't too many arguments. We decided to go into town the next day to get them all haircuts so they'd be ready to start back at school. Without my realizing what he was doing, Trevor had sneaked out in his slippers as he didn't want to wear his trainers or shoes, so he ended up having to buy himself a pair of trainers with his pocket money. We managed to get through the morning without further incidents.

Later in the afternoon, Andrew's social worker came to see him and asked him why he had been behaving the way he was. He said it was because his dad had told him that, if he behaved himself, he would always be in care and that would mean that his dad wouldn't be allowed to see him. The social worker explained to him that it was, in fact, the other way round. If his dad kept influencing him to engage in bad behaviour, then social services would have to look into the effect Andrew's contact with his dad was having, and contact may even be stopped. But if everyone worked together, there was no reason why he couldn't have contact with all his family members. This seemed to do the trick as his behaviour gradually improved. After a few weeks, his social worker was able to increase contact so that both he and his brother had contact with their parents together.

Trevor, on the other hand, was still playing up. I went to a counselling session with him because he still preferred to answer their questions by answering to me. This time, he revealed that he had been told that he would be moving to the same people who were carers for his older brother. When we got home, he told me that his brother's carers had told him. I then had a word with our support worker who knew nothing about this and said she would find out what was going on.

In the meantime, we had a new arrival. We were asked, on 3 January, if we could take Katie, a two-month-old baby girl who had sustained some nasty injuries. There were concerns over how she had received them. She was supposed to have rolled off a settee, but no one thought that could cause a fractured skull, fractured ribs, and bloodshot eyes. The situation had to be looked into, and in the meantime, they needed a safe place for Katie. She was so fragile, I couldn't remove her clothing. Each time I tried, she screamed. So at first, we had to make do with giving her a good freshen up without disturbing her too much. It was three days before I could change her clothes. Obviously, I had been changing her nappy and keeping her as clean as I could, but it was so nice to be able to give her a bath and get her really fresh. But we had to handle her very gently.

The first weekend after the holidays, I received a telephone call from a worker at Logan's school. She asked what had happened to the taxi. I said I didn't have a clue about anything to do with a taxi. She said that Logan was very upset because they had been expecting the taxi to collect him that afternoon, but it hadn't shown up. I still didn't have a clue what she was talking about. Then she asked me if my name was Margaret Brown, and when I said no, she asked me who I was. I explained that we were Logan's foster carers, but the people she had named had been his respite carers for a short time. She explained that arrangements had been made for Logan to stay with them that weekend, but the taxi hadn't turned up. The only thing I could do was to give her the Browns' telephone number. The school worker phoned me back after about fifteen minutes and said that the Browns had been expecting him but didn't know which taxi company was supposed to be doing the trip. She asked me if I would find out. I told her which company was normally used for Logan. She rang me back a bit later and said that the taxi hadn't turned up as no one had rung to confirm the booking. She had tried to get someone from the school to take him to the Browns', but no one was available. Would it be possible for one of us to go and collect him? I couldn't believe what I was hearing. I said no because the visit had nothing to do with us. If he had been coming to us, I would have made sure that I knew which company was being used and would definitely have rung both the school and taxi company to make sure that everything was confirmed. That is what I always did when arrangements were made over weekends or holidays. If it was to the Browns that he was going, then she had better sort it out with them.

We never heard anything until the following Tuesday when Logan rang to say that he was really angry and upset because of the weekend. He had been looking forward to coming home. I explained that he hadn't meant to be coming to us, so we hadn't been aware of any arrangements that had been organized until we got the telephone call on Friday night. He explained that they had promised him that he would be able to travel on Saturday, but then they cancelled that too, so he ended up staying where he was. I managed to calm him down as he was threatening to run away. But I told him that wouldn't get him anywhere; it would only make matters worse. I did say that I would have a word with his social worker and see if we could make arrangements for him to come to us, or if we could go to see him like we did before. I couldn't get in touch with his social worker the next day, but on Thursday, she rang me to say that we weren't allowed to see or speak to Logan as we had upset him so much on Tuesday that he tried to run away. So they thought it best if he didn't have any contact with us at all. I explained that he had been promised a weekend visit to the Browns and it had not worked out due to bad planning, leaving him very disappointed and angry. Might that have more to do with his behaviour than talking to me? Also, he had been told he couldn't come to us at Christmas because no one else went home, and then when Christmas arrived, he realized that there was only one other boy left there along with him. She said that had all been sorted, and he wasn't upset about any of that. He was angry only after talking to me. Here we go again—more back covering at Logan's expense.

We later found out that Logan had tried to run away on numerous occasions, especially after he wasn't allowed contact with us. One particular occasion we thought was really funny. It happened when they all went for a walk over the hills. Logan asked if he could go to the toilet in the bushes. At first he was told he would have to wait until they got back to the school, but he said he was desperate and couldn't wait, so they gave him permission. When he was hidden in the bushes, he tied a piece of string to one of the outside branches. As he gradually moved away, he let the string uncurl, making sure to tug it slowly every once in a while so people would see the bush move and think he was still there. The teacher eventually got suspicious when the movement stopped, but when they went to have a look Logan was nowhere in sight.

In the meantime, we carried on as normal. It was history repeating itself, and all we could do was to keep asking how he was and when would we be able to see him. We said that we could do the same as last time again. We weren't expecting social services to foot the bill; we were quite prepared to pay our own way as we felt it was important to Logan that we have contact. But they still kept refusing, saying that it was more important for him to have contact with the people he'd had respite with than with us, whom he regarded as his family because we had known him since he was two. But what did we know? They were the professionals, as they kept reminding us. We weren't going to just give up, so we lodged complaints. Again, we had to wait for their convenience.

David's mum and stepdad had moved from the hostel to a two-bedroom house. We thought that might settle David down a bit and enable him to come to us maybe once a month instead of every weekend. It had taken them a while to get the house because the first house they had been offered was the one in which David's dad had died. The council said they couldn't see a problem because all traces of the fire had been removed, and the whole house had been redecorated inside and out. Social services wrote letters to say that David still had memories of living there with his dad and was very aware of what had happened there. They couldn't possibly condone him moving back there. His doctor wrote a letter as did the mental health team. His parents were eventually offered another house far enough away from the old one. We started cutting his visits with us down to every other weekend to give them a chance to decorate his bedroom and get the rest of the house on order.

My niece Julie's husband had just been stationed at RAF Chicksands, which was just down the road from us, so Julie took over our babysitting. We said we may as well pay her as someone from the baby sitting company called Sitters. Although they had been very professional and reliable, they weren't always known to the children, whereas they would know Julie.

While all this was going on, we decided that we would have to change our car as the Albany had been registered as a taxi vehicle and the insurance was costing us around £800 a year. My brother-in-law was looking out for something else for us.

Also, I had been suffering with ingrown toenails for years, and they continued to be very sore and infected, so my doctor arranged for me to have them removed. The date I was offered was 29 January. It was only a one-day procedure, so we didn't have to organize any care for Andrew and Trevor as they were at school. Our friends who were carers looked after Katie. The procedure went well, and I came home feeling only slightly uncomfortable. Robert went to collect Katie, and everything was back to normal apart from me not being able to wear shoes, so I wasn't able to go out. And as luck would have, it my brother-in-law found us a lovely Toyota Lucida and brought it to us two days after my operation. But I couldn't drive it for a few weeks. Robert enjoyed rubbing it in that only he could drive our new car.

Trevor loved having Katie with us. The first thing he would do when he came down in the mornings was go to her crib to say good morning to her and give her a kiss. Then he had to give her another kiss before he left for school. And the first person he would look for when he came home was Katie—to make sure she was okay. Andrew, on the other hand, couldn't have cared less. He acted as though she didn't even exist. He would come down in the morning and completely ignore her. He never took any notice of her at all, and he never offered to help.

Cal was pregnant, and her pregnancy was going well. She was soon showing, so everyone knew she was expecting. When she had her scans, she and Dean wanted to know what sex the baby was, and they were overjoyed when they found out it was going to be a girl. They had a name picked out for her ages before she was born. I must admit I think we would have preferred not to know—not that it mattered as we were still excited. But we had months to wait.

Katie's routine was going well. Contact with her parents was organized for several times a week, but it was under supervision at a family centre and would continue like that until a thorough investigation had been completed.

My support worker found out that the people who were fostering Clint, Trevor's older brother, had asked if they could also foster Trevor, which would be lovely, but they shouldn't have said anything to Trevor until all the legalities had been sorted and confirmed. No way at that moment was Trevor ready for such a move until a lot more work had been carried out.

David was coming over every other weekend, and we were still having Baby-Marie at odd weekends, so we nearly always had a full house. The three boys got on well together and would play either outdoors if weather permitted or up in their bedrooms. There weren't too many arguments—just the normal disagreements, which we could handle. It seemed very peaceful after the previous year.

We began to prepare Trevor for his move to Clint's house. He had very mixed feelings about the move. He wanted to be with his brother, but he also wanted to stay with us. He said the ideal solution would be for us to buy a house where we could all live together. In the end, he started to look forward to moving. We had arranged lots of tea visits and weekend stays before his final move in April. We had a surprise party for him the evening before he moved. He was really pleased and, as he said, sad at the same time, but it was lovely to see him going to live with his brother. We just wished that more moves could be as positive.

One little person who missed Trevor very much was Katie. In the mornings when she heard Andrew coming down the stairs, she would get all excited, but when Andrew appeared, she would try to look around him for Trevor. It seems a shame the children's feelings can't always be taken into consideration. It affects them all when others move on.

Andrew was still bouncing between seeing his parents, his grandparents, and his older brother. That was the pattern that his life took for at least the next year.

Trevor was no sooner gone than we had a new placement, a fifteen-year-old girl called Stella. It was only a two-week placement, which was a shame as she settled in really well, got on well with Andrew and David, and fell in love with Katie. She was really good with Baby-Marie and got on well with all the adults too.

Cal was having a rough time with her pregnancy. We thought it would be nice to all go for a Chinese meal before Easter as we were going to Wisbech for the holidays. We had a good evening apart from poor Cal having to visit the bathroom between different courses. She wasn't coping very well with keeping food down, but bless her, she never complained; she just got on with life.

We set off to my brother's on a Thursday night after Katie's contact visit. On Friday, we took the children to Hunstanton for the day. They had a great time on the amusements and rides. On Saturday, we went to

Wisbech town. As the children had requested, we went to the butterfly farm on Sunday, and on the way home on Monday, we stopped at the fun farm. We all arrived home Monday night absolutely shattered. We hadn't had any problems with Katie at night as she had slept from about eight in the evening until around seven in the morning from her first week with us, so we were assured a restful night's sleep.

It was with mixed feelings the next day that we said goodbye to Stella, as she was going home. We were pleased for her, but we knew we were going to miss her as she had been a lovely girl and caused us no problems at all. We had enjoyed having her.

It was about this time that we had a knock on our door one Sunday evening. When Robert went to answer it, Logan was standing there. We were delighted to see him, but our first thoughts were that he had run away. But he said that he had been to the Browns' and wanted to come and see us, so he had asked the taxi driver if he would do a small detour and call in to our house. It was lovely to see him. He couldn't stay long as he had a long journey, but we got lots of hugs before he set off.

Andrew found it a bit difficult to amuse himself in the evenings when he was on his own; he had always been used to someone else being with him. But he soon settled down. We booked him to soccer lessons in the holidays, which helped pass the time. He looked forward to David coming at the weekends if they coincided with the weekends he was with us, as he was spending a lot of time at one or the other of his family member's houses.

He still wasn't concerned about Katie being here; he took no notice of her at all.

By now we were getting fed up with Logan's social worker determination that we were not to be allowed to see him. We even had to go to a post placement meeting, which is a meeting that takes place when a placement breaks down. The meeting chairperson wanted to know why more hadn't been done to help us make the placement work. They felt it should have been Trevor who was moved as Logan was supposed to be our long-term placement. More credence should have been given to that fact than any other. It was determined that no blame should be put on us because the facts showed that we had so much pressure put on us that it was no wonder we couldn't cope. The chairperson wasn't surprised that I had slept for three days after Logan had been moved. She realized I had been suffering from exhaustion. Nothing had mattered to those who had been in charge except that they were right and everyone else was wrong.

We felt that, while we were fostering for social services, our hands had been tied. If we wanted to fight for our right to see Logan, then perhaps we needed to think about fostering for a private agency. So we applied to a private company. That company began an assessment of us. At first we kept it quiet because we weren't sure if we would be accepted or not. As it turned out, we needn't have worried because we knew the person in charge of the private agency, and there was no problem with us working for them. But obviously they had to do all the checks for legal reasons, which we understood and had no problem with. In the meantime, we carried on as normal.

Andrew wasn't aware of anything but his own life, and Katie was getting very attached to me. But at her age, that was expected, and actually a good thing because she wouldn't have bonding problems when it was time for her to move on. Social services were still waiting for her court date, so any future plans could not yet be made.

In May we were presented with a long-service award at a party organized by social services. We had been fostering for them for nearly twenty-six years. It was a wonderful evening. They started off by giving bouquets of flowers to people who had been fostering for five years, then ten, fifteen, and twenty. We came under the twenty-five category as they were now going to start doing this every two years to thank their carers for the difficult jobs that they did. It was also a nice way to meet other carers and meet up with some whom we hadn't seen for a long time. It was just nice to have our work recognized.

Also at this time, we were given the good news that Marie was expecting again; she was due around Christmastime.

On Sunday, 1 June, we got a telephone call from EDT. We were asked if they could bring over a young lady whom they thought was about seventeen. They didn't have much on her background. She wasn't English, and they weren't sure if she was in the country legally or not. But they wouldn't be able to do much work on the case until the next day. Never before or never since have we had a placement who tried to make me sit down while she did the housework! I didn't get a look-in with Katie. Fran was dangerous around the town with the pushchair—she saw a space and went for it. Robert and I would cringe as we walked behind her. Her bedroom ended up looking like a showroom. We just weren't used to that. It was wonderful, although we tried not to let her do too much in case we were had up for child labour. It was great when we went out with Baby-Marie and Marie as it freed me up to have more time with Baby-Marie, and we had to remember there would be two grandchildren in a few weeks. I always wonder where the time goes. All too soon, the authorities had found her family, and her uncle came to collect her. We had a tearful goodbye as she had been happy with us, and her uncle couldn't thank us enough for everything we had done for her. I would certainly miss her, but we now had the birth of Chris, Dean and Cal's baby, to look forward to and Baby-Marie's birthday. It was a race to see which was going to be first.

Shortly before either event, we had a very short placement of a young girl of fourteen who was waiting to go into residential but had to leave home. She had to stay only from 18 to 20 June, so it wasn't too long. Chris managed to put in her appearance three days before Baby-Marie's birthday, so it was double celebration. Chris was born on 22 June and Baby-Marie was two on 25 June.

We were still having contact with Megan and her mum; sometimes they would come over to our house, and other times I would go and visit them. They were getting on really well. Things were working out well for them, which was lovely to see.

We were now seeing more of Dean and Cal as we now had another little granddaughter to get to know.

Our assessment by the private agency was still being carried out, which meant that an independent social worker came and talked to us and to our family members. This meant they had to interview Marie and Dean. Also, Donna gave us a glowing reference as did Chris.our ex-foster son

Because we did a lot of socializing with another set of carers, we sometimes helped each other out, and if we needed someone to look after one of ours, we would rather send them to someone they knew. This worked the other way too; we would have some of their children it. It was a lot easier that way as the children were more comfortable knowing who they were staying with. Well, at the end of August we had three children here for a weekend—Nigel, his sister, and an older girl. It was lovely as they all got on well together, and Nigel's sister wouldn't let me get a look in with Katie.

The summer seemed to fly by, Andrew had lots of contact, and again we got him into soccer lessons. Marie and Baby-Marie were at our house most days. David came over at the beginning of the holidays and kept saying that he didn't want to go back home. He even told this to a social worker who used to come to take Katie for her contact. She was getting rather worried about it as he was getting more upset as the holidays were coming to an end. She went back to the office and reported it. When they came to interview him, he was very adamant that he didn't want to go home because, now that his mum and stepdad had another baby, he wasn't wanted at home, and they were going to turn his bedroom into a room for the new baby. We couldn't confirm or deny any of this as we didn't know what was going on. We only knew that we were being phoned more regularly at the weekends before the holidays to come and pick David up for the weekend as they couldn't cope with him. Towards the end of the holiday, it was decided that he was to stay with us until something could be sorted. We didn't want payment, but I asked them to organize a school taxi as I couldn't get him to school. We kitted him out in a new school uniform, and he looked really proud as he set off on his first day back. Social services did talk to his mum and stepdad. They had various meetings. Then a meeting was organized that included David along with his parents. He decided that he would go back and live with them. As they blamed us for David not wanting to go home, they then refused to let him have any contact with us, which we did understand. We hoped that, in time, things would sort themselves out.

We had a few more visits from Logan, which was wonderful, but we were still a bit worried that he might get into trouble, so I told our support worker because I also felt that someone should know how he felt. But the only reaction I got was that we shouldn't be encouraging him. I explained that we weren't, and we never knew when he was going to call as it was always a surprise. Nothing ever happened, so we assumed that nothing had been said to his social worker.

We now had to let social services know that we had applied to the private agency because the agency needed a reference from them. They weren't happy about it, but they couldn't refuse, and the agency said it was protocol that they work with us during the hand-over as we needed to finish the placements that we already had. Andrew's placement was going really well, and it was decided that he would be going to live with his older brother as his carers would have a vacancy coming up in January or February, and it made sense that both brothers were placed together. So we at least had a reasonable finishing date. Katie's court case was going well as her grandmother had put in an application to have her full time. The only drawback was the distance she had to travel to build up a relationship with Katie, so social services paid for her to stay in a motel several times so she could come and meet Katie and get to know her. But again, we had to wait until we were given a court date, which looked as though it would be after Christmas, which fell in nicely with Andrew's dates. So it was agreed that we could carry on until these placements came to a natural ending. In the meantime, we should carry on as normal. We were allowed to have short placements.

We had two sisters in September for two weeks while their carer had a holiday, and in October we had Andrew's brother for two weeks while his carers went on holiday. Then we were finally put before a panel on 30 October. We had to go to Stanmore and meet them. It was an experience that we'd never had before as we had always had our yearly reassessment placed before a panel without us being there. But it was okay. We did think it was going to be a bit daunting, but actually it went well. They put us at ease, and we felt quite comfortable in the end. We were given the news that we had been accepted, and we couldn't accept any more placements from social services, but we were still involved with Andrew and Katie.

It wasn't too long before the agency placed a girl with us. Suzie fitted in well and got on with Andrew, although he wasn't here much as most of his time now was spent at either his brother's or his dad's. Suzie was also spending weekends back at her mum's, so we took advantage of this and tried to spend a bit more time with Dean, Cal, and Chris. Katie was no problem. Her contact was during the week, which didn't cause any disruption.

Social services were keeping a close eye on David's situation. His social worker was having meetings with other professionals, and I was invited to attend as we had known him for so long and knew him better than anyone else. We were able to relax some with the situation knowing they were still keeping an eye on him.

We now had to attend support groups in Milton Keynes, which we found strange as we knew our old group so well. And we also had to attend training courses in Milton Keynes. Heather came over to see us a few times, so we knew she was coping well.

Baby-Marie had started playgroup, and I had to go with Marie to meet her teachers as I was down as her emergency contact. If they couldn't contact Marie, or if Marie had any problems, I would collect Baby-Marie from nursery. Marie's pregnancy was going well, and we were all looking forward to the birth.

Christmas was fast approaching. Everything seemed to be flowing nicely. We decided that, straight after Christmas, we would make an appointment with a solicitor to find out what we had to do to gain contact with Logan. He was still calling in on odd Sunday evenings. But we would bide our time and get through the holidays first

Normally social services would have a very informal Christmas party for their carers in their office in the evening. It was a good time to catch up with people we hadn't seen for ages, but this year was going to be different as our new agency had organized a more formal party. We had a sit-down meal. The children were catered for in a separate room, and entertainment was provided for them. This gave us adults time to mix. We found it a bit daunting as we didn't know anyone else, but we got through it and had a nice time. Everyone was given a present before we left. Andrew and Suzie had a good time. We felt we enjoyed the social services gatherings more, but then we knew an awful lot of people and social workers there, but we would get used to our new situation in time.

Arrangements had been made for Andrew to go to his family for the Christmas holidays, and Suzie was going to spend some of the time with her dad and some of it with her mum, so it meant we would have only Katie over the holidays. On Christmas day we went to Willie and his wife for dinner, which made a nice change. On Boxing Day we went out for a meal for my birthday. Then we had a few quiet days until the thirtieth when we had Baby-Marie because Marie went into labour and had to go to hospital. Laura was born at about 9.23 that evening. She was about the same weight Baby-Marie had been, but she seemed a lot smaller; in fact, Marie didn't have any clothes that fitted her properly, so Robert and I had to go shopping before we went in to see her the next day. We managed to get them home in time for Katie to have contact with her mum and dad. When Baby-Marie went home, she was really excited to see a baby smaller than herself and was very gentle with her. This year we didn't worry too much about seeing the New Year in as we had no children with us—only Katie, and she was too young anyway. So we had a very quiet end to the year.

Chapter 32

We had a busy start to the year 2004. We went to a friend's for tea on New Year's Day. It felt weird being there without a load of our kids. They were foster carers, and all theirs were there. They wanted to know where everyone was, but we still enjoyed our time with them as we knew them all really well.

On the second, we went to my sister Elizabeth's in Wembley. It was nice to relax there this time and not have to worry about the telephone ringing and us having to head off home for an emergency placement, which had happened in the past. And we didn't have to worry what time we left. Usually we had to leave to get the kids home as they would have had enough and would be asking to go home early. So it was nice for Robert to be able to go out for a drink with my brother-in-law.

On the third, Julie and her husband came to us for tea. They would soon be moving to Northern Ireland as his time in Chicksands was coming to an end. They normally had moves every two years, so we wanted to make the most of their time living close to us.

On the fourth, Andrew came home as he had to get ready for school. Other than that, it was a quiet day.

I took Andrew to town to get new trainers, and we got a surprise in the evening. We had a telephone call from a social worker asking if they could bring David over as they had just had a call from his grandmother asking if she could put him into foster care. She couldn't cope with him because of failing health. We said of course they could bring him, and they could explain everything when they got here. They arrived about 7.00 in the evening, and David ran into our arms. The social worker explained that, apparently, things hadn't been going very well for them before Christmas, and by his birthday his mum and stepdad decided they couldn't cope with him any longer, so his stepdad took him to his mother's and left him there saying they didn't want him back. If she couldn't cope, she could ring social services. She managed until the holidays ended, but had finally called to say she couldn't manage him. She asked them to come and collect him. The social worker said they would sort out the paperwork the next day, but I explained that we were no longer working for social services. Even so, we would still like to keep him with us even, if it meant that we didn't receive any payment. Money didn't come into it with David.

Andrew started back at school the next day, and I received a call from social services to say they were having a meeting with other professionals that morning regarding David. They asked if I would like to come along. I left Katie at another carer's and went to the meeting. It was decided that, if we were prepared to have him on a private basis, then they would let him stay. His social worker would visit him regularly, and I could also attend any meetings for him. I agreed. After David and I went to collect Katie, we had something to eat, and I just about had time to get to a meeting at Andrew's school. We then returned home to let Robert know the news—or at least David told him he was going to be staying with us.

As we still had on-going placements with us, we were asked if we would like to attend the New Year's party organized by social services, which was great as it also gave us the chance to say goodbye to other carers we had known for years but hadn't seen for ages.

David's social worker came to see him and asked if we could take him to see his grandmother at the weekend. Although she couldn't manage him, she would still like to see him. As we think it is important for the children to keep up contact with as much family as possible, we agreed to take him over on Saturday.

Suzie was now back from her holidays and back into the normal routine of school, home, and visits to her mum's house after school and occasional evenings. We now had four social workers coming to see the children, and Katie was now seeing her grandmother several times a week as this had to be increased so that Katie was used to being with her. Grandma was coming to the house and feeding, bathing, dressing, and putting Katie to bed. Then she would come back early in the morning to give her breakfast and get her ready for the day. We didn't have a minute to ourselves.

David also had to attend counselling sessions, which I had to take him to. I sometimes participate if he asked me to.

On the weekend of 7 and 8 February we took Katie to her grandmother's and left her there while we went to stay in a motel overnight. We went back the next day and had lunch with them. It was nice to see them all comfortable together, and we were very happy to make the arrangements for Katie to move there permanently in a fortnight.

Andrew's move came first. We had a special goodbye tea for him on Friday the thirteenth and then waved him off the next day. It was a lovely positive ending to his time with us.

The fortnight soon went by, and Katie's social worker came to pick us up. The three of us set off with Katie for the last time. The transition went very smoothly, although it was quite an emotional experience for us as we drove away to see her waving bye-bye. We did leave her a life-story book that I had done for her, which I had thoroughly enjoyed doing. I was told later by her grandmother that they often sat and looked through it.

We now had another problem. Although we already had one placement from the agency, they refused to place another child with us because we had David, and he hadn't been with us when our assessment had been carried out. So either social services would have to place him officially with us through the agency, or he would have to be moved. Well, there was no way that was going to happen. Social services said they were not prepared to pay the agency as they could place David with other carers in the local area. We now had another decision to make. Well, as far as we were concerned it was no contest. We rang social services and asked if there was any way we could come back and foster for them again. And keep David. We were told they had been expecting our call, and we could certainly be registered with them again, but in the meantime all parties agreed that we could carry on with the one placement from the agency. And if we were prepared to keep David without payment, they would find a child who could be placed with us from social services through the agency. It seemed funny to us that they could place another child through the agency but not David. It was explained to us at a later date that this was the way they knew that they could get us back. Apparently there had been a big cheer in the office when someone called out that we were coming back.

There was some sad news in March. My brother Sean's partner died from cancer, which upset all of us. David knew her well because they had often visited us before going off to Tenerife and leaving their house keys so we could go and stay at their place in Wisbech. We knew we would miss her and felt for Sean as he was now on his own and living a fair distance from the rest of the family. But we would still go up and see him when we could, and he knew he was welcome to visit us at any time.

In early April, a social worker brought 14 year old Stefan to meet us. He had been moved around a lot in various foster homes and children's homes and wanted somewhere that he could settle. On the thirteenth, Stefan came to spend the day with us, and he moved in the following day. He and David got on well. He didn't have much to do with Suzie as she spent most of her time either at her mum's or her dad's.

We went to Wrest Park for Saint George's Day festival, and Stefan joined in the fun enthusiastically. He even volunteered to dress up in medieval warrior's clothing, which I think he slightly regretted as it was a boiling hot day and he looked ready to drop. But everyone had a good time. It was lovely to go out and enjoy ourselves without the usual petty arguments. David took Stefan to youth club where he met some of the other kids in the village.

Suzie went to her mum's for the May bank holiday, and we decided to go to Wisbech as my brother had left us his keys again when he went to Tenerife with Doreen's daughter.

Everyone had a good weekend, and as it was Stefan's first time there, we warned him about the mudflats because they were very slippery. But we should have known what to expect as we didn't have to wait long before he ended up on his back in the mud. We had a lovely job of trying to clean him off before letting him in the car. Apart from that, the weekend went off well, and soon it was time to come home. Stefan and David went swimming with Marie and Dave on Monday after we got home.

It was back to normal on Tuesday. David's social worker came to see him in the evening. There had been no changes. On Wednesday we had a review for David at his school; he had settled down and was happier at school since he was staying with us.

On Thursday, we had a family network meeting at the offices regarding David. His mum and stepdad attended along with his stepdad's brother. They were quite adamant that they didn't want David staying with us. They didn't mind where he was placed as long as it wasn't at our house as they saw that as David winning. The social workers and school officials wanted to know what they meant by that as they couldn't understand what David was winning. Both his stepdad and his brother both said that he could do with going to a boot camp as he needed to toughen up. The professionals who were there asked if they understood that David was special needs and no amount of bullying was going to make him any tougher than he already was. All were in agreement that David would be staying with us for the foreseeable future.

Friday was a little less hectic. Everyone was at school. We only had a doctor's appointment for Stefan in the evening. On Saturday, we dropped David off at his nan's and took Stefan for his opticians appointment. Then we returned to pick David up later in the evening.

Stefan was now going to youth club every Monday with David and seemed to be getting on there, which was good as he had trouble at school with other pupils bullying him. It was nice for him to go somewhere with other kids at not be bullied.

The rest of that week was fairly normal. We had one highlight when Megan's mum brought her back for a visit. Apart from that, it was the usual routine. The next week was busier. We had Stefan's looked-after child (LAC) review at his school on Monday, which went well. Everyone was pleased that he appeared settled and was doing well at school. We had David's child protection meeting (CPC) on Wednesday. It was unanimously agreed that he would stay with us under the conditions already agreed upon until our updated assessment was finalized.

Then he would be placed under normal conditions of a placement.

Stefan had his weekly meetings at Child and Adolescent Mental Health Services (CAMHS) on Thursday. We knew Suzie would be going home the following week, so we had a night out at the dogs then to the cinema. Finally, the night before she was due to leave, we had a special goodbye meal. Her social worker came after school to collect her and her things on Thursday. We knew we would all miss her as she had been a lovely placement. She had got on well with everyone and was very pleasant to have around. Now we were down to just David and Stefan until we went before the panel at the end of June. Nigel came swimming with us on Sunday and stayed the night as we were having the two other boys from his placement for the day on Monday. We took them all back Monday evening.

It was now half term. It was agreed that David could see his mum and stepdad for a few hours several days through the holiday. Both visits went well, so it was decided that he could go there after school several evenings a week.

As we had only the two boys, we decided that we would have a holiday with them. We made arrangements to go to Ireland. We went to Belfast and stayed with Don and his family for the first weekend at a camp there. Then we went further up north to stay with Julie and her husband, Frosty, for a week. Julie had made arrangements for some of the other families' kids to come and call for David and Stefan while we were there. They hadn't been out for long when Stefan came home on his own and went straight upstairs. When we asked him why he was back so quickly, he just said that he didn't get on with the others and would rather be on his own, so we left him to it. When David returned, we asked him what had happened, and he said he wasn't sure as one,minute, things were okay and the next Stefan was having an argument with one of the girls. After that, he'd just run home. We couldn't get to the bottom of it, so Julie said she would ask the girl next time she saw her.

We had a lovely week there, and the last week we went down to Mayo to spend time with my brother Dermot, which was lovely as we knew he had cancer, and we didn't know how long he was going to be around. While we were there, Stefan wouldn't do anything with David. He refused to play football or anything unless either Robert or my brother went with them. When we went up the mountain at Croagh Patrick, he ran off on his own. He was very unsociable for the whole week; we would have to sort it out when we got home.

Soon we were into July, and our papers went to the panel. We were passed as carers for social services once more. David's papers were now filled out, and he was a full-time placement with us. Stefan's placement was changed from the agency to social services. It was as though we had never been away.

We missed Baby-Marie and Laura, so we had to make up our time with them when we got home. Baby-Marie told us off for going away without her, so we promised that next time we went, we would take her with us. We managed a weekend to go see Katie and her grandmother. David came with us.

When we were back to normal at home, Stefan became very unsociable with David. He wouldn't do anything with him. On one particular Monday, they both went to youth club, and Stefan came home early and went straight to his room. When we asked David what had happened, he said he wasn't sure except that all the girls had been having a go at Stefan. He wasn't sure why. I managed to get hold of one of the girls who lived in the village and asked her what had happened. She said that Stefan had gone up to one of the girls and started calling her names very quietly, so every one of them had a go at him. The same thing also happened at school. We had a word with him the next day, and he admitted what he had been doing. We asked his social worker to call around and explained the situation to him, and Stefan confessed that, when he did that and people bullied him, he liked it when the teachers felt sorry for him and made a fuss of him. So I said that, in future, when I was told that he was picked on, I would want to know what he had done or said to whoever was having a go at him. The bullying seemed to ease off a lot after that.

We had a little three-year-old for a week while his carers went on their holidays. Everyone enjoyed having him, especially as it was for such a short time.

We had a new placement arrive in august. Denise was very nice, but I found it a bit difficult at this time because our dear friend Trudie had been taken into our local hospice, and the prognosis wasn't very good, so I wanted to spend as much time with her as possible. Unfortunately, Denise had to go with me, which couldn't have been very nice for her, but she said she didn't mind. She settled down really well. After the first few weeks, her dad and his partner asked if she could stay with them for the weekend so they could have her brother at the same time. Their visits to see him hadn't been very successful as his carers wouldn't even let them in the door, so it didn't give them much of a chance to see him. They often visited with Denise, coming to our house to have a cup of tea and spend time with her, but they felt that they would like to see the two children together and hopefully prepare them for going to live with them when they got their accommodation sorted.

The summer holidays were soon at an end. They had been filled with more meetings for everyone for various reasons, days out with Jane and her placements. Baby-Marie and Laura stayed with us occasionally, and I continued to visit Trudie. Unfortunately, she never saw the end of August; she passed away very peacefully. Her loss was going to leave a big gap in our lives as she had been such a huge part of our family.

It was decided that Denise would attend the same secondary school as Stefan. Her dad and his partner were going to be living locally, so she may as well start off at the beginning of the year.

We had our usual village fête. We went to collect Dean, Cal, and Chris and had them over for the day. The only cloud hanging over us was Trudie's funeral on Monday, 6 September. It went off without a hitch, but it was so sad. The only consolation was that she was now going to be with her Alan.

Denise's placement settled into a routine. She would be with us during the week and at her dad's house at the weekends until the end of her placement in December.

We decided that we needed a break, and three respite placements were organized. Denise went to a carer in Stotfold, Stefan went to Jane's where he was very happy to go as he knew them very well, and David went to another set of carers. He too was quite happy to go, as he knew these people.

We went to London for a long weekend and stayed in the Bonnington Hotel. We lost count of the number of miles we walked doing all the sightseeing. We needed a rest by the time we got home.

While we were away, David had to start his medication for ADH, but when his carer gave him his first tablet before he went to school, he complained of a buzzing in his head, so I told her to not to give him anymore until I spoke to his consultant. I learned that there would be some side effects, which would disappear after his body got used to the medication. So, he had headaches for a few days, but they soon stopped so he carried on with the tablets. The school workers noticed a bit of improvement in his behaviour, but a lot of David's behaviour was a habit of just ignoring the rules to do what he wanted. It was something that we had to work with.

It was Katie's birthday on 10 October, and we received an invite from her grandmother to go to a little party she was organizing. Stefan went to his grandad's, and Denise went to Jane's. We took David and Marie with us as they were also invited. We had a lovely time, and both David and Brooke were pleased that Katie remembered them.

Stefan was doing well at school now, and in October we attended an awards evening in Hertford organized by Herts and Minds, an organization that provides mentalization-based treatment (MBT) for children in foster care. There he was presented with a certificate for his improved achievements in school. He looked very proud that night and rightly so as he had worked hard in the last six months.

A few weeks after we had come back from our London break, one of my knees got so swollen I could hardly walk on it. We put it down to the amount of walking we had done, so I just rested it for about a week before the swelling went down. Then shortly after that, I got a sore mouth, which lasted for longer than I thought it should. I went to the doctor who then sent me for a barium X-ray as a sore mouth is one of the symptoms of Crohn's disease. I then had to go and see a consultant at the hospital who said he would put me on steroids as it look as though the Crohn's was coming back.

Life went on as normal with review meetings for all three children, medicals, counselling sessions for Stefan and David regularly, school meetings, and after-school activities.

Finally, Denise went to live with her dad and his partner just before Christmas, which was a lovely end to a very pleasant relationship with both Denise and her family. Logan had another change of social worker, and his new one actually listened to him and asked if he would like to come and see us, which he did. She felt it would do him good to spend some time with us as he had been moved from one boarding school to another. Finally he had been asked to leave altogether, so he had been moved back to our local area to live with the carers who had been having him for respite.

In the meantime, David had spent a weekend with Chris our ex-foster son and his partner, which he really enjoyed, and permission had been given by his stepdad for him to visit his little sister twice a week. He was over the moon with this. He and Stefan went to Bancroft youth club weekly which they both enjoyed. Arrangements had been made for Logan now 15 to come and spend a weekend with us just before Christmas, which David was looking forward to. I went to collect him and brought him back here, but as soon as I got home there was a phone call from one of the Support workers to say that his carers had said that they didn't want him back so could we take him to the offices on Monday morning without telling him. We felt this was wrong, but we had no choice. I asked what was going to happen to him and was told that social services would have to find an emergency placement for him, but I asked if he could stay with us until something was sorted as we didn't like to think of him going to strangers for Christmas. We could have a meeting after the holidays.

The weekend went well, but we didn't feel right knowing what was going to happen on Monday morning. We took Logan back to the offices. He thought it was just us that we needed to talk to someone, so he went in without any idea of what was about to be said to him. He came out of the room very quiet, which was understandable. He was okay with coming back with us, but he was still shell-shocked over how it had been done, as were we.

Christmas arrived. Stefan had gone off to his mum's on Christmas Eve and was going to stay there until the twenty-seventh, which was a normal arrangement. So we just had Logan and David. It all started off well. On

Christmas morning both boys were pleased with their presents. Marie and family arrived for dinner, and just as they were about to leave, we had a phone call from EDT. We were asked if we could take and emergency placement. We agreed that would be fine. Stuart aged 10 arrived about 7.00 p.m. We put him in with David as it was the only bed available. David said he would look after him. Everything went well that night, but when we got up the next morning, Stuart did nothing but complain about having to share. We explained that was the only option available in an emergency, but as soon as the holidays were over, he would be found a suitable placement nearer to his home as a lot of people won't take emergency placements over Christmas, but would be available after the holidays. He still wasn't happy about this and started picking on David and trying to accuse David of bullying him, which we knew definitely wasn't happening because David was the last child who would bully anyone. In fact, he would go out of his way to make sure that a new placement would feel at home. But the thing we were worried about was that we could see Logan getting wound up every time Stuart said nasty things to David, and we didn't know how much longer he would hold on to his temper. He and David were very close, and the last thing Logan would do would be to stand by and see David being hurt, so we had to get on the phone to EDT and explain the situation. They did find Stuart somewhere else to go, but it meant that Robert and my brother had to take him to Watford. So much for my birthday, but better that than having something erupt between the boys.

It was David's birthday on twenty-eighth. He had asked if he could take some of his school friends for a game of bowling. We sent out nine invites and received nine yes please answers. We asked our Dean if he would come with us as the thought of trying to look after ten of David was giving us nightmares. As it turned out, it wasn't too bad. We took them for a MacDonald's first and then got them all to the bowling alley. Dean had to keep an eye on one that kept disappearing into the machine arcade every chance he got, and one of them—a wonderful six-footer—followed me around so that, every time I turned around, I was bumping into him. One of the others kept calling Robert Bob the Builder ever so loud, but we managed to get through the day. Logan and Stefan had opted to go to the cinema to keep out of the way, bless them. All the parents turned up on time to collect their children and were appreciative because they didn't normally get invites to parties. They were a lovely bunch, and as much as we were all shattered, we had a really good time. But we wouldn't be doing it again next year.

The following days went by without any mishaps. It was Laura's first birthday on the thirtieth. She and Baby-Marie came over to us New Year's Eve so that Marie could go out and see the New Year in. We popped over to Jane's in the afternoon. Nigel came back with us and we saw the New Year in with the kids.

Chapter 33

The Year 2005 came in nice and calm especially after the fiasco at Christmas. Baby-Marie and Laura were here until Sunday the second.

David had a rocky January. He had an appointment regarding his eyesight during which he was told that there was nothing that could be done to improve his sight. He had to have his medication changed as he started hearing voices, so I stopped him taking it and made an appointment to see his consultant. He wasn't getting on very well with his twice-weekly visits to see his sister as he was made to play with her the whole time and not allowed to do anything else. Near the end of the month, after one of these visits, he came back very upset and in tears. When we asked what was wrong, he said his stepdad told him that they had got rid of all his belonging as he was no longer part of their family. In fact, they were thinking of having another child to take his place, which really upset him. We had a word with his social worker who went and had a word with both of them.

Stefan had a good month as he was in a school play and was attending rehearsals. Robert took David to see him in his play, which was very good, and Robert said he should be proud of himself as he seemed like a natural on stage.

Logan had a friend sleeping over a few nights and stayed at his house few nights as well at weekends. He wasn't attending any education facility, so his days were a bit long and tedious. He hadn't been able to see Stefan in his play as he had the flu.

We had Logan's review near the end of January, but he refused to take much interest as he said he no one ever listened to him or gave him a choice of what he wanted to do. But he did agree to go to Educational Youth Services EYS which is an educational programme being run locally. He would be collected every day and brought home. This program tries to get teenagers who can't cope with school at least to try to get some education. Although the next morning he couldn't remember agreeing to it, he said he would give it a go as it was getting boring being at home all day and he might meet other young people that he could mix with.

I was feeling wonderful because the doctors had me on steroids. I was still waiting for tests, which would take a little time, but in the meantime, I was able to cope.

Jim, my brother in Australia, was making arrangements to come home sometime in May, so we were going to organize a family reunion. It was decided that it would be held here in the village as it was about the most central location for everyone, and we could use the village hall, so that was something to look forward to.

Stefan had a letter from school. They were organizing a skiing holiday, and he wanted to go. We had to get permission from his social worker, but that worked out okay. It was going to be in March. We thought the rest of us could go on a holiday to Ireland while he was away with the school. He had been getting on our kids' nerves a bit recently by being silly and doing odd things when they all went to youth club once a week.

We went to a meeting to get the rest of the information we needed about the trip and a list of things that he would have to have. The date was given as 17 March. We booked our holiday for next day so that we would be able to see him off and get back the day before he was due to come home. We thought it would be nice to take Baby-Marie with us, so she was really looking forward to it. Logan decided that he wouldn't come with. He said he would probably be bored and would ruin the holiday for the rest of us. It was agreed that he would stay with Jane. We booked the cottage and airline tickets along with car-hire. The date was fast approaching when the school sent a letter of confirmation, but the dates they gave us differed by a week from the one we had booked I got in touch with the school and they told me that they had sent a letter home with all the students to let everyone know of the change of dates. When we questioned Stefan, he said he remembered getting a letter but hadn't thought it important. He'd thrown it away. We then had to arrange for him to go to another carer while we were away, and she had to see him off, but obviously we would be back for him to be picked up by us when they returned.

With only a few days to go, Laura was taken ill, and the night before we were due to leave, she was rushed into hospital. Marie and Dave were going to stay with her. We went to see them and say bye-bye. It was a horrible sight to see this little girl attached to all sorts of tubes. In some ways it was a blessing that we were taking Baby-Marie, as it gave Marie and Dave all the time they needed to be with Laura. It was awful for us to have to go away not knowing how she was going to be. But we couldn't have done anything if we had stayed. Marie phoned us the next day after we arrived at the cottage. She put our minds at rest; Laura was going to be fine but would have to spend a few days in hospital.

In the weeks leading up to this holiday, David had been having contact with his family, and after his social worker managed to have a word with them, they started changing their attitude. David said they were now saying to him that they wanted him to go home. They would do his room up and put a television in his room for him. David was torn between wanting to come away with us and returning home, but we explained to him that he wouldn't be able to go home as quickly as that. Any permanent move would be built up by going for a couple of weekends with everyone keeping an eye on the situation, but he was getting very annoyed that he couldn't just go home. People were saying to him that no one could stop him if it was what he really wanted. We managed to get him to agree to come away with us. Then we could concentrate on getting him home as soon as we returned from the holiday. Well, I wish we had let him go there while we went away because, every chance he got, he phoned his mother and stepdad. And every time he came off the phone, he asked us to take him home straight away as they were saying that is what we should be doing if he wanted us to. Everything we did on that holiday was done with bad grace and moods with a few tantrums thrown in. Apart from that, we had a good time. Baby-Marie enjoyed herself.

When we returned, the first thing David wanted to do was go home, so we arranged through social services for him to go home for a week. But he had been there for only a few days when we got calls asking us to go and collect him. They'd had enough and couldn't cope with him. He came home annoyed saying they hadn't decorated his room and there was no television, and all the promises they'd made had been forgotten. So David was back.

Laura was home again with Marie and her family and doing well. Stefan and Logan were home, so everything was back to normal. Logan had been to the educational centre and hated it. He didn't want to go back, so I had a job to get him up in the mornings. Nothing new there.

As we went into April, Marie came over to tell us that she and Dave had decided to get married. We were delighted. We asked when, and they said 19 May. Great, five days after our family reunion! Well I suppose we could organize both events in six weeks. Marie had been in touch with the registry office, but they were redecorating and couldn't guarantee that date. Marie and Dave needed to get in touch with the town hall as that is where all their bookings were being arranged. People in charge there told them that was the week that they were handing everything back to the registry office. So it was back to the registry office. They agreed to take the booking, but they told Marie to ring the week before to confirm it. Just what we needed to hear. Marie was happy for a friend to drive her to the registry office on the day of the wedding and back to the village for the reception, but we felt that wouldn't be right, so we managed to book a wedding car. The next six weeks flew by. I finished the last of my steroids and didn't think to go back to let the doctor know. Boy did I suffer. It felt as though someone had hit my legs with a sledge hammer. But there was a wedding to organize, and a reunion, so I just got on. I could go to the doctor when everything quietened down.

When the day of the reunion arrived, the weather was unbelievably hot. Just over a hundred family members turned up. It was fantastic, and everyone had a marvellous time, the last ones eventually going home very late at night. I had done the catering for that, but the pub would do the catering for the wedding as I really wouldn't have had the time to do much that day. Laura was full of cold but managed to get through the day, Baby-Marie looked wonderful and made a gorgeous bridesmaid.

We had permission to take the photographs in the manor grounds. It was a beautiful background. Then it was back to the village hall for the reception.

Bride and groom went away the next day, and Baby-Marie and Laura stayed with us, which pleased the boys.

I had to take Baby-Marie to school every day and collect her each evening. She was always worried in the mornings that she was going to be late, but we managed to get her there in time.

Logan had decided that he didn't want to go back to the EYS. I had such a difficult time getting him up in the mornings, and when he did finally get there, he caused so much disruption that it was decided that it would be better for him not to continue the education program. It was back to the old routine of either staying in bed most of the day or spending his days on the computer.

Life went on very much as normal. At the beginning of June, Logan's social worker managed to get his belongings together from the various places he had been. She kept it together at the offices. We said we would pick them up after we had met Dean and spent most of the day with him. By time we were ready to come home, we had forgotten to call to collect Logan's belongings. We only remembered when we got home. I said I would go back the next day as it was too late to go right away; by the time we got back, there would be no one there. He got really upset and angry, which I could understand, but there was nothing I could do about it that evening. In his temper, he put his hands around my throat, which really panicked and upset David. But as soon as Logan realized what he had done, he pulled away and shot upstairs. I had to spend a little time trying to calm David down, but in the end, everyone settled down. Apologies were made and accepted. We went in the next day to collect everything. There were quite a few things that we thought he should have but were missing, but they never did turn up. There was a plate that his mum had given him, a book that some friends had printed with a story that he was part of, all his Thomas the Tank engine toys, a few other bits and pieces, most of which I can't remember now. But at the time, we felt these treasures should have been put away somewhere safe for him as they were things that had been part of his life, but we just had to say goodbye to them as did Logan.

Logan's behaviour started going downhill and he kept saying that no one listened to him, and he wasn't asked if he wanted to come back with us. He'd had no say in it, and he now wanted to be asked what he wanted to happen to him in the future. I totally agreed with him and said it wasn't fair. I suggested a meeting to get things sorted and to determine that he should be allowed to make some decisions about his own future. He couldn't come up with where he wanted to go, but his behaviour with us was deteriorating and was a threat to everyone. We felt everyone would be safer if he was moved to a halfway house until something for the longer term could be organized. So he had to pack his bags yet again.

Life was so unfair we were going to miss him terribly because, with all his faults, we thought a lot of him and only wanted him to be happy. He did leave a few boxes of his belongings with us, which we still have. I keep asking him if he wants to sort them out, but he always says no, he would just like them kept where they are, which we have done and always will for as long as he wants us to. We feel that this is his home ground.

Rose and Nigel came to stay for two weeks while Jane and Baz had their holiday. David was pleased. We all went to the pictures, they all went swimming, and we managed a night at the dog races, which they all liked. We ended up taking them for a meal the night before they went home.

Three days after they went home, we had another boy for several weeks while his carers went on holiday. We were all missing Logan. Nigel and Rose made the new boy feel welcome and went swimming and to the pictures with him so that he didn't feel left out. Stefan was practising with Snappy G's youth club for Rhythms of the World, an annual musical festival.

David was getting ready for his school sports day, also his dad's sister got in touch with us and asked if she could see David. We thought it would do him good to have some contact with his dad's relatives as they hadn't been in touch since his dad's funeral, so contact was organized. He enjoyed seeing her and, through her, his grandmother asked to see him, so I took him to her house, and he spent time with her. We didn't have a regular meeting schedule, but we did usually take him several times a month. At last David's sports day arrived. Robert took the day off work. Marie, Baby-Marie, and Laura went with him to cheer him on. I couldn't leave the house as both my feet were so swollen that I couldn't get any footwear on my feet. It was two weeks before they were down enough for me to get into town to buy something comfortable that would fit so that I could go out.

School holidays began, and within a few days we had a new placement, 15 year old Emily arrived on 1 August. She was lovely and got on with the two boys straight away Emily was very sports minded, so we had to fit in taking her to all sorts of activities over the summer. Both David and Stefan did the usual rounds of going to the pictures and having days out with their youth club, going swimming, and participating in contact visits. Stefan did have one bit of trouble at the youth club. He had been hit on the nose by another boy. The police had been called, and it was a police officer who brought him home. Our immediate thought was, *What now?* But as it turned out, it was a misunderstanding over another girl, so we soon got that sorted.

We had a lovely visit from Toni and the twins, Linda and Veronica. It was great to see them. Megan, her mum, and Megan's older brother came over one of the days. David went to stay with Andrew, who had moved with the carers who fostered his older brother.

Emily had a few days at home, but I think as much as it went well, we could feel that they were all glad that it was only for a few nights. We had to make a visit to her school to make sure that it was okay for her to start back in September. Owing to an illness, she had missed quite a bit of schooling. It was considered that as she was very intelligent. If she applied herself, she would have no problem catching up. So it was agreed that she could start back at the beginning of the new term.

There had also been a lot of catching up to do with her family. There was a few meetings to work out what level of contact should be agreed on, as no one wanted it to fail. It was decided that she would start going back for weekends. If that went well, then eventually a return to home would be in her best interest. I also asked her mum if she would like to come with Emily and I when we went clothes shopping so that she would be involved in more practical matters. Also it was a way for me to get to know her mother better and for them to spend some time together doing something nice.

David had some sad news. His aunt on his dad's side died. She was the last person who had truly taken an interest in him. We made sure that he went to her funeral. Even today when we manage to take him to his dad's grave, he pops over to visit her grave. On these visits to his dad's grave, we noticed there was still no marker on the grave. So we took David to the stone mason's and got him to choose which headstone he would like put there. We paid for it ourselves as a gift to both David and his dad.

Stefan had a steady girlfriend now and spent a lot of time back and forth to her house. They had met at youth club. She was very nice, and it was lovely to see him so happy.

David also had a girlfriend. He used to stay at her house occasionally at weekends to keep her company while they babysat for her sister's child.

We had to take both Stefan and David back and forth. Very rarely did it work out that they required transport on the same night or even the same time, so we felt more and more like a taxi service, but they were happy.

David was also having to go up and down to Great Ormond Street Hospital in London for injections and tests for growth hormones. The process eventually settled down and was able to be administered by our local GP, thankfully. The nurses there got to know him very well, and even now when I see them, they ask how he is.

Mr and Mrs Jim were still interested in how we were doing and would stop and ask how things were. They would often ask if I had thought of writing a book of our experiences. I said that I might get around to it one day, but all my time was taken up with the kids and childminding for Marie while she was having driving lessons. Someone had to look after Little Marie and Laura, and I was very happy to do it We all enjoyed having them. If we went out anywhere for the day, they were automatically included, and we wouldn't have had it any other way.

My brother Sean had a timeshare in Tenerife and had been offered a deal on it, but it meant going over there, which he didn't want to do on his own as it would have been too hard without Doreen. He had been back a couple of times since she'd died, but it was with either with Doreen's daughter or my sister Mary. No one else could go with him, so he asked if I could go. Robert had to look after the kids while I went, but as they were all mostly independent, he would manage.

It was the first time I had gone there. It was beautiful, I thoroughly enjoyed it and was quite full of it when I returned and suggested that, if we ever got the chance, Robert and I should go.

The rest of the year went by in the usual round of sports, youth clubs, doctors, dentists, reviews for all of the kids school meetings, contacts with families, going to the dog racing and the pictures. It was actually a nice change to get through a whole term without any of the children being excluded.

Soon Christmas was upon us, and as usual Stefan went to his mum's. Emily went to her family, so we had only David. Logan came back for Christmas day, and Marie, Dave, little Marie and Laura came for dinner. We had a lovely time.

Marie had arranged for Robert and I to go to the pub for a meal by ourselves for a change, although I must admit I did miss everyone, and it was only for one and a half hours. When we got home, she had a birthday cake waiting for me. David had his birthday on the twenty-eighth, and Laura had hers two days later. Little Marie and Laura stayed with us while Marie and Dave went out. We stayed up to see the New Year in with all the kids, as by now they were all home and safely tucked in.

Chapter 34

The year 2006 came in nice and quiet. Not much was happening apart from Stefan appearing in a school play. This time I did get to go and see him, and he was very good. On Saturday, 21 January, they all went off with the village youth club to Ally Pally (an entertainment and sports venue in London formally known as Alexandra Palace). They went for the all-night ice skating and arrived back at about six in the morning. They tried not to wake us as they let themselves in but our alarm went off at that time, so we were awake anyway and were pleased to hear them come home safe and sound.

Emily was still going to her parents' at the weekends, and as it was Roberts birthday on 30 January, we asked if we could have a bit of respite. Stefan said he was quite happy to go to Jane and Baz's, and David said he would like to stay with a carer with whom he had stayed before and liked. Then he could get to see his friends. They all went off straight after school on Friday. On Saturday, David rang and said he didn't feel well. He asked if he could come home. As we were out shopping in the morning, we didn't get the message until late afternoon. We went there to pick him up. He didn't look well, but as he had just had a bath, we all felt it would be best to leave him in the warmth and come back for him the next day. That evening, Marie and Dave came around for dinner. We picked David up the next morning. He went straight to bed. So much for our relaxing weekend, but that was par for the course. We could never fully rely on getting much time to ourselves, but David really wasn't very well. He could hardly talk, which was a sure sign that he wasn't well. But he was back to his very noisy self in a few days and returned to school that Wednesday, so we were all back to normal.

My sister Elizabeth and my niece Kate came up for the day the following Saturday. On Tuesday the fourteenth, David was supposed to have contact with his mum and sister. The taxi was a bit late getting to our house, and by the time he arrived to the meeting place, his mum had gone. The taxi driver took him around to his friend's house. His mum phoned to say that she would pop around to see him, as it was only around the corner from where she lived, but then she never turned up, so by the time we went to collect him, he was very angry and upset. He cheered up the next day as Logan came for the day to spend some time with him. This was a good thing as a social worker brought Anthony for a visit. He was a little boy we had fostered when he was a baby. She was doing life-story work with him, so we sat and went through all the photos that we had. Then we showed him around the house and visited a bit of the village. We talked about the time he had spent with us and some of the places we had taken him. Both David and Logan remembered him, so it was nice for them to be able to share their memories of his time with us.

The next several months went by in the normal fashion with meetings, contact with families, and after-school activities. Emily was doing really well. She was enjoying her music lessons, had settled back into school extremely well, and was regularly attending homework club, her after school activities, and enjoying her time at the Youth Club she was going to. Her weekends at home seemed to be working well, so it was agreed that she could go home full time, which she was happy about. On 12 April, we took her out for her goodbye meal. She packed all her belongings on Thursday night, and I took them to her mum's on Friday during the day so that Emily could go home straight from school in the evening. I won't say that they have had smooth ride, but she is still living at home. They all keep in touch, and we have seen them quite a few times, so it is great when placements have a positive ending.

David and Stefan now had the house to themselves but no one knew for how long. Jane and Baz needed respite for a weekend at the end of April so, with Emily going home, we were able to have Nigel and his sister with us. Logan came back for the day on that Sunday and spent time with them. They all went over to the cricket field reminiscing about old times and seeing if their camp was still there.

Dean and Cal were finding it difficult to live in a nearby village. The cost of public transport made it very expensive to go anywhere. They put their names on the register to do a swap move, so we were trying to see them as much as possible as we didn't know where they would end up. They were looking at all options and even considering places in Devon or Cornwall as they thought it would be nice to live by the sea. We did try to point out that there were also downsides to living in remote areas wherever they went, and if it was that far away, then we wouldn't be able to see them as often as we would like. But it would be their decision, and we were prepared to support them whatever they decided. Now that Julie and Frosty were back in the area, we were seeing a lot more of them. Julie would sit for us when we went out as we still had to attend our support groups and the fostering forums with other carers and directors of the fostering team. Generally we were home at a reasonable time because they all ended at about 9.30 in the evening. The fostering forums were held in our county hall, and we were supposed to finish at 9.00 as that was the time the caretaker locked everything up. One Monday evening, however, we didn't think it was any later than 9.00, but when we went to leave, we found that we were locked in. It took about half an hour to find the caretaker and for him to let us out. Needless to say, we tried to be on the ball after that, but it did happen one other time. We did always manage to get home eventually.

Stefan had his sixteenth birthday. He went to his mum's after school to celebrate with his family. He then started to seriously look for a Saturday job. We would take him into town so that he could call into shops to see if there were any vacancies, but he didn't have much luck. His personal hygiene was getting worse. Laura would refuse to sit at the table with him, so we had to keep asking him to go and have a wash. His room was getting so smelly that we couldn't let him keep his door open. If he did, the rest of the house was overtaken by the smell. We were constantly having to send him in to clean and tidy it.

On one particularly nice weekend, we got him to empty the room out and disinfect everything. His room was downstairs by the front door, which meant that every time anyone came to our door, the first thing they could smell was Stefan's room. On the other hand, his room was near enough to the door that we could move all his furniture outdoors so we could attempt to clean the carpet. When asked why he wasn't trying to keep himself clean, he said it was because he was frightened of leaving care now that he was sixteen. He also knew his social worker was leaving, but we assured him that he didn't have to leave until he had finished his education, and the course he was on wouldn't end until he was eighteen, so he still had at least two more years with us. Also, everyone responsible would work with him to help him get ready for when he did leave.

We took him into town one Saturday so he could put in an application form for a Saturday position in Clark's, the shoe shop. But when we asked him later in the day how he'd got on, he said it was no good as they wanted someone for the whole day, I looked at him and asked what had he put down and he said quite seriously ten to two. I was speechless.

The next time he filled in a form, I made sure that I looked at it before he handed it in. I now knew why he wasn't getting anything. I explained to him that no one would take him on for a few hours. All Saturday jobs would be all-day jobs. He was still attending his counselling sessions and still needed them. As the weather was getting warmer, I bought some ice creams and lollies to keep in the freezer. A few days after I'd bought them, we had little Marie and Laura around. David asked if they could have some ice cream as it was a lovely warm day. Of course I said they could. David asked me where they were, and I said they were in the usual place in the freezer. But he said they weren't, and when I went to look, I couldn't believe that there wasn't one there! When I asked Stefan if he had taken any, he said he had been getting up at night and helping himself to at least four or five each time. So we then had to go out and get a lock for our freezer. I explained to Stefan that it wasn't fair to all the others if we couldn't keep any cold treats in the freezer over the summer. We couldn't just go down the road and get them. Sometimes we just had to find a way around things so that no one missed out.

David was still having health problems. His doctors were still trying him on different medication, trying to find one that worked. But nothing seemed to make much difference. He was still loud and noisy no matter what, and I think Robert and I and all the family members had resigned ourselves to this fact. But he was also having a growth problem, so we had to take him to a London hospital to see a specialist who said he would need a course of monthly injections for two years. David wanted to know if it had to be injections as he was petrified of needles, but unfortunately injections it had to be. I had to bribe him. I told him that, every time he had an injection, I would give him £1. It worked every time. The nurses at our surgery still remember him and ask how he is getting on. I think everyone in the waiting room knew when David was in for his injection, but he did manage to get through the course in one piece, and so did I and the nurses.

I was still attending the hospital for Crohn's disease and arthritis. My ankles and knees kept swelling, and most of the time I had a problem with walking. I was now using a walking stick to get around, but there was nothing they could do. I just had to live with it. I was on medication for the Crohn's. It would be a long-term treatment, but the medical providers were keeping me monitored.

Nigel would come over for the odd weekend to keep David company, especially if we were going out to places like the Imperial War Museum in Duxford, or dog racing. Sometimes he and David would go to the pictures or swimming and he would come out for meals with us.

Jane and Baz were having their holidays in the middle of June, so we had Nigel and his sister. Jane and and Baz were expecting another placement when they got back, but like all things in fostering, things rarely never work out as planned, and the weekend they were due back we got a call from social services. The social worker explained that the placement they were expecting had broken down. The boy needed to moving that day, which was a Friday. She asked if we could cope with an extra one until they got back on Sunday. It turned out it was Anthony, the boy who had been back to visit us while doing his life-story book, so it was lovely for him and us that we knew him. You can imagine how Jane and Baz reacted when they got home to be informed that, although they had left us with two of their children, we were returning three to them. We still have a laugh about it, but we did have a fun-packed few weeks with all the kids here.

Donna and John had moved to Florida and asked us to go and have a holiday with them, which we readily agreed to. We started making arrangements to go in October.

In July we had another placement of a girl who was having problems at home, but it couldn't have been too bad because, when she went home for a family visit, she ended up staying there. We'd had her for only eleven days, but she had been lovely while she had been with. Sometimes we wondered what problems some people have, because when the children were here with us, we could find no problems with them. We actually found ourselves wishing many of them could have stayed longer. But it was always nicer when they ended up going home.

Stefan was still having problems getting a Saturday job. His mum got married in August. Stefan went along to the wedding and was pleased to be able to meet up with some more of his family members. He came home having had a good day. His social worker had arranged a week away for him. He went off to a place that specialized in teaching drama and music. He had a thoroughly good time and asked if he could go again the following year. His social worker said she would see what she could do when the time came; in the meantime, he had to get his head down and study.

David went to Mersea Island with the town youth club. The workers weren't too pleased with him; they said that he had been smoking and hanging around with unsuitable older people. They would have to think seriously before taking him again next year. I confiscated the packet of cigarettes I found in his bag, which didn't go down too well with him.

Dean and Cal had finally sorted out where they were going to move to, so Julie, David, and I helped them to move to Chesham. We were pleased that it wasn't too far away, although it was still going to take us nearly an hour to get there. But that was better than six hours. It was a lovely house, and they seemed to like it. It was closer to a much better choice of public transport.

I received a phone call from social services. They asked if we could take an emergency placement. Jospeh was a twelve-year-old boy who was supposed to be going to a boarding school in September. All the arrangements had been made, but his placement where he was at the moment had broken down, and he needed somewhere to stay until he could start school. It was agreed that it would be okay as he would be gone by the time our holiday to Donna's was due. He arrived later in the day with his social worker, who said that he didn't know the date the school would be open for him. But they knew all about him and, if I phoned the school headmaster or secretary, he or she would let me know the schedule. Then he asked if I could possibly take him there. I agreed to phone the school and make arrangements, but when I finally managed to speak to someone, I discovered that no one there had a clue what I was talking about. I then couldn't get hold of the social worker. My support worker suggested that I try to speak to the headmaster, which I did. He said that they had Joseph down as a day boy, not as a full-time boarder. Again I had a problem trying to reach his social worker. My support worker said to get Joseph ready for school and start him off on days. In the meantime, she would have a word with his social worker's senior. Transport was organized, and he made a good start. In the meantime, my support worker managed to talk to his social worker and explain the problem. He said that he thought the boy could just stay with us and go to school every day. My support worker told him that wasn't what had been agreed upon, and we had our holidays booked. He must find Joseph somewhere else to go as we lived too far away from the school. He said he would see what he could do. He was reminded that he had only about three weeks to do this.

David, in the meantime, was getting restless and decided that he wanted to go and live in town because that was where his friends were. Robert and I, along with his social worker, told him that they would start looking for somewhere. It was a reasonable request at his age, but it could take a while to get the right place for him as he was becoming known, and most people refused to have him. He was becoming more disruptive at our house, and when Robert had a word with him, he said he thought that if he could disrupt this placement then he would be moved. But we explained that, while it might get him moved faster, to go. Indeed, he could end up being sent miles away.

Stefan was settled and giving no problems. He was looking forward to a family reunion that was being arranged at our house, as Dermot was coming over from Ireland and everyone wanted to see him.

In the week before the party, Joseph's social worker rang to say that arrangements had been made for him to have contact with his dad on the following Sunday, and could we take him to Watford? I explained that we were having a family party and most of my family would be here, so we couldn't do any running around. They would have to organize something else. He rang on the Friday to say he had organized a taxi to collect Joseph at about 10.30 in the morning and bring him back afterwards. I took down the details of the taxi and said that would be okay.

On Saturday, Robert took the children to Shuttleworth to give me space and time to get things ready for Sunday. Joseph appeared to be in a good mood, but when it was time for them to go to bed, Joseph refused. He started swearing and threatened to walk out. He packed a bag and left it by the back door. He found an iron bar and started to walk around the outside of the house banging the bar against the side of the house. Then he started going in and out of the house shouting and swearing. He walked up and down the village. By now the villagers would be saying, "It's only one of Marie and Robert's." He eventually calmed down and went to bed in Stefan's room. Stefan was quite happy to leave him there.

We all got up to a beautiful day on Sunday. The weather couldn't have been better. We got everything ready in the garden. Joseph got ready for his taxi. We thought it was good timing as it meant he would be out of the way when everyone arrived. But like so many of our plans, it wasn't to be. The taxi never arrived by 11.00. I rang them up, and the employee said the social worker hadn't confirmed a time even though he had told me he had. The taxi person said they would get one out asap, but it had to come all the way from Watford. I couldn't get hold of Joseph's social worker on his mobile as it was switched off. He should have left it turned on knowing there were contact arrangements going on that day. By now, Joseph was getting antsy and picking fights with some of my nieces and nephews. Luckily, they didn't take too much notice of him, and two of my brothers were keeping their eyes on the situation as they could see he was upset. The taxi finally arrived at 2.00 p.m. We didn't know Joseph's dad was going to still be there or what was going to happen, but we daren't stop him from going, as he would have tried to get there himself, and we could do without that on that day! He returned in a good mood as his dad had waited although the visit had lasted for only half the time they had expected. He was fine until about 9.30 when a lot of the family members with small children started going home. Those who were left divided up, the men going to the Raven, and the women opening a few bottles of wine and sitting out in the garden. David and Joseph went up to their rooms to watch television. Joseph's room overlooked the back garden, and when he looked out of the window and saw us sitting there, down he came and wanted to join in. We told him that this was our time, but we would allow him to stay awake a bit later and watch television with David so he wouldn't be missing anything. Well, off he went again. He found the iron bar again. The swearing started. He followed the men as they walked to the pub. They ignored him. He went in after them, but as no one took any notice, he came back out and returned to the house. We could hear him long before we saw him. Iron bar in hand, he was banging it off the walls of the house. When that didn't get him attention, he said he was going to go back up the village and start banging all the cars with the iron bar.

We thought now might be a good time to try to stop him, but he went hysterical. In the end, we called EDT, but no one there knew what to suggest except to call the police which we did. When the officers arrived and Joseph saw them, he curled up on the front garden. I managed to get him to sit up while the officers spoke to him. They asked me if I wanted him to be taken away. I said I would rather he wasn't, but if he didn't go to bed, then I might not have a choice. So the officers took him to his room. Just as they were going up the stairs, David was coming down ready to join in with Joseph, but when he saw the police, he shot back into his room and got into bed. Joseph went to his room and promised the officers that he would stay there all night as he didn't want to be arrested. The officers told him that, if he did that, he wouldn't see them again. But if he came down once more, then I was under instructions to call them. That was the last we saw of him that night. I peeked into David's room, and there wasn't a sound out of him except heavy breathing. I went back down to find that the men were all back from the pub and ready for tea or coffee. When they were all finally leaving at around midnight, they all wanted to know what entertainment I would be providing for them all next year and would it be as good as this year. Sadly, that was to be the last big reunion as the following year we were to lose two of my brothers.

Joseph got up the next morning and went off quite happily to school. I rang his social worker to tell him what had happened, but I didn't have to say much as he was able to tell me more or less how it had gone because this was what always happened when he had contact at the weekend. That was the reason he had his mobile turned off so that we couldn't get hold of him. I asked why either we or our support worker hadn't been told, and he said it was because he thought that, if he had warned us about what usually happened, then we wouldn't have taken him. I said we should at least have been told the truth. That way we would have been prepared. But all he said was that was the reason that Joseph's last placement had broken down. I then asked if he had found somewhere for him to go while we were away, and he said he hadn't even started looking. So how we were to work with someone like this was beyond me. I truly felt that the problems were as much the fault of the social worker as they were of Joseph.

The following week, Joseph settled down again, but my mouth got very sore on Friday evening, and because of my history with Crohn's, we thought it advisable to go to the A&E on Saturday. The doctor said I had an abscess and put me on antibiotics. I had a nasty reaction to the medication, and my whole face became swollen. I could hardly talk or eat which everyone said was an improvement. But we were going on holiday soon, so my support worker said she would get them to move the boys to their respite carers a bit sooner to give me a chance to sort myself out. I went to the dentist when the swelling went down, which was only a few days before we were due to go away. She said that, if the abscess hadn't cleared in time, then I wouldn't be able to fly. She couldn't lance it as it was over one of my capped teeth. The only thing I could do was either cancel our holiday, or she could remove my tooth and put in a temporary one until we came back, which is what we agreed to do.

While this was going on, Joseph's social worker still hadn't found him another place to go, so my support worker said the only thing I could do was, on the day that Stefan and David were due to move to their respite carers, I should pack Joseph's belongings and send him off to school. She would get in touch with his social worker and EDT to let them know, and they would have to sort something out. It wasn't the way I would have liked the placement to end because it went against everything we liked. But I was in pain and we were quickly running out of time. I didn't really have much choice as his social worker didn't want to know what was going on. I felt awful sending him off to school and saying goodbye.

In the next few days I went to the dentist had my tooth removed and the abscess lanced, which gave me immediate relief. The dentist installed the temporary tooth on Friday, and we were off on Saturday. Happy days, as soon as we arrived at Donna's my tooth fell out! I spent the next two weeks going around with a great big gap in my front teeth, but it didn't stop me from enjoying myself.

The two weeks flew by, and soon we were home. Robert was back at work on Monday. Stefan and David returned after school. I had been to their respective placements and collected their belongings. They were both pleased to be home and even more pleased to receive their presents. David said he really missed us and would try harder to make the placement work with us.

We were soon back to normal with Stefan and David going to school and youth club meetings and spending time with their friends. Soon half term was upon us. We spent a week going places with Jane and her family. Andrew came over for a few days, which pleased David.

After the school holidays, David's school organized for him to have extra maths lessons with a tutor who would work with him at home once a week after school. Most of the time he played up and wasted the tutor's time, but these things have to be tried and given a chance.

We were going along nicely with only Stefan and David, which gave me time to get my tooth sorted. It was just as well that Robert keeps reasonably well.

Near the end of November, we were asked to have Billy, a thirteen-year-old boy who was at present living with his father, who presently was having a hard time keeping him out of trouble. It was felt that a move far enough away from his friends might help the situation. Billy arrived with his social worker on a Monday night. He had no school for the rest of the week as he had been excluded. I was to take him back the following Monday. He got on well with David; in fact, a bit too well, which can sometimes cause problems when they get too friendly. But it was early days. Billy's social worker actually took him to school on Monday, but it wasn't long before they were back home as he had been excluded for a further week. His behaviour had been totally unacceptable from the time they walked through the school doors, and the school personnel weren't prepared to put up with it.

Billy social worker organized day care with Jane, as sometimes having them at home can cause problems with the others. They feel that, if one is off school, then they should be able to have time off to hang around with them. Billy had to go off in the taxi the same time the others had to leave for school, and he returned at about the same time in the evening. Being out of school can also put a big strain on the placement as the kids can get very bored and aggressive if they are not receiving attention or being run around to see their mates. The following week Billy's social worker made another attempt at taking him to school, but the same thing happened, and home he came again. He was allowed to stay at a friend's house for a couple of days, but soon his friend's mum was on the phone saying she was sending him home and didn't want to see him again this side of Christmas.

Billy's social worker had another go at taking him to school. This time, Robert and I followed in case the same thing happened. This time his social worker didn't have time to do the return journey. However, this time, his behaviour was worse. As soon as he arrived, he started swearing at the teachers, throwing stones in the car park at the teachers' cars and at the school windows. The headmaster had no option but to exclude him permanently. His social worker was so different from our last one. She organized day care for him as Jane was having problems of her own and it would have been more difficult for her to have Billy. Also, she had things to organize for Christmas.

Stefan's social worker arranged for him to have a weekend at home before the holidays which he was really pleased about, so that left David and Billy at home together. They asked if they could go for walk. We thought this would be fine as normally they just walked around the village or down the lane around the block. But, oh, no. Not today. They decided they would walk to town, but not by road as that would be too dangerous. They decided it would be safer to go across the fields, but they promptly got lost. They fell down a ditch and ended up phoning the police, who had to track them by their mobile phones and rescue them and bring them home.

The rest of the time to Christmas was rather uneventful. But on the twenty-sixth, Billy accused David of stealing £4 and his tobacco. We managed to stop Billy from strangling David. The following day, David returned Billy's £4, and they went off to town together. We went to collect David as Billy was going to see his dad. When we got there, David was upset because Billy had thrown his mobile phone away. We couldn't do anything as Billy was away until after the New Year. His friend's mum returned him to us on New Year's Eve, but we thought we would leave any sorting out until the next day so that we could see the New Year in without any fights. So ended another uneventful and peaceful year.

Chapter 35

New Year's Day 2007 was very subdued as I wasn't very well. I had the flu, so everyone was walking around very quietly. The boys were waiting for something to happen regarding Billy throwing away David's mobile phone, but I just wasn't up to it at the moment. I didn't normally get coughs or colds over the winter, but the medication I was on for the Crohn's was an immunosuppressant, so I ended up with a very severe bout of flu. Nothing happened over the next few days until Billy's social worker came to visit, and it was decided that, as both boys had been to blame in one way or another, they would go halves on a new mobile phone for David. And as they were having problems with each other, it was decided that it may be in everyone's best interest to move Billy. As soon as the social worker had left, Billy came to me and apologized for everything. He said that he really wanted to stay with us, and he would improve his behaviour. So we agreed that he would be on a month's trial. We rang his social worker, and she agreed that it might work. We would have to wait and see what happened.

David played up a bit as he thought that he would be moved if he did, but we said that, as long as he met us halfway with things, then he would be okay with us. He still had issues getting up in the mornings, but that was par for the course with most of the children. He played up at youth clubs and was banned for a while. He stopped taking his medication and seemed a lot calmer without it, so I rang his doctor. She said it would be okay to let him go without until his next appointment with her.

David's social worker arranged for all of us to go to a special college to have a look around. We were all impressed with what we saw and agreed that he would enjoy being there as there were a lot of hands-on lessons that we knew he would enjoy. So at least he would have that to look forward to. As long as he was accepted, all he had to do was keep his head down at school.

Stefan was going along nicely giving us no problems. He came home from school one night and noticed his mobile phone was missing from his room, and when we asked the two boys if they had seen it, they both got very verbal. But we couldn't prove anything, so we replaced it for him and told him that, if he wasn't taking it with him when he went out, he should leave it with me, and I would look after it for him.

Billy decided that he didn't want to go to Bishop's Stortford. He was running out of friends there, so it was arranged that he would go to day care in town, which he wasn't very pleased about. But he managed a few days until he eventually refused to go. He expressed this by throwing a major wobbly. He started kicking our door and back garden gate. When I got hold of his social worker, she told me to ring the police. Also, she would have a word with him on the phone. But when he couldn't get her to do what he wanted, he threw our cordless phone across to the other side of the road, shattering it. Luckily, it was one of three. When the police turned up, he went very quiet and docile, but they weren't pleased with his behaviour and asked if we wanted to charge him with criminal damages. We said no as we were used to it. We explained that sometimes these kids didn't have any other way of venting their feelings. His social worker spoke to them and asked that he be removed. She would arrange someone from the emergency care to meet him there. So he was taken to a crisis centre.

A few days later, we had a phone call from the care centre. The worker asked what we did to calm him down when he went into one of his anger modes. I said we tried to leave him alone until he calmed down, and we intervened only if someone else was in his firing line. The worker told us they had major problems with him and wondered how we managed to keep him for two months. They didn't think they could cope for a few weeks! I wished them luck.

It was time to get the room ready for whoever we would get next, but in the meantime, we still had David and Stefan to look after.

Someone from the youth club in Hitchin phoned me to say that they were a bit worried about David as he kept going out to smoke. They couldn't take responsibility for him unless he was prepared to stay indoors. We also had problems with his smoking and his fascination with lighters and matches. We had the safety officer from the fire brigade call around to check out the smoke alarm situation at our house and upgrade it if necessary. They installed one in each bedroom. We already had them in the stairwell, both at the top and bottom, and in the dining room. The firefighters had a word with David regarding the safe use of cigarette lighters and matches. They told him to keep them outside the house as he wasn't allowed to smoke indoors anyway. So he agreed to give them to me to look after until he needed them.

Stefan was going along well. We'd had no problems from him. He just needed to get his head down for his school work. But he was enjoying youth club and seeing his girlfriend.

Nigel came for a week's respite while his carers went on holiday, but we never had problems with Nigel. He got on with both Stefan and David, so Easter went as smoothly as David would allow. Logan even managed a visit, which was lovely. We had a few days out with Marie and the girls.

David was getting the bug to go to his mum's, and he started with the tactic of making as much noise as he possibly could, asking for money for cigarettes, saying his mum and her partner would buy them for him if he was living with her. He spent the few days swearing and shouting. He got up one day swearing and being abusive, demanding to go the youth club with money to pay for fish and chips instead of eating what I had cooked. He finally calmed down and ate his supper before we took him to the youth club. When we went to pick him up, he came out swearing and shouting. He continued with this as well as kicking the back of Robert's seat until we got home. When he came in the back door, he started kicking the furniture and doors and saying he wanted to go to his mum's as she had promised him his own room and would give him pocket money. We rang his mum, and she agreed to have him back for a few days. He then got a few things together, and I took him to them. He eventually calmed down, and they said that it would be only temporary as he couldn't live there on a permanent basis, so I came home leaving him there.

It was so calm in the house with only Stefan. We did eventually get a phone call from social services asking if we could take Manny, a thirteen-year-old illegal immigrant until they could sort out what to do with him. When they arrived with him, he was very confident considering he couldn't speak any English. He settled really well. We managed to understand each other with sign language. He wanted to learn English, so he listened very carefully when we spoke to him and pointed things out to him. It wasn't long before he was using basic words. He liked to watch *EastEnders* and said he picked up a lot of English from the program. He was very bright, which made having him with us very easy. Social services managed to trace his brother, who came to see him but said he couldn't have Manny live with him as he was only in lodgings. He would be quite happy for Manny to stay with us, and he would visit him. Manny could go and stay with his brother for one or two nights only, but he would support any decisions that we made. He was found a place in the secondary school and was very keen to go as he wanted to learn as much as he could because he was hoping to stay in this country.

Manny seemed to settle down okay, although sometimes he would get frustrated over certain decisions as he felt that he was being treated as a child. He was supported at his meetings by an interpreter so that he would understand what decisions were being made and why. He had problems with not being allowed to stay out late at night. It was explained to him that, in this country, a thirteen-year-old was expected to do homework and be home at a reasonable hour on a school night. Sometimes we got the feeling that he was a bit older than he claimed, but officially he was thirteen.

Unfortunately, we had a phone call from one of my nieces. Her husband had died very unexpectedly, which was a shock for everyone. We knew he had been ill but hadn't realized that his illness was so threatening. The boys had to go to respite carers overnight as we had an early start for the long journey to attend the funeral.

Manny had meetings with a solicitor and appointments at the home office as his status here needed to be looked into. Hopefully they would allow him to apply for citizenship, but he would have a long wait. And there would be lots of meetings to get it all sorted. He sometimes got a bit upset because he wasn't seeing his brother enough, and the reason he had come to England was to be with his brother. He thought everyone was trying to keep them apart. It had to be explained to him that he couldn't stay with his brother as he was living only in lodgings, and it wouldn't be appropriate for him to be there longer than a few days. He wanted to know why he couldn't get lodgings there too. He partly understood but said sometimes he felt frustrated and thought everyone was dragging things out.

In the meantime, David had to be moved from his mum's, and because they thought that we had enough on our plate with Manny, they arranged for David to live with carers to whom he used to go for respite. He had got on well with them. We had him back here for a weekend. He and Manny got on well together—probably too well.

Logan came back for another visit, which always pleased us as we still missed him. But was nice to keep up with how he was doing and where he was living.

Everything was going smoothly at the moment, which was a lovely change. Towards the end of July, we were asked to have a nine-year-old girl whose mum was in hospital. Sara arrived with her uncle and her social worker on a Friday night. Marie was here with the girls, and they asked if they could stay and keep Sara company and help her to settle in. Laura stayed one night, but little Marie stayed several nights, but as it was the summer holidays, we had days out together.

Again, David's placement broke down. He was now placed in a bigger town with a private agency. We ended up having him for a few days to give his carer a break.

Stefan was now old enough to get join the Scoots Wheels-to-Work Project, which helped qualified young people procure 50cc scooters to use as transport to and from their jobs. This was great as it gave Stefan more independence and stopped us from having to taxi him everywhere. Because he was now sixteen, I told him that he had to start getting ready for independence. Instead of asking me if he could go somewhere, he was now to tell me where he was going, what time he would be home, and if he wanted a dinner saved.

He was a bit slow at first in taking on the responsibility of his own life, but he soon learned. There were a few ups and downs. He forgot to take his driving licence with him on his first lesson and had to go back another day. And he broke the key in the lock of his bike, getting knocked off it by a passing car, but not with any serious consequences. The bike situation was the worst as he had to get the bike replaced with a new one. In the whole he coped well.

We had the usual summer holidays, taking the children to multiple places. Marie and the two girls usually came with us. On one day we took an outing to Whipsnade Zoo along with Jane and all her foster kids. Luckily, they all got on together as they were used to mixing when we used to go there for coffee or Jane would bring her kids to our house for the day and let the kids go over to the woods while we enjoyed a coffee break.

Sara had been with us for only three weeks when it was agreed that her mum was now well enough to have her home. We took her out for a meal the day before she was due to go home. Everyone was a bit sad as she had been a lovely placement and would be missed. Little Marie probably missed her most as they had got on really well together. Several weeks after she had gone home, I received a beautiful thank you letter from her and her mum, which was lovely. We had visits from Megan and her mum during the holidays, and I was still attending hospital appointments with David and his career, as he wanted me to go with them because I knew his history and the doctors at the hospital. He was also coming back

337

to us so I could take him for his monthly injections as he would have them done only if I was with him.

We also had more bad news in the family. At the beginning of September, my brother Martin, who lived in Birmingham, had been diagnosed with cancer. He was taken into hospital for tests and scans, and he died suddenly while in the hospital. He was going from his bed to the bathroom but never made it to the door. His funeral was on 24 September. We hired a mini bus as Tony had managed to make it over from the States, so we thought our family members would be happier travelling together rather than taking two or three cars. George very kindly drove the bus for us so that we didn't have to worry. Martin's death had been so sudden and unexpected that we couldn't believe it had happened. He had been diagnosed only a few weeks before; in fact, knowing his sense of humour some of us expected him to rise out of the coffin and say "Fooled you!" But sadly, we had to come to terms with it. And if that wasn't bad enough, six weeks later my brother Sean had an aneurism and died on the operating table. I think everyone in our family was in shock.

Luckily, Stefan and Manny weren't giving us much trouble. Manny had a job to get a pair of shoes as he wouldn't even look at the youth shoes. He was determined to get an adult pair, but it wasn't easy to find a small size six. Eventually we ended up in a very expensive shop that had only one pair in his size, which he agreed to have. I told him that, at that price, he had better look after them and not play football in them.

Stefan's teachers decided that he wasn't taking his A levels seriously and would never get a pass with the work that he was producing, so they downgraded him to doing a business tech course, which he said he would put more effort into.

Manny had made a new friend when he went to stay at his brother's and asked if he could stay there some weekends. Consent was given as his brother knew the family. One weekend he came home very quiet and asked to speak to his social worker. He wanted to put in a complaint, saying that he didn't want to be stopped using his phone in the middle of the night. As it was his phone, he felt he should be allowed to use it whenever he wanted to. He also said that we should be putting credit on his phone whenever he needed it; £10 a week wasn't enough pocket money; we weren't buying him enough clothes (we should be getting him something new every week); he was not getting enough money to take to school; and to top it all, he was made to wash his coffee cup after using it, and he didn't want to do that because it was our job. We had a long discussion, and he said that he would like to move somewhere else where the people would give him all that and more! His social worker said she would have a word with our support worker to see about getting him moved.

The following day, he had a phone call from his new friend who wanted Manny to go to London the next day to help him celebrate his birthday, so he told me that he would not be going to school because he would be going to London. I told him it didn't work like that; he couldn't just take time off school to go wherever he wished. He could see his friend at the weekend without any problem. Reluctantly he agreed that he would go to school, but he wasn't happy about it and would be speaking to his social worker.

We did get a two-week respite during September and October; both boys went to respite carers. Stefan went to Jane's as usual, and Manny went to another carer not far from the school. When we got back, Stefan was fine. He and Jane had had no problems, but when I went to collect Manny's clothes, it was a different matter. This carer had had no end of problems with him. He was late home from school and went to London. She'd had problems getting him home. He wouldn't do anything to help around the house—washing up, making his bed, putting his clothes in the wash. And he just kept demanding more money all the time saying I gave him more. But luckily, we had already talked about money with the carer before Manny went there. The bottom line was that she would not be having him back again under any circumstances.

Manny started a pattern of going to his brother's every weekend and coming home late on Sunday. Then he wouldn't want to get up for school. He'd want to stay in bed for the day. He was very sullen in school and rude to the teachers. On one Monday, I had to collect him early as they wanted him suspended for the afternoon. I had a word with his social worker who came to see him and said that, if he was finding it too tiring to go to his brother's every weekend, then it should go back to once a fortnight as school was more important. If he wanted to stay in this country, then he must be more positive with his education. He admitted that he was trying to break the placement with us, thinking that he would be sent to live with his brother. But it was explained to him that, even if his placement with us broke down, he would not be going to live with his brother. He could even end up living even further away if they couldn't find foster carers in the area. So he agreed that he would ease off. His behaviour improved for the rest of the term as he was going to his brother's for Christmas.

Stefan was still having problems with his schoolwork. School authorities said that, unless he worked harder, he wouldn't be getting either a pass or a merit. He said he would try harder. The man from Scoots rang to say that Stefan hadn't paid any money since he started on the scheme, so I had to have another word with him. I knew he was getting enough money to cover most things, and we were saving his clothing allowance for him. He said he didn't know what he was doing with his education maintenance allowance (EMA) money or the money he was getting for his Saturday job, but would go to the bank and sort it out. I settled the Scoots debt with his clothing allowance and then made him go and set up a direct debit, which he did.

Christmas came and went quietly for a change. On 30 December, social services called to ask us to take a little girl whose mum had been arrested for drunk driving. When the police questioned her, she admitted to having a child at home whom she needed to get to, but the police needed to keep her in overnight. So, at 11.00 p.m., the police arrived with a ten-year-old. She was very quiet and tired, so I put her straight to bed. The next day, two social workers arrived. They spent most of the day at our house on the phone finding out what was going to happen to the child. When it was agreed that the police were letting her mum go, the social workers took her home to her mum's.

That was another year over, a very sad one for our family. We could only look forward, hoping the next year would bring better things.

Chapter 36

The year 2008 started quietly, but it didn't stay that way for long. As some of the kids were away for a few days, we managed to get to my sister Elizabeth's for a few days, which was nice and relaxing. Manny arrived home from his brother's at about 8.00 p.m. He was a bit tetchy, but we put it down to being tired. The next day after school, I met him and took him to the dentist, and on the way home, he asked about sleeping at a friend's house at the weekend instead of going to his brother's. But I explained that we would have to check it with social services because they might need to do a check on the family before he would be allowed to spend over night. So he said that he would not be going to his brother's; instead, he would be staying home at the weekend, which was okay with us.

On Friday we took them all to the fish and chip restaurant along with little Marie and Laura. They all said they had a good time.

The following week a worker from Scoots rang to say that Stefan had been involved in an accident at the beginning of December and hadn't told anyone. His scooter now needed a lot of work done, and the claim for the other person's car would have to go through the insurance as it was too late to do it privately. This would now cost Stephen an additional £250, and he would also be losing the deposit that he would have got back at the end of the contract. Also, If at any time Stephen didn't keep them or us informed, then they would be cancelling the contract.

When we went to our January support group, we left Manny to get his own supper. We came home to a sink full of dirty dishes. Definitely words would be had the next day.

Stefan had to be brought home by one of the teachers on Friday as he had lost his keys sometime during the day. I also had a phone call from one other teacher asking if he should push Stefan's bike inside the building to make sure of its safety, to which I said would be a good idea. We took him to Scoots on Saturday to pick up a spare key for the scooter, and then dropped him off at work on the way home.

Manny's parents' evening on the following Wednesday was not very positive. All of his teachers said that he had the ability to do the work but his attitude let him down.

January wasn't even over when we had a call from David's social worker asking if we could pick him and his clothes up as he would be coming back to us. They also asked us to please sort his clothes out as they were all in a mess. Two-thirds had to be thrown away as they were too small, and the few track suits he had were much too large. It seemed that he hadn't had any new clothes since he left us.

The only problem with having David back was that he and Manny thought they could stay awake half the night chatting. But then they didn't want to get up in the morning and go to school or college. David wasn't too bad as he could manage only one or two late nights before wanting early nights. Manny, on the other hand, had no such problem and was very stubborn when we asked him to leave David's room and let him sleep. He repeatedly kept asking to be moved to somewhere where he would be allowed to do whatever he wanted as he didn't like rules and didn't care about anyone else. He only wanted what he wanted. Luckily, he was going to his brother's at the weekends, which did give us a break from his stubborn attitude.

David asked to go to another town. We said that was okay, but later on we received a phone call from him to say that he was lost. He did manage to get back to our local town, so Robert had to pick him up.

Stefan, in the meantime, was behaving himself and getting into a regular routine of school, seeing his girlfriend, and attending youth club.

David was back to normal, and it wasn't long before his college rang to say that he had been caught drinking alcohol on the premises. He would be excluded until further notice.

We had a meeting the following week at the college. College administrators said they would take him back, but if there were any other incidents, he would be excluded permanently. With this threat hanging over our heads regarding David, we could never relax. Life with David was like a roller coaster, only we never knew when we would be on top.

At half term, Stefan went to work in a cafe in town where the people who worked there were very good at looking out for him and would let us know of any problems. So far, he was doing well there. Manny went to his brother's, and David stayed at home. On one of the days, his girlfriend came over, and on another day we met up with Emily and took her and David to the pictures and something to eat. Then we took Emily home. It was like old times as Emily came over on Friday and ended up staying the night. We dropped both David and Emily at the train station. David returned home on time on Saturday.

David was attending Child and Adolescent Mental Health Services (CAMHS) regularly, and I had to pick him up after each session.

Manny had an options evening, which was a waste of time as he said he wouldn't be going to school for much longer. But we had to go through the motions. He also said that one of the teachers had made a racist remark, so we told him to speak to the head of year. He was getting more and more aggressive in his arguments both at home and at school, still demanding to be able to do whatever he wanted. He felt that we should be there to taxi him wherever he wanted to go and whenever. School teachers were having real problems trying to keep him interested in lessons, but they said his behaviour was bordering on insolence, and he could be looking at an exclusion. His looked-after child (LAC) review was scheduled for the end of February. His social worker said she would put in a referral for him to be moved to a carer nearer to his brother, so all we had to do was wait. But he wasn't happy with having to wait, so he tried everything he could think of to break the placement—getting detention at school and getting banned from youth club. I asked him what he was trying to do, and he admitted that he was trying to break the placement. I explained to him that we could ask for him to be moved, but he wouldn't get a place nearer to his brother as there wasn't one; otherwise, he would have been moved there by now. We told him he could end up anywhere, even further away. So he said he was sorry and he would try to behave himself and wait.

Things did quieten down after that. Easter went well. Manny went to his brother's, Stefan divided his holiday between his job, his girlfriend, and home. We had one of Jane's foster boys, Nigel, for a few days as he was going off to cadet camp while Jane was on holidays. That was only until Good Friday. On Saturday, David came to Santa Pod Raceway dog racing with us, Marie, and family. Nigel returned from camp and quickly got ready to go for a course called Aim Higher.

David went to town on Easter Monday and brought a friend home with him. His friend said that he had been kicked out and had nowhere to go. We checked with EDT who said that hadn't happened. They said, if we kept him overnight, they would arrange to have him picked up in the morning as we were going to our Dean's for the day. The rest of the holiday went okay without any mishaps.

It was time for some work to be done with Stefan to help him get prepared for leaving care. Several couple leaving-care social worker came to see him after school one day and told him what to expect. One of the first things they said was that he must start looking after his room and his belongings because, if he kept his room in the same condition that it was now, he would be evicted. Also, no one would put up with getting him a new bed every year.

There was a lot of work to be done with him. He could do a bit of cooking himself, but that was as much as we had managed. His financial abilities left a lot to be desired. He knew he had lots to do, and he said he would try to work with us, and we couldn't ask for more.

David and Manny were going around together. We took them both out a few evenings to the pictures, bowling, and for meals. Often when they went out on their own, one of them would phone us to say they'd had an argument and he needed to be picked up.

David had his looked-after child (LAC) review at college. It was agreed that he could stay on there until the end of term, but somewhere else would have to be found for the new year. Additionally, he was not allowed to go off the grounds for any reason.

One evening Robert smelled smoke. He went upstairs into Manny's room. The window was wide open and Manny had his head out. David was lying on Manny's bed. A pack of cigarettes was lying between them. We gave them a talk on safety in the house and sent David to his own room. I had a job to get Manny up for school the next day. I eventually got him out of the house. When he came home, he said he had two detentions to go to and therefore wasn't going to school the next day. I soon put him right on that one. He went to youth club that night. When we went to pick him up, we caught him outside smoking with some of the others. He still denied that he was smoking, but he eventually backed down and admitted that he had been smoking in the house.

Manny came home from school one evening very quiet. At around 9.00 p.m., he wanted to talk about how unhappy he was. He felt that we shouldn't have our winding-down time at nine; we should let him stay up until he wanted to go to bed. And if he wanted to go out, then we should be prepared to take him wherever he wanted to go. He should be allowed to smoke in his bedroom (even though he was denying that he still smoked). Finally, we got him to go to bed.

The next evening Manny and David asked if they could go swimming. We said that would be okay, and we would pick them up at about 7.30. We could all go for something to eat. We finally got hold of them at about 9.55 and asked them to meet us at KFC. But we were there for a little while when they came sauntering across the car park. By the time we got them home, the car must have been blue with the language that had come from both of them. David finally came and apologized and went off to bed, but Manny stayed in the back garden for ages before finally coming in and going to bed. When we went up a little later, we could smell smoke coming from his bedroom. When we went in and checked the smoke alarm, we discovered that he had removed the batteries. The next morning he refused to get up to go to school. I got in touch with his social worker, who organized for a specialist company to come and pick him up and take him to an emergency foster placement in town. When I cleared his bedroom up, I found cigarette stubs under his bed in a paper bag and marks on the wall near the window where he had been putting his cigarettes out. Several weeks later he phoned me up and asked if I could go and see him as he wanted to ask me something. When I did, he asked if he could come back and live with us again. He hadn't realized how happy he had actually been with us. He promised that he would change, because where he was, he wasn't allowed to go out on his own or ever be taken anywhere. He was not given much pocket money. Obviously I wasn't going to take a chance on him. I couldn't risk the fact that he kept taking the batteries out of the smoke alarms, and we had to consider the safety of our grandchildren and any other foster children who slept at our house. After that, he did keep in touch with us, saying that he still thought of me as his surrogate mum as I was the first person to be a mother to him in this country.

Things quietened down for the next few weeks. Stefan was no problem; he was just going through life normally. David, however, was a different story. Several weeks after Manny moved, our support worker suggested a week's respite. Stefan, as usual, went quite happily to Jane's. David went to his mum's. They both went on Friday straight from school and college. On Saturday night, the police rang to say that David had been reported as missing. I gave them the phone numbers of his friends, thinking he might be staying with one of them. We were on constant phone calls with the police until 2.30 in the morning. I rang the police the next day, but he was still missing. I went on his Microsoft Network page, but none of his friends on there had seen or heard from him. Finally Robert and Marie went to his mum's to see if she was okay, but on their way they spotted David walking down the road looking as if he didn't have a care in the world.

He said he had been in town and had met a friend whom we didn't know. He had gone back to his friend's place, got drunk, and stayed the night. He'd awakened with a bad hangover, had been sick, didn't think about making phone calls, and was only just sober enough to make his way home at about four in the afternoon. We rang the police and told them he had been found. We went around to his mum's in the evening to see that they were all okay.

On Monday we took a spare mobile round to David's mum's for him. He rang us in the afternoon to ask if he could go to Jane's and get his youth club money that day instead of the next. We told him that would be okay. Jane rang to say he was there and asked if that was okay. I said it would be all right. His stepdad rang in the evening to ask us to cancel the taxi for the next evening as David had spent all his money, which I did. The next evening, his stepdad rang to say that David was creating a scene outside his house and refusing to go indoors. I told him to ring EDT. David rang me to complain about his stepdad. I told him to ring EDT and sort it out with them as I was supposed to be having respite.

My support worker rang the next day to say that David was put in a B&B. The following day, I rang his social worker to find out where he was as we were to pick him up on Friday. So much for our rest. We took him and Nigel's sister to an ice-skating show on Saturday. The following week we confiscated from him two roll-ups of weed and destroyed them. We took him and a friend dog racing one weekend, which they enjoyed as his friend had never been before. Everything went quiet until the middle of June when he had a new girlfriend, Sandy. We took him to her house and then dropped them both off in a local shopping centre. At about two in the afternoon, Sandy's mum rang to say that there had been an incident in the town and could we collect David as they had to stay in the police station with Sandy.

When we arrived home with David, we asked what had happened. He said he wasn't sure as Sandy hadn't been feeling well. He had left her with some of their mates while he went to get her something to eat and a drink. When he got back, there was a police car there, and Sandy was getting into it. That was as much as he knew.

There wasn't much we could do then as there was no reply from Sandy's house, so we just had to wait until we heard from them. Sandy's mum rang in the evening to say that she was still at the police station giving a statement as she had been raped. David was shocked and felt a bit guilty at leaving her, but it was something he couldn't have foreseen. We told him not to blame himself as he thought he had been doing the right thing by going to get her a drink a something to eat. As there was nothing we could do, we went to bed hoping to hear something in the morning.

But, as with all things that happened with David, we didn't have to wait all night. At four in the morning, I was awakened by a loud knocking at the front door. Out of our bedroom window I could see police lights flashing. I went down and answered the door. Outside were two large policemen. I asked them to come in. Another two came from around the corner. They asked for David, and I told them he was and was upstairs fast asleep. They told me they had come to arrest him. He had been accused of raping a girl, and they would like to go upstairs and get him. I told them they couldn't just barge in on him as they would frighten the life out of him because he was special needs. I would go first and wake him up to which they agreed.

Up I went and woke him and explained what had happened. He went as white as a sheet and looked terrified. The police said he would have to go with them to the station, but under the circumstances, I could go with him. We had to gather up all the clothes that he had been wearing during the day as they would go to forensics. So off we went in a large police vehicle. They did turn the flashing lights off. We were taken into the back of the station where we had to fill out a load of forms. Then David had to be bodily examined by the on-duty doctor. Then we were taken to the cells. The police were very gentle with him. They left the cell door open all night and kept offering me cups of tea or coffee. Later in the morning, Robert got permission to bring us a McDonald's breakfast. Then they gave us permission to switch places so that I could go home and freshen up.

I hadn't long been home when Robert rang to say not to bother going back as two detectives from a larger police station had arrived and were taking them to that police station because that was where the offence was committed, and they had all the information there. All I could do was wait. Eventually, in the early evening, Robert rang to say that I could go and pick them up as the police were letting David go. They explained that they had arrested two boys, and the girl said it was the other one who had raped her, not David. The police would get in touch with us if they needed any more information.

It was a few days before we received a telephone call from the police. The case was being dropped as the young lady was known to have made these allegations in the past and had admitted that the sex had been consensual between her and the other boy while David had gone to get her something to eat.

Things got back to normal again—school, college, mental health checks for David. This time they were trying him on Risperdal to see if that would be any help. But nothing seemed to make any difference, so we just carried on putting up with his outbursts and trying to ignore them as much as we could. Stefan was working over the summer and seeing his girlfriend. He even went on holidays with her family.

Nigel came to stay for a week while his carers went on holiday. A few days before they were due back, we got a call from social services saying that Nigel's carers were expecting another placement when they got home, but the placement he was in had broken down, and he needed to moved rather quickly as he had gone around the house and cut all the electric cables from the television, DVD player, and anything else he could find. So we made room for him. It turned out to be young Anthony, who had been with us when he was a baby. Jane was a bit surprised when we not only brought Nigel home to them, but an extra child as well.

We had a break from David's tantrums when he went to Mersea Island for a weekend with his youth club. The rest of the summer went on as normal with David popping between our house and his mum's, keeping appointments with Child and Adolescent Mental Health Services (CAMHS) or sessions with Adolescent Drug and Alcohol Service in Hertfordshire (A-DASH).

Finally, in September, it was time for them all to go back to college, and we had two weeks respite—a week away in Tenerife and a week back in the village to enjoy the peace and quiet in our own home.

On our first day back, we had a call from David's college. He had been excluded until further notice. When we attended a meeting regarding the decision, they said they would not be taking him back as he was too loud and abusive. He then spent his time going back and forth to town and coming home drunk and aggressive. Eventually, late in October, he rang to say that he was going to Scotland with a couple of friends who would look after him. I tried to talk him out of it, explaining how far away it was, but one of his mates said to me that they were taking him home with them to get him away from where everyone was taking advantage of him and either getting him drunk or giving him drugs. I told social services, but they said there wasn't much I could do. They would get in touch with social services up there when he told me where he was. Several days later, he rang with his address, which I passed on. Then I had a call from a Scottish social worker who told me that she had been in touch with David as his friends had brought him to the offices asking for help for him. They had found him somewhere to stay and had taken him to the charity shops and bought him some more clothes, as he had only what he was wearing. They would be happy to look after him up there. She spoke to his social worker here who said that neither she or I could give him permission to stay. Permission would have to come from his mum, but when she was contacted, she refused to give her permission, and he had to be sent back. He finally arrived back feeling tired and hungry. He was okay with us but very angry with his mum. She then said he could stay at hers for a few days, but when he got there on Sunday evening, she said that he couldn't stay there because he hadn't turned up in the morning, so we had to collect him.

He spent the next few weeks in the town, at his mum's, and with us. He made lots of abusive telephone calls asking for money. His social worker said they would be moving him to somewhere where he wouldn't have such easy access to town. Finally, on 14 November, he was moved to somewhere in Hemel. He rang a few days later to say that he was okay and was quite happy where he was, but he wanted to stay in touch. We said we expected that and had no problem with it. The house seemed really quiet and unnatural, but lovely. Stefan was no problem. He was getting to and from town by moped as he had been accepted onto the Scoots program, which was brilliant and got him used to being semi-independent.

On 19 November—I will always remember that date— two letters arrived from Saint James' Palace. I opened mine, but I had to read three times before it sank in. The writer asked if it would be agreeable to us to accept an MBE award (Member of the Order of the British Empire).

The letter also asked us not to say anything to anyone. Well, I had to hold myself back from making phone calls. It was the hardest thing I ever had to do, and when Robert came home at lunchtime, I handed him his letter and told him to open it. He told me he'd open it after lunch. I said, "No. Open it now." And when he did, he had the same reaction I'd had. We had to carry on as normal when inside we wanted to share the news.

We had another new placement arrive a few weeks before Christmas, which took our minds off our letters—only just a bit. Stephen went to his mum's for Christmas, so we had only Declan with us. Christmas went smoothly. We saw a lot of little Marie and Laura. We even managed to see Dean, Cal, and Chris.

The day before New Year's Eve, I got a phone call from our local radio station asking how we felt about our award. They would be announcing it the next morning. I told him we were over the moon. Then I thought that we had better tell Dean and Marie before they heard it on the radio. What a way to end the year!

Chapter 37

I lost count of the number of phone calls we had at the beginning of 2009. I felt as though I was still in a bubble. Our family members and friends were all ringing to congratulate us. I didn't even know that half of them read through the awards section.

Newspaper and radio reporters were ringing us to do interviews. A reporter from the *Sunday Telegraph* asked if they could come out in a few days to take photographs. They asked if we could we organize some of our foster children so they could be included. I was frantically ringing around to catch some of them, and we did end up with a bunch of them who could make it. The funniest call came from our local radio station. They rang early one morning to ask if they could do an interview. When I said that would be okay, they asked which house in the village was ours as they were already outside the pub. I directed them down to us. They arrived in a small van with a rather large antenna on top. Robert came home because one of his workmates had asked him what was going on in our house as there was a big van with a great big thing sticking out of. But when he walked in, he was told to be quiet as we were on air. We still laugh about it now. Then the letters started arriving from our local MP, the head of the department of education, the Countess of Veralum, and the chairman of Hertfordshire County Council.

Robert and I were told we could take three guests each to the awards ceremony, which worked out really well. We could take Dean, Cal, and Chris, and as Marie had just split up with her husband, we were able to take Marie and her two girls.

In the meantime, it was back to normal. Stefan was still giving us no problems; it was actually lovely having him around. Declan, on the other hand, was having a lot of problems at school, so there were a lot of educational meetings at school because of his behaviour and his refusal to do his work. He had a few exclusions in January, and each time I had to take him back in on his first day back. We had a break in the beginning of February as it snowed so much that they couldn't get them into school, so he and Stefan went off up the local hills or to the cricket field and built an igloo with the other children in the village.

After they'd been back at school for several days, an administrator from the school rang to say that they had a hygiene problem with Declan. Some of the other children were complaining. I explained that he had a bath every night, but I couldn't go into the bathroom with him to check that he was washing properly. I did understand as we had the same problem with him at home, and I was constantly nagging him.

Just when we thought it was going too well with Stefan, had a call from Scoots to say that they wanted Stefan out of the program because he was constantly lying to them.

He had come off his scooter and didn't tell them. Then he had continued to ride the scooter, creating more damage. We made arrangements for a meeting the following week. They were very good and said they would give him one last chance, but if he ever did anything again and didn't tell them, they would have no alternative but ask him to leave. His social worker came to see him and do some work on his getting-ready-to leave care. I had been getting him to do his own washing, but he was doing only half of it. The social worker took one look at his room and had a fit. She told him he had to get into a routine of cleaning and tidying his room before they could move him into independence. Then he settled back down again.

Declan still had a lot of problems at school. The school administrators said he would have to be excluded. My support worker wasn't happy as she felt that it wouldn't be good for him to be at home all day. And his social worker agreed, so day care was organized. I had to take him to a nearby village every day and then pick him up every evening. The school had sent some work for him to do. On top of the school problems, Declan also had to attend court, which resulted in his having to do community service. The first Sunday he was supposed to do three hours at the local police station, but when we got there, they didn't know anything about it. So on Monday, we got in touch with his social worker, and they organized for him to spend his time with the youth offending team who arranged for him to attend their sessions where he enjoyed himself making bird tables.

It wasn't too long before we received a phone call asking us to have another boy. This encouraged Declan to clean up his bedroom so we could actually get into the room.

Nick arrived on 4 March. He seemed a lovely lad and settled in quite nicely. We went through the house rules with him, and he appeared to accept them. The only thing he asked was if he could have a light on all night as that would make him happier. That was okay with us. Then he and Declan went off upstairs to unpack his belongings.

The next morning, Nick went off to school quite happily with his packed lunch, as that was what he was used to. It was parents' evening that day, but his dad attended that and brought him home afterwards. The next evening, Nick had an appointment with the orthodontist, and again, his dad took him. On Saturday, we all went to the pictures and had a fish-and-chip supper, which everyone enjoyed. On Sunday, both Nick and Declan went swimming together. It was lovely having two of them who got on well together. On Monday, Robert and I attended the fostering forum with the director of fostering placement team. This was a good idea because we could take any problems to the top and at least have a chance of having them sorted out.

On Saturday, all three boys went for a walk up the hills. Stefan rang me to say that two of them had an argument, and Nick had run off. But before we could get out to meet them, he rang again to say that they had met up and were now walking back through the manor grounds together. So when they got home, I gave them a lecture on how dangerous it was to separate like. I told them to try to stick together.

On Sunday, Stefan went to see his girlfriend, and Nick went with his dad to see his sister and his nan. That left

Declan on his own all day, so he just wandered around the village.

The two boys had to stay at Marie's house for the night on 16 March as we had to go to my brother-in-law's funeral the next day.

On 20 March, it was Nick's birthday, so he brought one of his friends home. We all went out for a meal and then took his friend home. On Saturday, we took him shopping to get his roller boots, and when we got home he and Declan and Stefan all got their boots on and went off around the village on them, and they played up when out of sight. Robert's boss took him to one side and told him that there had been complaints about three boys shouting abuse at cyclists coming through the village and also that the two of them were going around the manor grounds trampling all the daffodils. So needless to say, they were asked not to go near the manor grounds again.

As Nick's contact with his family had gone so well, it was decided that he could go home. He and Declan went for a walk up the hills before his dad came to collect him. We were sad to see him go as he was a really nice lad, and Declan would miss him. But it was nice to see things working out. When his dad brought him back to collect his belongings, they brought me the most beautiful bouquet of flowers and thanked us all for everything that we had done.

Now it was back to normality for Stefan and Declan. By the beginning of April, things were going really badly for Declan at school. On one Thursday morning, there was an important meeting with our support worker and David's social worker along with some other professionals.

It was agreed that he was a very damaged boy and needed more input than a foster placement could give him. A therapeutic assessment might be helpful.

In the afternoon, there was a meeting with school officials who said there was a strong possibility that Declan would be a permanently excluded because heof Declan consistently made unprovoked attacks on the other pupils. He also flung constant verbal abuse to the other children as well as staff members. They would let us know their decision after the Easter holidays. In the meantime, he would remain excluded. But as it happened, he had an appointment at Great Ormond Street Hospital and had to appear at the local magistrates court another day.

Declan came with us to see *Dancing on Ice* on Easter Saturday, and we stayed overnight at my sister's. We had a good weekend, but he made up for that on the following Wednesday.

We took him to the magistrate's court again. After the court proceedings, he had do his community service. We collected him at about one o'clock. He went straight out for a walk and didn't get back home until 8.00 p.m. He was a bit narked because we hadn't gone looking for him. I had taken the telly out of his bedroom because of the mess. He was upset about that and tried to tidy his room. He was still going up and down the stairs at 9.30. He then got annoyed because we asked him to stop going up and down and leave it till the next day. He put all his rubbish on the dining room table and went out into the garden. He got frustrated because we didn't go out to make him come in. He then went upstairs and laid on the floor half in and half out of his bedroom. He got fed up and went into his room, slamming the door because he was being ignored. He said he wanted to be moved somewhere else, so I said he could ring his social worker and ask. He then went off to bed in a bad mood.

Declan got up the next morning. The first thing he did was apologize for the night before. I explained that we don't keep prisoners at our house, but we do expect anyone living there to keep the few house rules that we do have. Any time he wanted to, he was welcome to ring his social worker to ask to be moved. But we would like him to stay because, apart from his recent behaviour, or in spite of it, we did like him. He stayed at home for the rest of the day.

Stefan hadn't come home the night before, but it wasn't the first time that he had spent the night at a friend's house without telling me. His girlfriend rang asking to speak to him, and I told her he wasn't here. Her mum then came on the line and explained that her daughter was worried as Stefan had rung her last night and arranged to meet her at the youth club in about ten minutes' time, but he never turned up. I tried ringing his phone, but it was turned off, so I rang the local hospital to see if there had been anyone admitted the previous evening due to an accident, but there hadn't been anyone either there or at the Queen Elizabeth II Jubilee Hospital. I rang social services and explained to them what was going on, and the social worker there told me to report him missing to the police, which I did.

Then at, at one o'clock, he rang to say that he was at a friend's house in one of the other villages and had been there all night. They had been so engrossed in computer games that he forgot to go to the youth club and to ring us. I explained that I'd had to report him missing to the police and they may have to go around and see that he was okay, but he arrived home about three and stayed home for the rest of the day.

Things got really bad for Declan at school towards the end of April. During a meeting with professionals, he was told that he would be leaving his present school and going for an interview at a school that was especially for children who had difficulties at a normal school. There would be smaller classes and more time for one-to-one teacher-pupil time. At first, he was upset, but when he went along to meet the headmistress and have a look around the school, he began to look forward to the move.

Declan also had an Attention-deficit/hyperactivity disorder (ADHD) assessment, which determined that he didn't have ADHD. They knew this because he always knew exactly what he was doing and did it on purpose. At this time, he was spending a lot of time over at our cricket club as the people there had taken an interest in him when they found out that he was being fostered. They gave him free lessons and a cricket bat plus some clothes. He spent most of his evenings and weekends going back and forth, and it was nice for him to have something to do.

In the meantime, we were still having our David come and go as we were taking him to music therapy and to the doctors for his growth hormone injections as he wouldn't go with anyone else. On top of that, I was looking for an outfit to wear to Buckingham Palace as we didn't yet know the date when we would be going. I was also going shopping with Marie and the girls to get their outfits.

Dean managed to get a new suit, and we got Chris a dress when we got little Marie and Laura's. Cal sorted herself out with Dean's help. It was such an exciting time.

We found out that, when Declan let us believe that he was going to the cricket field, he had actually been breaking into the old chapel where the playgroup stored their toys. He had also been asked not to go to the village hall tearooms and arts and crafts centre as things had been going missing. I had a word with his social worker and explained the problem we were now having. He was running out of places to go in the village, and he was beginning to get a bit angry at not being allowed his freedom. On a Thursday in May, he came home from school in a really bad mood because he had overheard someone saying that Declan would not be allowed to go on the school trip to the zoo. He had been looking forward to it, so I said I would ring the school in the morning. But that didn't calm him. He went through his usual routine of slamming doors, kicking chairs over, running outside and knocking things out of his way. Luckily his social worker was at our house and witnessed this behaviour. Declan shut the door in our faces when we tried to go out and talk to him. I managed to calm him down when I said that I would do him a packed lunch the next day anyway in case he got to go.

I rang the school first thing next morning. They said there had never been an issue; in fact, it was another Declan who wasn't being allowed to go. I thought our Declan would be in a better mood when he came home, but as soon as he walked in, he started shouting, slamming doors, and pushing things over. He took his shoes off and walked around the kitchen in his smelly socks. All of this he kept up until bedtime.

He got up early on the Saturday and accused Stefan of strangling him and threatening him with a cricket bat. He started shoving things off the worktop, and he slammed the doors on his way out to the cricket field. I rang EDT and warned them that we were possibly reaching a crisis point and we may need some help when he came home, but when he did arrive home, he was very quiet and said he had a headache, so I gave him some headache tablets and he went off to bed.

He was in a foul mood when he got up the next morning. He went to the cricket field and came home at about two in the afternoon asking for some money so he could go to the village hall. I had to explain to him that he wasn't allowed to go there. He got very angry and went up to his room saying he was going to tidy it up. Marie took the girls home in case he decided to kick off. As soon as they were gone, he started swearing and kicking things over. He punched Robert on the arm. When he calmed down, I asked why he had kicked my garden lights over, and he said it was because he was angry and he did things like that. I said it wasn't acceptable for him to damage other people's things just because he was angry. He swore very loudly and threw a bottle at me. Then he rushed out and threatened Robert on the way. As he kicked the dustbins over, I rang EDT. They would send someone from a residential home in Enfield to pick him up, as it was unacceptable for us to cope with that sort of behaviour. I didn't tell Declan in case the news might cause him to do any more damage than he'd already done—or cause him to try to run off down the lane or into the woods. EDT personnel arrived at about 10.00 p.m. We got his belongings packed, and he went off quite happy with them. It's always sad when a placement ends in this way because the carers try to think of anything they could have done differently.

We now knew the date for our appearance at Buckingham Palace. Up to this time, we had still been going to fostering forum meetings and recruitment venues. We'd been keeping up with David's music therapy and organizing how we were going to get to the Palace. We had several offers from within the village, but we had to get eight of us there, so we thought we may as well treat ourselves and hire a limo. My sister suggest we arrange for it to collect us from her house in Wembley, and we could all stay the night before, which is what we did. All we had to do now was wait until the second of June and hope the weather would be good.

What can I say? We went to Wembley the night before the ceremony as we had arranged with my sister. We got up early and we were actually all ready and waiting when the limo arrived. Everyone had a camera! My sister from Ireland and her husband had come over as well, which was lovely. While we were having photos taken, Robert spoke to the driver. He had actually come down from Luton as that was where the company was based, so we could have been picked up from home, but it was lovely to be with two of my sisters. Soon we were all ready to get into the limo and start our journey. With a final wave to everyone, we drove off. We all loved being together in the big car. The children thought it was fantastic. We soon arrived at our destination. As we pulled up outside the gates of Buckingham Palace, it seemed that we might be the first to arrive. The police guards told us where to park until the gates were open. We sat patiently just enjoying being there, but it was amazing how many people knocked on the windows to talk to us and ask if they could have a look inside the car. We let them all have a look, and they all wished us well.

It wasn't long before the gates were opened. Yes, we were the first through. After our driver drove inside and stopped the car under the pillars at the entrance, we all got out onto the red carpet. As we all walked in, a woman standing at the top of the stairs asked us for the name of the recipient. We said there were two of us, and she said our names. I thought, *We are famous at last!* We were escorted up the stairs, and then Robert and I were directed to go one way while Dean, Marie, Cal, and the kids were ushered in another direction. Robert and I were taken to a large gallery where all the MBE recipients were to gather. It was really interesting to talk to some of the other people and find out what they were receiving their awards for. We all mingled there until an official called us over to explain what would happen and how we were to respond. After another little while, we were called to form a line in the presentation hall. As we were led through, someone clipped a hook onto our clothing. This is where Her Majesty would hang our medals. As we were joining the queue, one of the officials called Robert and I to one side and explained that, as there were two of us, we would be going up together, so our ceremony would be slightly different. We had to practice walking straight side by side.

Then we were to turn together and face the queen, who would then place our medals on our hooks. Thinking that we'd got it right, we joined the queue to await our turn. While we were waiting, we were able to see the friends and relatives of all the recipients sitting watching. We managed to see our family members, who were giving very low-key waves to us. When our turn came, we managed to keep together and make a perfect turn. We then were supposed to either bow or curtsey, depending on our gender. Well, I managed to curtsy, and so did Robert, but I don't think anyone noticed. Her Majesty placed our medals on us and then asked us what we were receiving the award for. She asked how long we had been fostering and how many children we'd had over the years. She then put her hand out, and that was the sign that it was time for us to move on, which we did. Again, we had to turn together, keeping a straight line, and walked off to the side where we were greeted by yet more officials. These people removed our medals and the hooks. They then placed our medals in beautiful padded boxes. Finally, we were allowed to go outside where we had to wait for our families. When they met us, we all trooped out to wait our turn to have the official photographs taken. It was a boiling hot day, and we were roasting as the square we were in was a closed area—a sun trap. But better that than rain.

We were then escorted to our limo where the driver was waiting patiently. He said what an honour it was for him to actually be allowed inside the Palace. We had all had a wonderful time, but now it was over, and everyone was hungry. We were trying to decide where to get something to eat. The children wanted a McDonald's, so that was where we went. The driver pulled up in front of the restaurant and said he would wait outside. We asked him if he would like anything, but he said that he had brought something to eat with him. We then paraded into McDonald's in all our finery, fascinators and all. When we had eaten, the driver took us back to my sister's, although on the way back, he made a detour, and we picked up a very special lady who meant a lot to us. Robert had known both her and her husband since he was seventeen, and they were like parents to him after he had left home. We took her with us to my sister's where an awful lot of our family members were waiting to help us celebrate. It was a wonderful evening. Our medals were passed around to everyone. Eventually they all went home, and we stayed another night. We returned home the following day along with a bottle of champagne that the limo company had given us.

The following few weeks were eventful. We hosted an open house on Saturday to which all the village came to congratulate us along. Some of our family members who hadn't been able to get to Tuesdays celebrations also came along with most of our friends. At some point, someone said there were well over a hundred people there at one time. It was lovely to celebrate our special day with all our friends and family members.

Not much later, we received an invitation to attend a soiree that was being organized in the name of the Lord Lieutenant of Hertfordshire, the Countess of Verulam. This would give us a chance to meet and talk with other honours recipients. It was a new idea to recognize the people of Hertfordshire who received these honours and bring them together every year. It was a lovely evening, and we met some very interesting people.

Life carried on as normal. We had an introduction to our next placement. He came along to our gathering on the Saturday to meet some of the family members and neighbours that he would be mixing with. It went well, and arrangements were made for 12 year old John to move in on Monday. He arrived with his social worker on Monday afternoon, settled himself in, and we took him to Cadets in the evening. The first week went fine; he got on well with Stefan. We had his seventy-two-hour meeting on Wednesday. He met Marie and the girls properly on Thursday. We met him after school on Friday and took him shopping to get him school shoes and a school bag along with anything else that he needed. He came to my niece's on Sunday and joined in with everyone. Everything seemed to be going smoothly both for John and Stefan. One Saturday, John's grandparents took him to Harlow for the weekend. He came home quite happy.

Arrangements for Stefan to move into independence were progressing. But he received a call from Orange and looked worried so we asked him what the problem was. He said he owed them £600. I rang his social worker who came over to see him and had a talk about the money he owed. She also explained that there would be a room available for him to move into at the beginning of July.

We had Chris and little Marie's birthday to celebrate as there were only two days between them. Also we attended the funeral of one of my cousins. When we got home, Stefan's room was empty. We hadn't expected that! It would have been nice to have been there to see him off, especially as he had been with us for so long, but we knew we would be seeing him again. We were now down to just John, but I was still going for blood tests every month. Also that July, a lot of family members were coming and going, so we were kept busy. We did have a placement for three days to give some other carers a break. The boy who came to us was a lovely quiet boy, and we would easily have kept him for longer if needed.

Towards the end of July, we had another placement arrive. We had to be careful where we let 14 year old Violet go as her father had said that he would be looking for her, and if he found her, he would kidnap her and take her back to his country. It was very difficult to watch her as she was very strong minded and felt that she could go where she liked and see whomever she wanted without our permission. We had her social worker explain to her that she had to be very careful and do as we asked, but she still kept arranging things with her friends and expecting us to drop everything and run her into town. She kept trying to stay weekends with friends but wouldn't let us meet them. I explained to her that I couldn't let her stay anywhere overnight unless I had met the people. For the first overnight, we usually liked the kids' friends to stay at our house. If her friends stayed with us, then we could work on letting her stay over at their house, once we had met both parents. But that wasn't good enough. Not that it mattered as she couldn't get to town without us driving her there anyway

She was very spiteful to both Marie and Laura. When we took them all out for the day, she would run off and hide, and the day would end up in an argument either between her and the girls or her and John. In fact, one night she came home and started shouting and wailing. Then she went to her room and started throwing her things on the floor in a temper. We told her that we could only allow her to go into town to see her friend during the daytime only, not over night. And there were certain areas we had been told we should keep her away from. We explained this to her, and when we went to collect her, she was exactly where we asked her not to go, so she had to be grounded for a few days. Things were getting very tetchy between her, John, and little Marie. Violet was saying spiteful things to Marie, and John was saying spiteful things both to her and about her to other people. John was gradually making friends with some of the other young people in the village, which was nice, especially over the long holidays, but that didn't stop him from coming out with us to parks, swimming, and the pictures.

John went to camp with the Cadets for a fortnight towards the end of August. Violet's guardian ad litem came to see her, and the news, as far as Violet was concerned, was not good: she would not be allowed to go home for quite a while, and a court case would follow. While John was away, we did let her go swimming with her friends with the understanding that she would not go anywhere else. While she was out, I took the opportunity to tidy both bedrooms. John's wasn't too bad, but in Violet's I found three Pepsi bottles full of urine, one on the chest of drawers and two inside the wardrobe. (I thought, *Here we go again. We have been here before.* When I asked her why she had them, she couldn't give me a good reason, but she told her social worker it was because she didn't want to disturb me when I was in the bathroom. While John was away, we took her to town to have hair extensions, which seemed to please her, but within a few days, they were gradually pulled out.

As soon as they were back at school there was a permanency meeting for John. The plan was that any family members interested would be assessed, and he could move to them. If that was not possible, he would be in long-term fostering, which he accepted.

There was an incident on the school bus with Violet. She was not liked, but it was important that she got on the bus as soon as she came out of school. She was not to linger in case her father was around watching for her. For that reason, it was important that she try to get on with people.

One Saturday, we let her go shopping in town with several of her friends. We received a phone call from one of the mums to say that they had been arrested for shoplifting. It turned out that Violet had not done any stealing, but she had asked one of the others to get her something, so both mums asked that we keep her away from their families, and we agreed.

On 14 September, we were to have an evening out to attend the Countess of Veralum's reception. While the summer was passing, we'd had a letter from our local paper to say that our names had been put forward as nominees for two awards—Parents in a Million and Service to the Community Award. This was a wonderful surprise for us as we were not expecting anything like that. We couldn't even think who could have put our names forward. The awards evening would be on 23 October.

In the meantime, we had our holiday coming up, so we had to do introductions for Violet to the respite carers. John was settled as he would be going back to the people who had had him before he came to us, and he was happy about that.

We took Violet along to meet the carers and explained the situation to them about Violet not being allowed in certain parts of town. Her social worker said there were to be no overnight stays with friends unless police checks were done. They assured us that they would cope just fine and wished us a good holiday.

We went to Lagos in Portugal and loved it. We had a wonderful restful holiday. Again, we had only a week away and then looked forward to having our week at home on our own. We had been back for only a few days when I made the usual calls to where the children were staying to let them know we hadn't forgotten them. We spoke to John, which pleased him, but when I phoned Violet's placement, she wasn't there. The carer asked me when we were due back. I explained that we were back but wouldn't collect Violet until the two weeks were up. She then asked if we could take her back straight away as they couldn't cope with her. She thought that Violet may have stolen a ring belonging to her, and also they'd had a job keeping her from going to town. At the moment, she was staying overnight with some friends in town, but they didn't know exactly where that was. I remarked that social services had been able to get the police to do a check in remarkably short time. But the social worker said that a check hadn't been done. The social worker had said that, because they were having such a hard time with her, she could stay overnight with friends. I said I would sort it out when our respite finished. (This was exactly what I needed to hear!)

The first announcement Violet greeted me with was, "I can stay anywhere I want to now, without any permission. And I will be staying at my friend's most weekends." Needless to say, the first call I made on Monday morning was to her social worker. When I asked why she had allowed Violet's carers to let her go to a family that had not been investigated, she said that the carers had had so many difficulties with her that she allowed it. But she further stated that I should go back to the way it should be done because I had been coping better with Violet. I told her that, as far as I was concerned, she had just broken the placement because with her decision she had taken away any authority I had. I told her that Violet now thought she could do what she liked with whom she liked. I then phoned my support worker and explained what had happened. She agreed with me and asked for Violet to be moved. She said they would start looking for somewhere else.

The next few weeks were very rocky. There were lots of arguments and temper tantrums as Violet demanded to get her own way. She believed that she had special permission from her social worker.

John had made arrangements for a friend to come and stay at the weekend. After we picked him up, we let them go around town. Violet refused to stay with us and ran off. We kept looking for her but didn't see her anywhere, so we came home and reported her missing to the police. We told them we would stay home by the phone. We then realized that we had our mobile phones for communication both ways, and we could go and have another look. When we parked behind Marks & Spencer, we noticed a police car parked outside. Robert stayed in the car while I went in to look for her. I found her sitting with a shop assistant and a security officer while a police officer was talking to the police station saying that there was no sign of her carer, and we had gone and left her. I tapped him on the shoulder to let him know that I was there. He came off his phone and asked me what had happened. I explained the situation to him regarding the last few weeks. He said that she should now go home with us. She stormed off out of the shop and got into the car. She spent the whole journey home giving John and his friend dirty looks. We had to stop at a supermarket on the way home, and when I came out, Robert said that she had assaulted John for no reason. When we arrived home, she avoided both boys until bedtime when she started winding them up until we had to go and separate them all.

The following day, Violet kept a low profile for a while, but then she started sitting in front of the telly while the boys were trying to watch something. On Monday, everything was fine until lunchtime when she tried to wind John's friend up by sitting on his chair, but when she got no reaction, she started swearing at him. She followed him out to the kitchen and gave him two really hard pushes. We managed to contain the situation by explaining to her that she could be accused of accosting him, and she should calm down.

I couldn't get in touch with her social worker, but I did manage to speak to her social worker's manager. I explained what had happened, and she said she would have a word, but as far as she was concerned, the placement wasn't working if Violet believed she could do as she pleased and didn't have to do as we asked her since her social worker have overridden the sleepover rules.

Things were very tense, and Violet kept insulting John and anyone else who came near her. She was still insisting that she could do as she pleased and she no longer had to ask for permission because that's what her social worker had said.

I managed to get hold of her social worker and said that she had to find her somewhere by Friday as I wasn't prepared to put up with her behaviour. And since the problem was down to her social worker, then it was up to her to get things sorted before Violet came to blows with John or our grandchildren. Violet packed her belongings on Friday morning, and her social worker picked her up about seven that evening.

While all this was going on, we received our invite to the Comet Awards evening. It was a well-organized evening, and it was nice to meet some of the other people who had been nominated. In fact, one of them had been David's teacher, so we were able to let her know how David was getting on. Marie and the girls were allowed to come with us. It was quite humbling to hear some of the stories of other people who had been nominated for all the different categories. We won the certificate and trophy for Parents in a Million and won runner up for Services to the Community. It meant a lot to us to know that someone had taken the time to nominate us, and we were very grateful for all the people who voted for us.

Into November, and it was just us and John, but not for long. We were asked to take a placement of two boys while their carers had their respite. They arrived on Friday, 6 November, and settled in quickly. In fact, they settled too quickly because, within a day, they were play wrestling with John in the bedrooms. I lost count of the times I had to go upstairs to stop them from damaging the furniture. I wouldn't mind, but we have a big garden and the weather was dry so they could have gone outside. However they were only here for the weekend, so it soon ended.

John was back to being alone again. He was having a few troubles at school, but nothing too bad that couldn't be worked at.

Halfway through November we had a placement of Lennie, a twelve-year-old boy. John showed him around and took him to his room. I went to see if he wanted anything to eat and found him sobbing. He said he wanted to go home or to be placed with one of his brothers, which I completely understood, but I explained that there weren't enough placements near his parents, and all the siblings had to go to individual carers. He cried until nearly 10.00 p.m. when I managed to get him upstairs. Then he was back down again sobbing. Eventually I got him back upstairs, and he said he was worried because he didn't have his medicine. I said we would get that sorted the next day. I put on a DVD for him, and he eventually cried himself to sleep. It's always hard for the first few nights when siblings have to be separated.

Lennie got up the next morning quite happy to go to school, but he was very adamant that he wouldn't be coming back at the end of the day. He wanted to say goodbye to us, but I told him to wait and see. When they were both gone off to school, I rang Lennie's social worker and explained how he was doing. He told me that he wasn't concerned about his medication, and the police were going to be interviewing him again that afternoon. He would be sent home in a different taxi. He came home with John in John's taxi and greeted me with a high-five and a cuddle. He was fine for the rest of the evening until bedtime when he started worrying about his medication again. But I managed to settle him again with a DVD, and he went off to sleep without any problem.

John had a bad day at school. One of his teachers rang me to say that he had been very disruptive in his science lesson and had to be removed. But he was no better when he was allowed back into the lesson. He would be put in isolation the next day and would also do two hours of detention either that Friday or the next. I had a word with him when he came home, not that it did any good. I received another phone call the next day. He had been in a fight with a year seven boy. His excuse when he came home was that the boy had said horrible things about his mum. I told him that sometimes it is best to just walk away. As difficult as it would be, it was the only way to deal with things like that.

Lennie went off to school, again saying he wouldn't be back to us after school as he would be going home. I tried getting hold of his social worker without any luck, and then tried to get hold of someone who could give me his doctor's details so that I could sort out his medication as that seemed to be his biggest worry. But no one got back to me, so that was another day gone without his medication. He was better but still anxious at bedtime.

On Friday, I managed to get hold of his doctor's details and arranged to pick up his prescription in the evening. We met up with one of his brothers at the surgery, which was lovely for Lennie. We made arrangements with his carer to meet up in town the next day, which pleased them. We stopped in the Four Leaf Clover on the way home for something to eat. He was a lot calmer going off to bed that night.

On Saturday, we dropped John off at his friend's house for the weekend and took Lennie shopping for shoes, trousers, shirts, underwear, socks, and lots of other things that he might need. We also had to buy him incontinent pants as one of his problems was soiling himself, which wasn't very pleasant for either us or the school workers. We met his brother, and they were able to spend a bit of time together. His carer and I swapped phone numbers so they could call each other. We had to go out that night, and he was still up when we got home as he said he couldn't settle when I wasn't there. But he went off to bed just fine after that.

He had a lie-in, and because he got up late, he refused to take his Concerta, which is a medication to control attention-deficit/hyperactivity disorder (ADHD), so he was on a high all day. He monopolized the phone all morning except when Robert took him for a walk around the manor to see the ponies. He was back on the phone again talking to his mum, so that gave me a chance to have a word with her to find out more about his medical needs as his social worker wasn't telling us much. He then wanted to keep ringing either his mother or his brother, and I explained that he couldn't keep using the phone all the time as we usually had a lot of phone calls ourselves. He then threw a temper tantrum and refused to eat his dinner. So I told him it was up to him if he ate it or not. The food was there, and he could help himself. After about fifteen minutes, he sat down and ate. He was a lot calmer afterwards, and we played board games with him until John came home. Then they watched television together until bedtime.

The week started off okay. There were no incidents with John at school. On Monday, Lennie was up and ready for school and went off again saying that he wouldn't be back that night. I was having a slight problem getting him to take his tablets as they were slightly different than the ones he was used to. But he came home again with no incidents.

Tuesday was slightly different. He actually packed his clothes, saying he wouldn't be back that night. But I managed to talk him around with the promise of tea and biscuits the next morning. That solved that problem. John's head teacher rang to say that they weren't very pleased with him at the moment and had made the decision to have him go to a special education center for the rest of the week as he had been involved in a very serious incident. He had assaulted another year seven boy, and it could not be ignored.

Wednesday was the same thing from Lennie although this time he actually took his packed clothes to school. When he returned in the evening, he was happier as his head teacher had told him that he would get him a place near his parents. I had to explain gently that his teacher shouldn't have promised him that because he would have no control over where any foster child was placed. That was up to social services, and they had already told him that he was on referral. As soon as a vacancy became available, he would be able to move there, but in the meantime, we were very happy to have him. He was still adamant that his teacher was going to get him somewhere near home, so there wasn't much else I could say to make a difference. We would just have to wait to see what the next day would bring.

At about 4.30 on Wednesday evening, two social workers arrived with a teenage girl who was having problems at home and needed a placement. She was a bit nervous, which was only natural, but she went with me to my doctor's appointment and was more relaxed by the time we got back home. They all settled down nicely for the night.

Where do I start to recount the following day, Thursday? Emily, who had arrived the previous day, went with her social workers to see her mum. The social workers came back without her saying that Emily didn't want to be in a foster placement. She had expected social services to provide her with a flat of her own. They explained to her that, if she wanted help and support, she would have to stay in foster care, but she and her mum decided that she could live with an uncle, so it was agreed that would happen.

Lennie went off to school okay. He was fine when he came home as his social worker was coming to see him. Lennie spent about an hour with him and kept asking to go back home. His social worker kept explaining that couldn't happen, but he would arrange for Lennie to be moved as soon as there was a vacancy. When it was time for his social worker to leave, Lennie followed him out to his car and kept trying to get into the passenger seat, but we had to keep pulling him back. It took a good ten minutes for the social worker and I to get him back in the house. The social worker shut the door on him, jumped into his car, and drove off. Just before he left, he told me to ring EDT if I had any more problems as he was going home (great, thanks).

It took three of us—Robert, John, and I—to keep Lennie from escaping. In the end, we had to lock the front door and the back door so that we could man the downstairs windows. He kept throwing himself against the furniture, and then he accused Robert of child abuse when he tried to stop the boy from hurting himself. John tried to help Robert keep him under control while I rang EDT to explain the situation. They said they could hear most of it over the phone. They also said that his social worker should not have gone and left him in those circumstances; however, they would send two workers from emergency care to help.

Lennie finally calmed down when they arrived. They took him outside and explained to him that there were no vacant beds near his home. He would have to stay the night with us. He said he would if they stayed too. None of us had a problem with that. They got him settled and up to bed. Then we got the emergency workers comfortable in our living room. We showed them where the tea and coffee were, and the bread in case they wanted something to eat. Then we went off to bed to have a peaceful sleep.

The next morning, the emergency workers got Lennie to take his Concerta tablet and got him into his taxi for school. When everyone was gone, I phoned our support worker and told her what had happened. She was not very pleased with the social worker. Arrangements were made to remove Lennie that day, but it would not be near home; unfortunately, he had to be moved to somewhere further from the area.

John was on his own again, but that lasted for only for a few days. We had another placement arrive the following week. John showed Jonathon his room, and the two of them got on well. Although Jonathon was sixteen, he was very easy going and got on with everyone.

It wasn't long before John started wrestling with Jonathon every time they went upstairs. Jonathon did keep complaining about it, but it was a job to get John to stop. He even tried to wrestle while they were on the computers in the dining room. It got so bad that I had to warn the pair of them that, if it didn't stop, their placements would be at risk. John just shrugged, but Jonathon said he was sorry, and he didn't want to go anywhere else. Unfortunately, he had to spend a lot of time in his room avoiding John. Apart from that, everything seemed to be going well.

At Christmas, Jonathon went to his dad's for several days, but he did ring to wish us a happy Christmas and to thank us for his presents. John tried to ring his grandmother, but couldn't reach her on either Christmas day or Boxing Day.

On 28 December, we all went for a meal to celebrate David's birthday. Everyone enjoyed it and behaved themselves. David stayed overnight again, and everyone got on well together,

On New Year's Eve, Jonathon stayed in his room avoiding John as he was still trying to wind him up, but he did come downstairs to see the New Year in with us.

That was another year gone, and we were still alive.

Chapter 38

I think we spent most of New Year's Day in 2010 thinking back over everything that had happened the previous year and how much had happened to us. But we were now into a new year and would see what that brought.

Jonathon was settled in nicely. He enjoyed going to school. Even when they dropped him back a year, he said that was okay as he said he had missed a lot of schooling the year before and needed to go over most of the work again. The school was very pleased with him, and he caused no problems either at school or at our house. In fact, he was lovely to have around, especially when he wasn't in his room avoiding John.

John was still having problems at school and wasn't that pleasant to have around the house. Both boys were stuck at home for about three days when it snowed and the taxis couldn't get through to us, so they made their own amusement outside in the snow.

Things went on as normal. John had to spend a bit more time on his own as Jonathon was still avoiding him, but he had no one to blame but himself. In fact, I was a bit worried that Jonathon had to spend so much time in his room just to avoid John. But he said he wasn't too worried as it gave him a chance to revise as they were going through his options for college courses, and he needed to get good results.

Towards the end of January, John wanted to go out with a group of his friends, so we took him into town. I went into the bowling alley and paid for their game, and then I gave them money to go to the pictures afterwards. I told them that Robert would pick him up when the film ended. It all sounded so easy, but when Robert got to the cinema, he was asked to wait until the police arrived as they wanted to interview John. He had been assaulted on his way out of the auditorium because they had all making so much noise during the film and John had been running up and down the aisle, which had annoyed a lot of people and ruined the film for everyone. In the end, nothing could be done as everyone else had disappeared, so Robert just brought him home. I must admit that John didn't get a lot of sympathy.

We took him to the pub for his birthday meal. Marie, the two girls, and David came over to help him celebrate. On Burns Night we all went to our village hall for a traditional Burns supper organized by some of the villagers—a traditional night to honour the poet Robert Burns. We had a really fun evening. Jonathon was as good as gold and really enjoyed himself apart from ignoring John, who kept on annoying him all evening and everyone else as well. It's a good job that we have such understanding friends and relatives.

Things just went from bad to worse with John's behaviour. One evening he didn't come home from school. A worker from the taxi company rang to say that he hadn't been there, so we had to ring EDT and the police. Just as the police arrived at our house, the worker from the taxi company rang to say they had just had a phone call from the mum of one of John's school friends. John was at her house, and she was a bit worried about how to get him home. I wanted the taxi company to send someone to get him, but the police officer said that they would go. John had told everyone a pack of lies. The police officer gave him a lecture about wasting police time. He basically told John it was about time he grew up. When they got him home, he went straight to his room and stayed there except for journeys to and from the bathroom, banging doors each time.

Our support worker said that she wasn't too pleased with his behaviour, and she would organize some respite for us. She arranged for him to go to a carer for a weekend, with the possibility that she could have him there full time as she had no one else, and it might work better for him as he did seem to cope better at our house when he was on his own. From her house also, he could walk to town or get a bus to visit his friends.

On Monday, I got a phone call from his social worker who said that he would be coming home that night as the new carer needed time to think about having him full time. When he was back with us, he was okay, but he was still trying to annoy everyone. After a few days, it was agreed that he could go and live with the other carer. He was okay about it as he could see the sense in living in a town. So we had a goodbye meal for him the night before his move, and we all ended as friends.

Jonathon was a lot happier now he could come out of his bedroom and enjoy the rest of the house. He was pleased on several occasions when David and Logan came to visit. Everything went smoothly apart from one incident at school. He was accused of sexually harassing one of the supply teachers. He was really worried. When I asked what had happened, he said that he had only very lightly placed his arm across her shoulder, and it was one of the other boys who had said abusive things to her. So I told him to go into school the next day, apologize, and explain what had happened. He had to make a statement, and eventually he was suspended for three days as punishment.

Jonathon was required to do work experience, and one of our friends in the village, Julian, had a landscape gardening company. He offered to have Jonathon work with him for the week. It went well except that they had a job to part Jonathon from his mobile phone; otherwise, they were pleased with him. One day I had to take him a second packed lunch as Julian's dog had eaten his when he wasn't looking. He came home shattered every evening, but he enjoyed himself.

In the first week of March, a most gorgeous three-year-old girl, Jennie, and her ten year old brother, Martin, arrived. Everyone fell in love with Jennie. Social services hadn't been sure if I would have her or not because of my illness, but thought I should be asked as they didn't have carers who could take both of them, and it's best not to separate siblings. I told them that they weren't taking her anywhere, and we would love to have them both.

Martin was very protective of his little sister, which I could understand as there was a big age difference. He didn't mind me changing her nappy, but at bedtime on the first night, he went to check on her after I had tucked her in and got her to sleep. He decided that he would wake her up to see if she was okay. He then had to stay with her and read to her until she went back to sleep. He was very anxious over the looking after of his sister. He told us he was used to doing everything for her, and anyway, he hadn't asked to come to our house. He wanted to go back to his mum. He refused his dinner. I had a chat with him, and we agreed that I would look after her during the day while he was in school, and when he came home, he could supervise her bedtime preparations and read to her until she fell asleep. He readily agreed to that, so things went a bit smoother after that.

He enjoyed his time with Jonathon. They went to the cricket field with their skateboards and a football, as Martin was football mad.

It was decided that Martin would go to the village school as he would be starting secondary school in September. We felt he may as well be registered in the village as they couldn't take him back to his old school because we were classed as a place of safety for him and his sister. There were several boys in the village with whom he became friendly, and he enjoyed going out and about with them.

After the first few weeks, Martin told me that, as he was out with his friends, he didn't mind if I put Jennie to bed as that gave him more time being outside playing. Jonathon got on well with him and often they would be playing football together. Martin was a really good player, and the school coaches wanted him on their team, which pleased him. The team would often go out to other schools to play.

Jonathon was also eager to play football, so we took him to a practise with a local youth team, but unfortunately, he was too old for the youth team, so that ended that. The coach gave Robert some telephone numbers of local teams for which Jonathon would be the right age, but it all came to nothing as he lost interest when he couldn't join the local team.

The following week started off with all of us quite busy. Jonathon had been excluded from school, so he went to work for Julian. Martin's personal education plan (PEP) was scheduled for lunchtime. It went well. Everyone was pleased with him and how quickly he had settled and made friends. They were also very impressed with his talent for playing football. Jen was looked after by a friend when I went to National Vocational Qualification (NVQ) training. Then it was dental appointments for all of them. Jen had to wear a brace on her foot every night, which she didn't like, but she accepted that she had to wear it. When she arrived, she was wearing a pair of shoes that fitted her good foot, but the other one kept slipping off, so I took her into town and bought two pairs of shoes in different sizes. She was delighted that she could wear a shoe that didn't keep falling off. We carried on doing for the time she was with us. We took her to Clarks' on one occasion to get her something really good, and when I asked for the two sizes, I was informed that, in such circumstances, they sold the second pair for half price, which was wonderful, so we kept going back there.

Every Wednesday and Thursday, both Martin and Jen got to see their mum. Because it was such a regular schedule, they settled down nicely to it. I would take them on most occasions, but if for any reason I couldn't, then a volunteer driver took them. She also fell in love with Jen.

Jonathon had friends stay over a few times, which was nice. There was never any trouble. They just hung about together each time and interacted with the rest of the family. Martin was okay with that as he had made friends in the village and was able to see them every evening and at weekends. Jonathon was having extra one-to-one lessons in maths on Saturday mornings.

We all had days out over the Easter with Marie and girls. Then, after the Easter holidays, Jen started playgroup three mornings a week. Just after Easter, Martin and Jen's social worker came to see them and make sure that they were both happy. She was pleased with the way they had settled down and were enjoying their time with us.

Martin and Jen had optician appointments. Martin's eyes were fine, but Jen needed new glasses as hers were now too small for her. Indeed, they must have been hurting her. They both had health assessments at the QEII Hospital. Both were deemed healthy. Martin wanted to use Microsoft Network, but he was told he couldn't. When I explained that he had to be careful whom he spoke to as he and his sister were now in a place of safety and no one must know where they were, he started telling me about what he had witnessed. But I had to stop him as he hadn't been interviewed, and he had to wait until that was done formally before he could talk about it.

Jen came with me to my hospital appointment. The gastric nurse was a bit worried as my health seemed to have gone downhill slightly, but she could see why as Jen was there with me. She said that she wouldn't ask me to have Jen moved, but I was to promise that, after the placement ended, I was to have a good break and make sure that I rested. I agreed, and in the meantime, they would keep a close eye on my blood levels.

David was now living in a hostel, so we visited him occasionally and took him out for a meal or brought him back to or house.

Jonathon started having overnight stays with his dad, which seemed to be going well. He even started talking about moving back home, but his social workers and school officials told him to think long and hard because, if he went home now at his age, then he would be more or less on his own. But if he stayed with us, then he could stay most weekends at his dad's, but while he was with us, he could carry on at college. His teachers said he was capable of going to university, so he had a lot to think about.

Jen and Martin's contact was going well, and there were hopes that, after the court case, they should be able to return to their mum sometime in September. That gave us a chance to start planning a break. We had already booked a short holiday to go to Ireland in June. Marie and the girls started coming over a lot more as they were going to move into our house while we were away as we didn't think it was fair to move everyone somewhere else for the week. Jonathon went to his dad's for the week. Everything went well. Martin and Jen were absolutely great for Marie, and they loved having the two girls here.

Jonathon came back from his dad's saying that his dad and stepmum wanted him to move back home. We had a few meetings to organize his going home, which was arranged for 1 July. His social worker tried to talk him out of it, but he said his stepmum told him there were plenty of jobs locally, so he could help with the running cost of the house. He was now at college, and they were very disappointed as they said he could have ended up at university, but he was now quite adamant, especially as his parents let him stay out very late at weekends. Although his move had been arranged for the first of the month, his dad rang and asked if they could postpone it until the tenth, which was fine. So, after a goodbye meal, Jonathon moved back to his dad and stepmum's on 10 July. We were very sad to see him go as he had been a lovely placement but also a very intelligent young man. He could easily have done well by continuing his education, but it wasn't our decision. We wished him well and hoped that things worked out for him.

Martin had really settled in. He was doing well at school, especially at sports. He wasn't so good with homework, but it was nothing that we couldn't help him with. An assessment contact was held towards the end of July to see how things were going. School broke up on 23 July. That year the parents of all the children who would be leaving the village school organized a disco and a trip in a limo. They all ended up at one of their houses for a "leavers' BBQ." We all shared the cost, and Martin did enjoy it, although he was sad to leave the village school as, in September, he would be going to the secondary school even if only for a short time while the court case was going on.

Jen had a teddy bears' picnic on her last day at playgroup, but she would be going back in September.

We did a lot during the summer break. We took them swimming and out to lunch. We went to animal parks with Marie and girls. We met Dean and Chris in town a few times. We took the children bowling, which Jen loved. David came over a few times. Martin and Jen even managed longer contact with their mum sometimes. We helped out at fêtes and fairs with the recruitment team, which we had been doing for a few years. I was still doing my National Vocational Qualification training, and towards the end of the summer, we went on holiday with Dean, Cal, and Chris for a week to Bacton, which everyone thoroughly enjoyed.

We were now taking Martin and Jen to contact, so it was nice to meet their mum. The court case began at the beginning of September. It all seemed to go well, but the judge wasn't happy about the little time the children had for contact and wanted that increased before he would let them go home. We were asked if we could increase the visits at weekends, but that wasn't possible as we had other commitments. We did offer to have their mum stay at our house two nights in the week. She could take over responsibility for them, and we would continue with our support meetings and forum meetings along with any recruitment, and we wouldn't need a sitter. So it was agreed that was what would happen.

On Martin's second day at school, he fell and broke his arm. He was taken to the hospital. I stayed with him until about 5.00 p.m., and then I had to return home and get together some paperwork. I had phoned his social worker and told her what had happened, and I asked if his mum could be told as he would have to stay in hospital overnight because he had to have an operation to straighten the bone. When his mum arrived at the hospital, it was agreed that she would stay the night with him, so I was able to go home and settle Jen for the night. The next morning, I phoned their mum to see how things were going. She told me that he was in theatre, but she would ring me when he came out. I had plenty of time to pick Jen up from playgroup, and by the time we got to the hospital, we still had to wait for him to be given his medication so we could bring home. His mum stayed the night, which pleased Jen as she was sharing her room.

We both took Jen to playgroup the next day, and I introduced her mum to the playgroup workers and explained that she would be bringing Jen a few days every week for a while. The contact was going well. Their mum would arrive every Tuesday and stay until Thursday. We took turns with the cooking and washing up so that life was as natural as possible for the children. The next court date wasn't until sometime in October, but things were working well, so there were no problems.

My family had a good family reunion in late September. My brother was over from Australia, and another brother came from America. My sister and brother from Ireland also came. This time it was at my sister's house in Wembley, but it was fantastic to get everyone together.

The guardian ad litem came to see Martin and Jen the day before the court date and said she was happy for arrangements to be made for the children to go home at the weekend. We were eagerly waiting for the phone call to say that everything had gone well, but the social worker rang to say that the case had been adjourned until sometime in November when they would have the results of some tests that the judge wanted. We had organized a goodbye meal for them, but it was all a bit flat as everyone was so disappointed for them.

It was back to school for Martin and playgroup for Jen. I was still doing my training, so Jen had to be looked after by another carer during the day when I had to do the work with the NVQ worker. Jen had an appointment at hospital to get measured for a new splint. She would have to go back to have it fitted, but her mum said she would make sure that it got done, as hopefully Jen would be back home by the time of the appointment. We were still waiting for a court date at the end of October.

We took all the children to a wildfowl park where little Marie fell over and hurt her wrist. Luckily, there was no damage done even though we had a journey to the hospital to make sure.

The day of the court case finally arrived. This time, we were waiting with a bit less excitement, especially after the last time; however, the children's social worker rang at lunchtime to say the judge had agreed that there was no reason the children couldn't go home. Their mum rang to ask if it would be okay to collect them that evening, which was fine with us as we knew how much everyone wanted it to happen. Both children helped me to pack their belongings so that they were ready as soon as their mum arrived. It was lovely to see them so happy. Finally they were in the car and ready to go by about 7.00 p.m. Despite the excitement and tears, we were so pleased with the way this placement had ended.

Chapter 39

Although we were pleased for Martin and Jen, we were sad in some ways to see them go, but now I was to have that break that the nurse had ordered. Our support worker had purposely not placed any other children with us so that we could have that break. We decided that we wouldn't accept a placement until after Christmas as we were into November, so we had time on our hands. We went to the cinema one evening just on a whim when Robert came home from work. We could go out with friends or just pop in to see people without having a trail of children or having to organize a sitter. We still attended our support group and helped with recruiting, which was something we both enjoyed. And we could actually make arrangements to have Christmas dinner with Marie and her family, which was great because they had had a son, Colm, on 7 November. Although we did take David there.

When the girls and David came around, they said it was very quiet, and they missed all the others. We were all ready for starting back after the New Year. I felt better and was more rested, but we went to see my sister

Terry as she wasn't too well. She had been diagnosed with ovarian cancer, which shook us. I decided I would like to spend more time with her as I had lost other family members without having the time to see them because of the fostering. This time I wanted to be there with Terry, so we spoke to our support worker who said she would put us on hold for another few months to see how things went. Terry seemed to look a bit better, but we weren't too sure that she was doing so well. I went back and forth to her house for a few months.

We were asked if we would book in a boy for respite for ten days in the following September. We said that would be fine. We should have been back a few months by then as we felt that we should be back in June sometime because Terry was not doing too badly at that time. We thought we could start fostering with limitations so that I wasn't quite so tied down.

June arrived, and with it the news that Robert's sister had cancer in her foot and would have to have her leg amputated. As she was Robert's only sister, it was only fair that he spend a bit more time with her. So we made another phone call to our support worker to say that we would be delayed for another while. Even so, she did want to make sure that we would still be able to take the boy for respite in September. I said that, as it was only for ten days, there would be no problem Robert's sister. Had her operation and was doing really well. Terry was okay, so we said we would have the boy and then start back as everyone seemed to be doing well at the moment.

14 year old Joe arrived in September. He was a lovely lad, and we had no problems with him. He went to school

just fine, and at the weekends, he had contact with his mum one day and his dad the next. He liked to see his friends after school in the evenings, which was okay, but since we had last had a placement, social services were having cutbacks, and they no longer provided taxis for the school run. Joe's school was fifteen miles away, and I had to get him there before 8.45 in the morning. And most nights I had to pick him up from one of his friends at about 8.00. I also had to take him to his weekend contacts with his parents and then pick him up. All of this meant we could make no arrangements for ourselves.

Joe was lovely, polite, and caused no trouble, and it was not his fault that I had to do so much driving. But having had nearly a year without having to do any running around, it came as a bit of a shock to be so tied down, and we had to have a long hard think about what we wanted to do. Normally we had three placements at a time, and there was no way I could get them all to school if they were in different directions. And during our break, it had been nice to be able to go out whenever we liked and to be able to watch telly without interruptions. Also, it was nice not to have our furniture kicked around.

We decided to have a word with our support worker and tell her how we felt. Perhaps the time had come for us to retire. She asked us to come to the next two support groups and make our last one the December one as it was our support Christmas party. We agreed to do that, and we attended both our support group and our fostering forum where they said they would have to find replacements for us, but it was agreed by the director that we should be

403

allowed to carry on helping with recruiting as we both enjoyed that.

The November support group was very subdued when they were told that we were retiring. They said that they would miss us, but we would say our goodbyes in December.

We attended the December meeting expecting the normal group, but when we entered the room, there were a few more social workers in attendance, and the director of social services was also there. We were greeted with an enormous bunch of flowers, and there were two chairs looking like thrones waiting for us. We were shown to the table, which was loaded with food. But in the middle was the loveliest cake we had ever seen. It was decorated with figures made to look like us, sitting in front of a coffee table on which lay our MBE awards. We were really choked up. One of the social workers had made it specially for us. Needless to say, it was a wonderful evening and a marvellous ending to our years of fostering. We were asked back to the New Year's party where, along with three other couples, we were presented with a beautiful pot plant, and we were all wished a happy retirement.

Well, that was finally the beginning of our retirement, and we can only say that we have no regrets about our fostering all those years. We made so many friends and cared for some wonderful children, some of whom are still part of our family and whom we think the world of.

We had some brilliant placements over the years that brought us lots of laughter and tears along the way, but we wouldn't have had it any other way. So many made us so proud of them.

Lightning Source UK Ltd.
Milton Keynes UK
UKHW012217030619
343799UK00002B/61/P